The Reaction Against Experiment in the English Novel, 1950–1960

RUBIN RABINOVITZ

The Reaction Against Experiment in the English Novel, 1950–1960

COLUMBIA UNIVERSITY PRESS

NEW YORK & LONDON

1967

Rubin Rabinovitz, an instructor in English at
Columbia University, is the author of *Iris Murdoch,*
one of the Columbia Essays on Modern Writers.

Copyright © 1967 Columbia University Press

Library of Congress Catalog Card Number: 67-14064

Printed in the United States of America

TO MY
FATHER AND MOTHER

Preface

THIS BOOK began as an attempt to discover the reasons for, and the manifestations of, an apparent change in English literary taste which occurred after the Second World War. The English had begun, it seemed, to be more and more vehement in rejecting the experimental novelists of the 1910–1940 era, particularly James Joyce and Virginia Woolf. At the same time there was, after the war, a revival of enthusiasm for the Victorian novelists which was apparently shared by the novelists of the postwar period.

After these impressions had emerged I compiled a bibliography in which I attempted to include all of the novels, critical books and articles, and book reviews by the following novelists: Kingsley Amis, John Braine, William Golding, Iris Murdoch, Alan Sillitoe, C. P. Snow, and Angus Wilson. I began by searching through the card catalogues of a number of major libraries, cumulative book indexes, and periodical indexes. This gave me a good list of novels and critical books, but, as I later found, the eleven periodical indexes I consulted listed few book reviews or critical articles by novelists who were not yet well known in the year in which the index was compiled. I therefore went through the bibliographies of individual periodicals which were published by the periodicals themselves, fifteen in all. Most of the monthlies and quarterlies, I found, had very adequate yearly indexes. So did some of the weeklies, like the *Spectator,* the *New Statesman,* and the *Listener;* other weeklies—the London *Sunday Times* and the *Observer*—had no indexes at all, and I was forced to go through these publications issue by issue. When I was finished, I found that I had a list with about 1,500 entries, including almost all of the publications of the seven novelists listed above as well as many items by other novelists and critics of the contemporary novel. I divided the bibliographies for the seven novelists into three parts: the first listing books by the novelist, the second listing his critical articles and reviews, and the last one containing critical articles about the novelist.

It became obvious, at this point, that it was necessary to eliminate some of this material. I finally decided to devote individual chapters to only three of these novelists—Amis, Wilson, and Snow—and mention the others in an introductory chapter. Though Snow had written novels before the Second World War, he did not write any literary criticism before 1949, nor did he begin to achieve his present popularity until that time. Amis and Wilson began to write both criticism and novels in the early fifties. I chose these three novelists because they all met the following criteria: all had, to some extent, been involved in an anti-experimental movement in their criticism, and this was also reflected in their fiction; all of them wrote novels which had been esteemed by both the critics and the English reading public in the 1950–1960 decade; all had written a great number of critical articles, many of which reflected their aesthetic ideas.

The bibliographies for these three writers contained about 650 items, and I read almost all of these. In addition I read about 500 books and articles which dealt with other novelists of this period. Many of these items were short book reviews; others did not seem relevant to my topic. About a hundred of the items on the bibliography were novels, and these, of course, I read in their entirety, and in many cases read more than once.

Using all of this material, I tried never to attribute an opinion to a particular novelist unless it could be supported by documentary evidence; even more, I attempted to permit these writers to give their opinions in their own words. This accounts for the great amount of quoted material in this book. I have also attempted to give a summary of contemporary critical opinion on certain important issues dealing with these writers.

The general cut-off date for the bibliography is 1962, though many important items which appeared after that date have been added. The bibliographies for individual writers have additions which were suggested by the writers themselves, and I am grateful to them for reading and emending the bibliographies which I sent them. I would also like to thank Professor William York Tindall for the advice, suggestions, and encouragement he gave me while I was writing this book.

RUBIN RABINOVITZ

Contents

ABBREVIATIONS

Com	Commentary	*Obs*	Observer
E in C	Essays in Criticism	*REL*	A Review of English Literature
Enc	Encounter	*Sat R*	Saturday Review of Literature
Ken R	Kenyon Review		
List	Listener	*Spec*	Spectator
Lon M	London Magazine	*Sun Times*	Sunday Times (London)
Nat	Nation	*Tex Q*	Texas Quarterly
N Repub	New Republic	*TLS*	Times [London] Literary Supplement
n.s.	new series		
NS	New Statesman		
NY	New Yorker	*TSLL*	Texas Studies in Literature and Language
NYHTBR	New York Herald Tribune Book Review		
		WLB	Wilson Library Bulletin
NYT	New York Times	*WSCL*	Wisconsin Studies in Contemporary Literature
NYTBR	New York Times Book Review		

CHAPTER ONE

The Novelists of the 1950s
A General Survey

FOR A LONG TIME, the English have been known for both their eccentricity and their love of tradition. Therefore the election of A. E. Richardson, a traditionalist, to the presidency of the Royal Academy of Arts in 1955 caused no great flurry in England. According to the *Sunday Times,* Richardson is a great admirer of the eighteenth-century architect, Henry Holland. So great is Richardson's love of the past that he lives in an eighteenth-century house lit by candles, "with oil lamps and gas here and there." To keep up the mood of the place, "he sometimes dresses up in eighteenth-century costume." He felt that the outstanding book published in 1955 was *English Dolls' Houses of the Eighteenth and Nineteenth Centuries,* by Mrs. Vivien Greene. In commenting on the appointment of Richardson the *Sunday Times* wrote, "Many have a passion for the past, but they do not identify themselves with it so exuberantly, so practically. It is this that makes Professor Richardson so suitable a successor to the Presidency of the Royal Academy of Arts. . . ." [1]

No one, of course, expects academicians to be leaders in artistic revolt. But this example does illustrate the great importance of the traditional in English art, and the consequent distrust of the new and exceptional. Avant-garde movements in England have very often had their origins in other countries, particularly France; even the word *avant-garde* is borrowed from the French. At times, however, the traditional aesthetic movements in England were strong enough to withstand the foreign avant-garde almost entirely; during the 1950s, when the *nouveau roman* was emerging in France, most English novelists had returned to traditional forms.

Though the English novelists of this period wrote about contemporary social problems, few of them experimented with the form and style of their novels; nor did they incorporate the techniques of Joyce, Virginia Woolf, or other experimental novelists into their own styles. Most of the postwar writers conscientiously rejected experimental techniques in their fiction as well as in their critical writings, and turned instead to older novelists for inspiration.

Some of the novelists of the 1950s, C. P. Snow and Angus Wilson, for example, felt that the novelists of the nineteenth century had influenced them most. Others, like Kingsley Amis and John Wain, went back to the eighteenth-century novel and the fiction of the post-Victorian realists: Butler, Bennett, Wells, and Galsworthy. All of these postwar novelists, along with many of their contemporaries—like John Braine, Alan Sillitoe, William Cooper, Pamela Hansford Johnson, David Storey, Honor Tracy, and Keith Waterhouse—rejected the experimental novelists of the early twentieth century.

---

[1] Mr. Richardson's choice of Mrs. Greene's book appeared in *Sun Times*, Jan. 1, 1956. The rest of the material in this paragraph was taken from the *Sun Times*, May 1, 1955 p. 3.

Two English critics have written about this eclipse of the experimental writers. Graham Hough, in *Reflections on a Literary Revolution,* is mainly concerned with the poets who were contemporaries of the experimental novelists; but he sums up the general literary climate in England by saying that "There is no avant-garde." [2] Stephen Spender divides the writers of the early twentieth century into two groups, the "moderns" and the "contemporaries," in his study, *The Struggle of the Modern.*[3] The first group, the "moderns," includes writers like Joyce, Eliot, Pound, Yeats, Lawrence, and Virginia Woolf; Spender's "contemporary" group is made up of writers who came just before the "moderns"—Wells, Shaw, and Bennett—and those who came after the moderns, like C. P. Snow, and to some extent, Kingsley Amis and John Osborne.[4] The "moderns" deliberately set out "to invent a new literature as a result of their feeling that our age is in many respects unprecedented, and outside all the conventions of past literature and art." The "contemporaries" are "at least partly aware of the claim that there is a modern situation. Yet they refuse to regard it as a problem special to art." The "contemporaries," furthermore, give more emphasis to the importance of scientific technology in our culture:

The "contemporaries"—of whom H. G. Wells was an early example and C. P. Snow a recent one—see the changes that have taken place in civilization as the result of the developments of scientific technology, and think that, on the whole, the duty of writers is to enlist their art to support the cause of progress. The "moderns," on the whole, distrust, or even detest, the idea of progress, and view the results of science as a catastrophe to the values of past civilization; nevertheless, opposite to this, there have been some moderns

[2] Graham Hough, *Reflections on a Literary Revolution,* p. 4.
[3] Stephen Spender, *The Struggle of the Modern,* pp. 71 ff.
[4] Though he refers mainly to C. P. Snow as a more recent example of a "contemporary" in *The Struggle of the Modern,* Spender uses Kingsley Amis and John Osborne as parallel examples in an earlier article on the subject, "Moderns and Contemporaries," *List,* 68:555 (Oct. 11, 1962).

who were sustained by the idea that, instead of progress enlisting art, artists might convert scientists to a modern aesthetic vision which would transform the external appearances of our whole civilization. . . .[5]

Spender, like Hough, concludes that the aesthetic theories of the "moderns" are presently on a decline, and that the ideas of the "contemporaries" have been more widely accepted in England. Both Spender and Hough are mainly concerned with the decline in avant-garde or "modern" aesthetics. The primary focus here, however, will be on the writers of the 1950s and on how this decline in avant-garde aesthetics affected them.

Three of the writers of this period who became leaders in a return to traditional forms in the novel were C. P. Snow, Angus Wilson, and Kingsley Amis. Snow began his career as a novelist well before the Second World War, but the peak of his fame and influence came a good many years later. Snow had always opposed the experimental novelists, but it was not until the early 1950s, when he became a regular book reviewer for the London *Sunday Times,* that he had an opportunity to put his critical views forward. Wilson was not so much an opponent of the experimental writers as a leader in the revival of interest in the nineteenth-century novelists. In 1952 he published a study of Zola, and in subsequent years he wrote a number of articles praising the Victorian novelists. Amis' first novel was *Lucky Jim,* published in 1954; he also published articles indicating his lack of sympathy for the experimental writers. Though Amis was, to some extent, influenced by the nineteenth-century novelists, his greatest affinity was with two other groups: the humorous and satirical writers of the eighteenth century, and the novelists of the early twentieth century whom Spender calls the "contemporaries," Wells, Bennett, and Butler. Amis, Wilson,

[5] This quotation, as well as the uncited material above it, is from *The Struggle of the Modern,* p. x.

and Snow all showed in their fictional styles the influences of those writers whom they had praised in their criticism. Because these three writers are so important to the central ideas of this study, they will be separately discussed in later chapters.

Many other English writers who first achieved fame, or first began writing, in the 1950s participated in a rejection of experimental forms and a return to a more traditional style. There were exceptions, of course—notably Lawrence Durrell, William Golding, and Iris Murdoch. It may also be argued that the realistic style of the nineteenth century had never really died in England, especially in the fiction of writers like Evelyn Waugh, Anthony Powell, or Graham Greene. An important difference between these writers and the novelists of the 1950s, however, is that the second group consciously opposed the experimentalists and argued in favor of a return to traditional forms, while the earlier writers usually did little more than ignore the experimentalists.

The novelists of the 1950s had a number of arguments against the experimentalists. A principal one was that the experimental novelists, particularly Joyce in *Finnegans Wake* and Virginia Woolf in *The Waves,* had baffled ordinary readers to such an extent that they had stopped reading novels altogether. Pamela Hansford Johnson (who was later to marry C. P. Snow) argued in this vein in 1949:

In the nineteenth century [the ordinary reader] was happy. Dickens wrote for him; and Trollope, and Thackeray, and George Eliot. . . . But today he is seriously worried. Reading some of the weekend literary columns, he finds himself urged to admire some work which, when he buys or borrows it, he finds arid, unenjoyable, and not infrequently incomprehensible. He turns back from book to review. He thinks, "Is this man crazy or am I?" He has been taught to respect the critic. If the lesson is well-learned he may start to lose faith in himself. If he preserves his independence of judgment he will say, when informed that *Finnegans Wake* is literature and that *The Old Wives' Tale* is not, "So much the worse for literature." He then takes refuge, more often than not, in the detective story. . . .[6]

Pamela Hansford Johnson urged a return to the novel which told a story, the novel in the tradition which began with Chaucer and continued through Fielding, Sterne, Smollett, and Dickens, culminating in Joyce Cary's novels. Novels should be intelligible, says Miss Johnson. "Writing is not a private game to be played at a private party." She finds signs of a "renaissance," however, in the novels of C. P. Snow and Joyce Cary.[7]

William Cooper, another novelist of the 1950s, would agree with Pamela Hansford Johnson. In an article on the experimental novel, he tells how he made plans to "run" avant-garde writing "out of town":

During the last years of the war a literary comrade-in-arms and I, not prepared to wait for Time's ever-rolling stream to bear Experimental Writing away, made our own private plans to run it out of town as soon as we picked up our pens again—if you look at the work of the next generation of English novelists to come up after us, you'll observe that we didn't entirely lack success in our efforts. . . . We meant to write a different kind of novel from that of the thirties and we saw that the thirties novel, the Experimental Novel, had got to be brushed out of the way before we could get a proper hearing.[8]

The experimental novel, says Cooper, concentrated too much on "Man-alone"; he was more interested in social themes, "Man-

[6] Pamela Hansford Johnson, *List*, 42:235 (Aug. 11, 1949).

[7] *Ibid.* A refutation of this and of similar arguments of Pamela Hansford Johnson is in Spender's *The Struggle of the Modern*, pp. 81–83. A discussion of both the argument and the refutation is to be found in David Lodge's "The Modern, the Contemporary and the Importance of Being Amis," the *Critical Quarterly*, 5:336 (Winter, 1963).

[8] William Cooper, "Reflections on Some Aspects of the Experimental Novel," in *International Literary Annual Number 2*, edited by John Wain, p. 29. The "literary comrade-in-arms" Cooper refers to is probably C. P. Snow.

in-Society." [9] In addition, Cooper wanted to return character, plot, and traditional forms to the contemporary novel. These, he felt, had disappeared from the novels of the experimentalists and the novelists who followed them, the French *nouveau roman* writers. The experimentalists eliminated character, Cooper says, because "writing Experimental Novels is a retreat from writing about Man-in-Society by novelists who are unable to adjust or reconcile themselves to society; it is a retreat into writing about the sensations of Man-alone by people who cannot stomach present day industrialized society." [10]

In an argument which echoes Pamela Hansford Johnson's, Cooper emphasizes the value of plot in the novel: "A notable slump in novel-reading in this country occurred in the thirties, when Experimental Writers began to eliminate the story. . . ." At that time, "intelligent men in the world of affairs began to write off the literary world as an enclave given up to playing a private game." [11] Cooper feels that experimental writing is motivated by a decadent impulse:

The impulse behind much Experimental Writing is an attack from the inside on intellect in general, made by intellectuals so decadent that they no longer mind if intellect persists—in fact some of them sound as if they would be happier if it didn't. . . . In any part of intellectual society the decadent are at the present moment of history immediately identifiable: they are plugging a theory that everybody really knows *won't work*.[12]

Some of Cooper's arguments are weak: the experimental novelists never completely eliminated character and plot from their fiction, nor were they as subversive as he suggests. As G. S. Fraser says, Cooper "seems naive in some critical comments he has made on experiment in fiction." [13]

---

[9] *Ibid.*   [10] *Ibid.,* p. 32.   [11] *Ibid.,* p. 33.
[12] *Ibid.,* p. 36. The italics are Cooper's.
[13] G. S. Fraser, *The Modern Writer and His World,* p. 165.

A more sophisticated view is put forward by John Wain, whose first novel, *Hurry On Down,* was published in 1953. Wain feels that the experimental novel followed in the tradition of the great nineteenth-century novels, and that it culminated in Joyce's *Ulysses;* after this, the only direction left to go was down:

Technical experiments could be made, but the results could never be as far-reaching as the results of that great movement towards complete dramatization, complete imaginative possession, which had been made by the generation of 1860 to 1910. There was only one major step left to be taken, and Joyce duly took it in *Ulysses* when he wrote a novel which dispensed with the central point of view and made each of his three main characters contemplate the same reality from different standpoints.[14]

Since the publication of *Ulysses,* says Wain, "there has been very little experimental novel-writing that strikes one as serious, or motivated by anything more than faddishness or the irritable search for new gimmicks." Wain considers the writing of Hemingway and Ivy Compton-Burnett and finds it more a "refinement in craftsmanship" than, in either case, an advance in experimental techniques. Beckett's novels, Wain feels, "are actually nothing more than adaptations of the method he has made so much his own in the theater," and hence do not really qualify as advances in experimental writing. The last "undeniable success" of the experimental novel was Flann O'Brien's *At Swim-Two-Birds,* published in 1939. "In reality," says Wain "the experimental novel died with Joyce."[15] Wain does not consider the work of the *nouveau roman* writers or of earlier writers like Faulkner in this discussion.

As might be expected, the novels of Wain, Cooper, and Pam-

---

[14] John Wain, *Essays on Literature and Ideas,* pp. 49–50.
[15] *Ibid.,* pp. 50–51. Wain does not mention here that Beckett's plays were written after most of his novels had been completed. Hence his novels could hardly be called "adaptations."

ela Hansford Johnson contain no examples of experimental techniques. Their styles are plain, their time sequences are chronological, and they make no use of myth, symbolism, or stream-of-consciousness inner narratives. Their prose is realistic, documentary, and even journalistic. Though Wain and other novelists of this period are also poets, there are no attempts at poetic novels or effusive style. Elaborate descriptions, sensitivity, and plotless novels are avoided; nor do these novelists try to develop an individual style. To display too much individuality in style would be egregious and in bad taste: the differences between these writers can be noted mainly in the diversity of the subject matter of their novels.

This reaction against the experimental novelists has been commented on by a great number of critics of contemporary English literature. William Van O'Connor, for example, after writing about Lawrence Durrell and William Golding, makes this point:

> Another group is represented by such names as Joyce Cary, Anthony Powell, L. P. Hartley, C. P. Snow, and Angus Wilson. Despite their mid-century preoccupations their novels seem related to the solidities of an older world, say the Edwardians, in some ways akin to Galsworthy, but not to John Braine or Kingsley Amis. Even so, one detects a similarity of another sort: all of them, Cary, Snow, Amis, or Miss Murdoch appear largely indifferent to the experiments of the twenties and thirties.[16]

Particular lists of writers may vary, but many other critics agree with O'Connor that most of the writers of this period have eschewed experimental techniques in their fiction. Indeed, some critics feel that the trend includes not only fiction, but poetry and drama as well. Raymond Williams, who often writes on the social aspects of English literary history, feels that "the 1950s could be fairly characterized . . . as a period of return to

[16] William Van O'Connor, *The New University Wits and the End of Modernism*, p. 148.

older forms, and to specifically English forms, especially by comparison with the most widely discussed work of the 1920s and 1930s, which was largely experimental in form and cosmopolitan in spirit." He does not limit this statement to fiction alone:

In the novel there has been as sharp a reaction against the methods of Virginia Woolf as between the wars there was a reaction, led by Woolf herself, against the "realism" of Bennett or Wells. In poetry, there has been something of a conscious return to native traditions and models, and this has had its counterpart in a growing criticism, now almost fashionable, of the disintegrating effects of Eliot and Pound. In the drama, the most widely successful plays—of Osborne, Wesker, and Delaney—seem to represent a return to a kind of naturalism which again reaches back beyond 1914.[17]

Some critics, in addition to describing this reaction against the experimentalists, welcomed it in the very years when some of the younger writers of the 1950s were still completing their first novels. A writer for the *Times Literary Supplement,* for example, said in 1952, "Enough—some would say more than enough —has been achieved in the way of experiment," and urged novelists to write about recent social changes.[18] A few years later J. B. Priestley helped to set an anti-Joycean mood, deploring "the fact, set down by Mr. Levin, Joyce's American enthusiast, that this disreputable author is today required reading in college courses. . . . (Anybody impressed by that can never have entered an American college.)" Priestley concludes, "Two questions still remain. Did he write like a great novelist? Does the intelligent reading public genuinely accept him as a great novelist? And the answer to both is *No.*" [19]

These comments helped determine the critical mood of the early 1950s. In the two years after the comment from the *Times Literary Supplement* appeared, Wain, Amis, and Iris Murdoch

[17] Raymond Williams, *Audience,* 8:76 (Winter, 1961).
[18] *TLS,* Aug. 29, 1952, p. xii.
[19] *Sun Times,* Jan. 2, 1955, p. 5. The italics are Priestley's.

published their first novels. The first novels of Keith Waterhouse, Honor Tracy, and Alan Sillitoe were published shortly after Priestley's article. Since it was inevitable that these first novels would be reviewed by the *Times Literary Supplement,* and possible that Priestley might review some of them, these critical comments are more important than general literary criticism might be. Nor are statements rejecting the experimentalists isolated; in addition to comments of this sort by Snow, Amis, and Angus Wilson (which will be given in later chapters), many other English novelists, critics, and book reviewers wrote in the same vein.[20]

As has already been indicated, along with this rejection of the experimental writers, many of the writers of the 1950s turned to earlier writers for inspiration. The older writers in this group, particularly Snow and Angus Wilson, were most attracted by the novelists of the second half of the nineteenth century. As Walter Allen has written,

It must be apparent by now that a significant shift in fiction during the decade has been towards a renewal in the influence on contemporary writers of the Victorians. Or perhaps it would be more accurate to say that admiration for the amplitude and plenitude of the great Victorians has led some contemporary novelists to question what has often seemed the main tradition of the modern novel from James to Joyce and Virginia Woolf and attempt a return to something like nineteenth-century modes.[21]

[20] A selection of articles describing or supporting the movement away from the experimentalists is given below. Emyr Humphreys, *List,* 49:557 (Apr. 2, 1953); Walter Allen, *NYTBR,* Sept. 17, 1961, p. 40; V. S. Pritchett, *NYTBR,* Sept. 13, 1953, p. 18; Stephen Spender, *NYTBR,* Aug. 1, 1954, p. 2; Paul West, *The Modern Novel,* I, 126, 146, 149; John Lehmann, editor, *The Craft of Letters in England,* especially the essays by Francis Wyndham (p. 44) and Philip Toynbee (p. 60); Bernard Bergonzi, the *List,* 70:415 (Sept. 19, 1963); John Holloway, *Hudson Review,* 10:424 (Autumn, 1957); V. S. Pritchett, *NS,* 49:76 (Jan. 15, 1955).
[21] Walter Allen, *The Novel Today,* p. 29.

Snow, Cooper, and Wilson, Allen feels, are primary examples of this shift. This renewed interest in the Victorians was aided by a general Victorian revival which occurred shortly after the Second World War. This revival encompassed not only literature, but painting, interior decoration, and women's clothing as well. In an article entitled "The Victorian Revival," published in 1948, B. Ifor Evans says, "It can be confidently affirmed that in the period between the two wars the literature of the Victorian age was a theme of attack in Great Britain, and with the same confidence it can certainly be stated that those years of hostile criticism and dreary vituperation are passed. The Victorian Age has come into its own again." [22]

As examples of this revival of interest in the Victorians, Evans mentioned an exhibition of pre-Raphaelite painting; a general reassessment of Tennyson's poetry; London houses, "where attention is paid to matters of taste," decorated with "looped curtains, fringes, and over-mantels such as existed in England in the later decades of the nineteenth century"; and even "the small straw hat, the bustle, and the full skirt," showing "the influence of Victorian fashions on women's clothes." [23] Many Londoners, says Evans, came to see an exhibition of the first editions of Victorian novels sponsored by the National Book League in 1947. The B.B.C., at this time, began a popular program in which sections of famous Victorian novels were dramatized. Film versions of Victorian novels—Evans mentions *Great Expectations, Nicholas Nickleby, The Mill on the Floss,* and *Silas Marner*— as well as the revival of a number of Victorian plays on the London stage contributed to a new interest in Victorian writing.

There was also a considerable amount of Victorian scholarship in the late 1940s and throughout the following decade. New editions, biographies, and critical works dealing with almost every important Victorian writer appeared during these years. Two examples from *Victorian Fiction, A Guide to Research* will

[22] B. Ifor Evans, *Britain Today*, Feb., 1948, p. 20.
[23] *Ibid.*, pp. 20–21.

illustrate this.[24] In the section on Charles Dickens, Ada Nisbet writes, "Exclusive of the *Dickensian* 50 more articles on Dickens were published in the 1940's than in the 1930's and 130 more in the 1950's than in the 1940's. And the *Guide to Doctoral Dissertations in Victorian Literature, 1886–1958* . . . indicates a parallel growth, showing a rise from 7 dissertations in the 1930's to 11 in the 1940's to 32 in the 1950's.[25] Similarly, W. J. Harvey says of George Eliot scholarship,

The body of published work on George Eliot may fairly be represented by the figure of a globe densely populated at its poles, yet at its equator but sparsely inhabited. On this analogy one pole represents the period beginning with the first reviews of *Scenes of Clerical Life* . . . and ending roughly with Leslie Stephen's *George Eliot* (1902). The other pole essentially represents a post-1945 phenomenon. Between lies a long desert of neglect.[26]

Surveys of the scholarship on other Victorian novelists show a similar increase. It may be thought that this increase in Victorian scholarship was caused by a general increase in postwar scholarly activity. Actually, it was not until around 1955 that, in a quantitative sense, postwar exceeded prewar scholarship; and this increase alone is smaller than the increase in Victorian scholarship.[27] In scholarship, as in other areas, there was a true Victorian revival at this time.

Many of the novelists of the 1950s contributed to this Vic-

---

[24] *Victorian Fiction, A Guide to Research,* edited by Lionel Stevenson. The companion volume to this book, *The Victorian Poets,* edited by F. E. Faverty, shows a similar increase in scholarship on the poets of this period.
[25] *Ibid.,* pp. 44–45.   [26] *Ibid.,* p. 294.
[27] As a general index of yearly activity in literary scholarship, a table was made of the number of pages in the annual *Bibliography of English Language and Literature* (Cambridge, England: University Press). This bibliography, similar to the American bibliography published by the Modern Language Association, annually lists the important literary criticism published in English (book reviews are excluded) and about writers in the English language. The prewar high came in 1937, when the bibliography had 286 pages. This was not exceeded until 1955–56, when the bibliography had 586 pages (mean: 293). The mean for 1953–

torian revival in scholarship. Angus Wilson, for example, has written three essays on Dickens, as well as a number of reviews of books dealing with Dickens. Wilson's interest is not confined to English nineteenth-century writers: in addition to a book on Zola he wrote the introduction to a novel of Zola's. Kingsley Amis wrote an introduction to an edition of Wilde's *Selected Works,* and an essay on Victorian poetry. John Wain, in various essays, has written on Dickens, Bagehot, Tennyson, Browning, Hopkins, and Housman. David Storey wrote the screenplay for the movie *Wuthering Heights;* Muriel Spark, in collaboration with Derek Stanford, has written *Emily Bronte,* a critical study. Few, if any, of these writers were unsympathetic to the Victorian writers they dealt with in their critical books and essays.[28]

Many contemporary English writers whose style is close to that of the nineteenth-century realistic novelists have indicated that these writers have influenced them. This will be dealt with more fully in later chapters, especially the influence of Dickens and Zola on Angus Wilson, and of Trollope and other Victorian novelists on C. P. Snow. Other contemporary writers have also indicated their preference for the nineteenth-century novel: Doris Lessing, for example, whose own fictional style follows the realistic tradition, has written,

---

54 was 198 pages for 1950–52 it was higher, 234 pages. The low point during the war came in 1942, when the bibliography had only 140 pages. After 1959 the bibliography always had over 300 pages, with a high point in 1962 of 418 pages. Beginning in 1935, the mean number of pages, by decades, is as follows: 1936–1945, 211 pages; 1946–1955, 234 pages; 1956–1963, 339 pages.

[28] Angus Wilson: "Charles Dickens: A Haunting," the *Critical Quarterly,* 2:101 (Summer, 1960); "Heroes and Heroines of Dickens," *REL,* 2:9 (July, 1961); "Dickens and the Divided Conscience," *Month,* 3:349 (May, 1963); *Émile Zola, an Introductory Study to His Novels;* Introduction to Zola's *The Kill.* Kingsley Amis: "Communication and the Victorian Poet," *Essays in Criticism,* 4:386 (Oct., 1954). John Wain: *"Little Dorrit"* and "Gerard Manley Hopkins: An Idiom of Desperation," in his *Essays on Literature and Ideas;* "An Introduction to Bagehot," *REL,* 1:66 (Oct., 1960); " 'A Stranger and Afraid': Notes on Four Victorian Poets," in his *Preliminary Essays.*

For me the highest point of literature was the novel of the nineteenth century, the work of Tolstoy, Stendhal, Dostoyevsky, Balzac, Turgenev, Chekhov; the work of the great realists. . . . I hold the view that the realist novel, the realist story, is the highest form of prose writing; higher than and out of the reach of any comparison with expressionism, impressionism, symbolism, naturalism, or any other ism.[29]

Similarly, Iris Murdoch "prefers nineteenth-century novels to new ones," and John Braine has said that Dickens is one of his favorite writers.[30] Pamela Hansford Johnson, in an article already mentioned, says that the Victorian novel was a high point in literature because the writer was so close to his reading public.[31] John Wain has written that "prose fiction is still dominated by Tolstoy and Chekhov, Stendhal and Flaubert, Dickens and Henry James." If, says Wain, "the Pantheon of European literature is substantially the same now as it was in 1910, that fact represents a great triumph of the critical spirit." [32] Another contemporary novelist, Emyr Humphreys, compares Joyce and the nineteenth-century novelists and feels that Joyce was too cold and objective about humanity. "The two greatest novelists of the nineteenth century," says Humphreys, "Tolstoy and Dostoevsky, had a concern for humanity of a kind which does not exist in Joyce." This makes the nineteenth-century writers more relevant for a contemporary novelist: today's writer "must arrive at a positive attitude to the human situation before he can begin to say anything worth communicating. He cannot continue forever to indulge himself in the quiet sport of technical experimentation. . . ." [33]

---

[29] Doris Lessing, "The Small Personal Voice," in *Declaration,* edited by Tom Maschler, p. 14.
[30] Interview with Iris Murdoch, *Obs,* June 25, 1961, p. 24; John Braine, "How I Write My Novels," *Time and Tide,* 43:23 (Oct. 4–11, 1962).
[31] *List,* 42:235 (Aug. 11, 1949).
[32] *Essays on Literature and Ideas,* pp. 133–34.
[33] Emyr Humphreys, *List,* 49:558 (Apr. 2, 1953).

In their fiction, the novelists of the 1950s show the influence of the nineteenth-century novelists by their realistic style and their concern with social and moral themes. This is true for virtually all of the writers in this group. In addition, many of these writers borrow techniques or idiosyncrasies of style from some nineteenth-century novelist whom they admire. Snow's chapter headings are almost exactly like Trollope's; many of Wilson's minor characters are Dickensian enough to seem almost like caricatures. The titles of two of William Cooper's novels, *Scenes from Provincial Life* and *Scenes from Married Life,* are based on the title of one of George Eliot's early novels, *Scenes of Clerical Life.* In general, John Holloway's comment seems accurate: "In the novel, we are reverting to our well-established nineteenth-century preoccupations: the detail of our provincial and local life; our elaborate and multiple gradations of money, influence, or power; and what has perhaps always been intimately linked with these, our processes of sexual selection." [34]

Holloway's mention of provincial life brings to mind another important group of writers who influenced the younger contemporary novelists: the early twentieth-century writers like Bennett, Butler, and Wells. Amis, Braine, Sillitoe, Wain, Waterhouse, and Storey all have, to some extent, been influenced by these Edwardian writers. Many of these younger novelists, whose protagonists are lower class and whose novels are set in provincial towns, owe a debt to Bennett. As Alan Sillitoe has written in an introduction to Bennett's *The Old Wives' Tale,*

if he was at the ending of a great stream of English writing, he was also in at the beginning of that more modern literature that has kept its scenery in industrial England. There have been many men from the north after him—many who are writing now, and are still young, novelists like John Braine, John Wain, and David Storey;

[34] John Holloway, the *Hudson Review,* 10:429 (Autumn, 1957).

playwrights like Shelagh Delaney and John Arden; poets like Ted Hughes.[35]

John Wain, who was born in Stoke-on-Trent (the setting for a number of Bennett's novels), has written, "Bennett has always seemed to me an excellent novelist, not so inferior to Lawrence as the current fashion would have us think." [36] Wain has a good knowledge of Bennett's novels, and, in an essay on Bennett, he does not conceal his admiration for him. At the close of this essay, Wain recalls Virginia Woolf's famous criticism of Bennett, "Mr. Bennett and Mrs. Brown," and says that the methods of the writers who followed Bennett also had their limitations. *"The Years* is an attempt in the same direction as *The Old Wives' Tale,* but," asks Wain, "can we honestly say that it is equally successful?" [37] Wain concludes with a plea for a new recognition of Bennett's importance: "Now, surely, his period of enforced quarantine is over, his passport is in order, and he should be allowed to land at the harbor of English literature." [38] To some extent Wain's plea has been successful; as David Lodge points out, Bennett "is now enjoying something of a comeback, assisted by the attention of John Wain, one of our leading 'contemporaries' in his *Preliminary Essays."* [39]

A number of critics have noted the similarities between Wain's fictional style and Bennett's.[40] Wain's novel *The Contenders* owes a good deal to Bennett. The protagonist of this novel, Joe Shaw, tells of the efforts of two of his school friends

---

[35] Arnold Bennett, *The Old Wives' Tale,* with an introduction by Alan Sillitoe, p. 18.

[36] John Wain, "The Quality of Arnold Bennett," in his *Preliminary Essays,* p. 122.

[37] *Ibid.,* p. 155.

[38] *Ibid.,* p. 156. Wain makes the same point again in an interview with Frank Kermode, *Partisan Review,* 30:77 (Spring, 1963).

[39] David Lodge, *Critical Quarterly,* 5:336 (Winter, 1963).

[40] Frank Kermode in *Partisan Review,* 30:77 (Spring, 1963), and Gilbert Phelps in *The Modern Age,* edited by Boris Ford, p. 490, are two examples.

to achieve enough success to enable them to leave their northern provincial birthplace. The town is "that place you stop at on the way to Manchester—the one where you look out of the train window when it's slowing down, and think, 'Well, at least I don't live *here*.'" Growing up in this squalid town helps to make its inhabitants competitive:

Being brought up in a town where everything was shabby, dirty, dwarfish, peeling, and generally lousy was another thing that helped to make most of us competitive. You looked round you as you stood waiting for the bus to take you to school, and you thought, "If I don't do well I might have to end up staying *here*." [41]

This theme, the attempts of young men to rise above or break away from the poverty and narrowness of provincial towns, occurs in a number of the novels of this period, such as John Braine's *Room at the Top,* Kingsley Amis' *That Uncertain Feeling,* David Storey's *This Sporting Life,* Alan Sillitoe's *Saturday Night and Sunday Morning,* Keith Waterhouse's *Billy Liar,* as well as in C. P. Snow's *Time of Hope.* All of these novels are written in a style as colorless as the places they describe, with a treatment of ambition, money, and success similar to Bennett's. What William Van O'Connor says about two of these novelists could apply to this group as a whole:

The books of John Wain and David Storey are not very different from Bennett's, and deal with their subjects in a manner he might have employed. They leap back of Mrs. Woolf and Joyce—to the pre-modern Bennett. And as we have seen some of their older contemporaries have done the same thing.[42]

There are also similarities between these writers and other members of the Edwardian group. The attitudes of Amis' protagonists toward social class, and Snow's interest in science, recall Wells's

[41] John Wain, *The Contenders* (New York: St. Martin's Press, 1958), p. 5. The italics are Wain's.
[42] *The New University Wits,* p. 149.

novels; the *Times Literary Supplement* finds William Cooper's style close to Wells's.[43] Paul West sees the influence of Wells and Gissing in Braine, Sillitoe, and other "new realists of the English novel." [44]

Samuel Butler is another Edwardian who has influenced these writers, as William Van O'Connor has noticed.[45] There is a good deal of similarity between Butler's *The Way of All Flesh* and John Wain's novel, *Strike the Father Dead*. An important theme in this novel, as in Butler's, is a conflict between father and son. Jeremy Coleman, son of a professor of classics, rips up his Greek grammar book, leaves home, and, to the dismay of his father, becomes a jazz musician. Kingsley Amis' satire is closer to Butler's *Erewhon*, and Amis has written an afterword to this book, praising it.

All of this merely reenforces one of Stephen Spender's major arguments: that the "contemporaries," or Edwardian writers, are beginning to occupy the place of esteem which the "moderns" held a decade or two ago. Spender makes one other important point. He recalls three writers who criticized the "contemporaries":

To Henry James, Wells seemed, with all his immense gifts of enjoyment and vitality, lacking in the consciousness of that separateness which alone can create individual values. To Lawrence it seemed that Galsworthy in his novels invented nothing but social units, described a life which had none but social standards. And to Virginia Woolf it seemed that Arnold Bennett saw his characters only from the outside. . . .[46]

To this list Spender could have added Virginia Woolf's attack on Wells in her essay "Modern Fiction." These criticisms of the "contemporaries" by writers who are closer to the "modern"

[43] "Uncommitted Talents," *TLS*, Aug. 29, 1952, p. iii.
[44] Paul West, *The Modern Novel*, I, pp. 126, 141.
[45] *The New University Wits*, p. 133.
[46] *The Struggle of the Modern*, p. 119.

point of view, Spender says, illustrate some of the deep-seated differences between the two groups. That the writers of the 1950s have chosen to defend the "contemporaries" from "modern" attacks can only illustrate the connections between these younger writers and the "contemporaries." In addition to Wain's defense of Bennett, which has already been mentioned, Pamela Hansford Johnson, C. P. Snow, Kingsley Amis, and Angus Wilson have all attempted to use Virginia Woolf's method in "Mr. Bennett and Mrs. Brown" (often referring to the essay) as a means of attacking Woolf herself.[47]

In addition to the Victorians and Edwardians, there is one more group with which the writers of the 1950s can be compared: the eighteenth-century picaresque novelists. V. S. Pritchett, for example, compares Amis, Wain, Braine, and Hinde to the Edwardian novelists, but also finds links between the first group and the eighteenth-century writers.[48] Generally, the streams of influence divide in the following manner: the older novelists (Snow, Wilson) whose main concern was social and moral were most influenced by the Victorians; the younger novelists (Sillitoe, Braine) whose settings were provincial were influenced mainly by the Edwardians; while an off-shoot of the last group (Amis, Wain) whose novels were satirical or picaresque was influenced by the eighteenth-century as well as the Edwardian group. Amis and Wain are both interested in the eighteenth century, Amis professionally, for it was his field of specialization as a university English instructor. Wain's first novel, *Hurry on Down,* is directly in the picaresque tradition: the hero holds half a dozen jobs in as many places before settling down, and his travels from job to job give the book an episodic character. Wain has also written a number of critical essays on

[47] Pamela Hansford Johnson, *List,* 42:235 (Aug. 11, 1949); the criticisms of Woolf by Amis, Wilson, and Snow will be discussed in later chapters.
[48] V. S. Pritchett, *NYTBR,* Apr. 28, 1957, p. 1.

eighteenth-century figures.[49] As will later be shown, Amis' novels show the influence of Fielding and Richardson. Braine's favorite novelists—Fielding, Dickens, and Wells—show that he too is interested in all three of these periods, eighteenth-century, Victorian, and Edwardian.[50] Wain feels that Bennett's novels are "at the end of that branch of English fiction which was begun by Defoe"; [51] if Wain is right, this provides another link between the eighteenth-century writers and the Edwardians, and helps to explain how the later novelists were influenced by these two groups, which are separated by over a century. Derek Stanford, however, feels that the two novelists who influenced Amis and Wain most are Fielding and Dickens.[52] A number of other critics place Amis and Wain in an eighteenth-century or picaresque tradition, without much reference to writers from other periods.[53] There seems little reason to assume, however, that influences from all three groups were not important to the 1950 group in varying degrees.

What may have seemed at first to be only a movement away from the experimentalists and back again to the nineteenth-century writers is actually more complex, since each novelist's literary taste played a part in determining the particular authors he would choose to follow. Though the 1950 group showed a greater unanimity in rejecting the experimentalists than in following writers from any one earlier period, there is still another series of factors which adds to the complexity of this reaction. This is the great number of changes in social, political, and intellectual life which occurred in England after the Second World

[49] Wain's *Essays on Literature and Ideas* contains pieces on Pope and Johnson, and an essay on Restoration comedy is included in *Preliminary Essays*.
[50] "How I Write My Novels," *Time and Tide,* 43:23 (Oct. 4–11, 1962).
[51] *Preliminary Essays,* p. 152.
[52] Derek Stanford, *Contemporary Review,* 191:238 (Apr., 1957).
[53] Some examples: S. Diana Neill, *A Short History of the English Novel,* p. 395; Walter Allen, *Tradition and Dream,* p. 279.

War, changes which influenced, and to some degree were themselves influenced by, this literary reaction.

Perhaps the most important social change to influence the postwar English writers was a partial breakdown of the class system and a corresponding strengthening of the bureaucracy. Straker, Shaw's "new man" in *Man and Superman,* had finally appeared—not, perhaps, as a mechanic, but in the more respectable role of engineer, scientist, or plant manager. C. P. Snow's novels (one of them is called *The New Men*) illustrate this trend: his lower class heroes rise, as Snow did himself, through universities, corporations, the government, until they are able to enter what was once exclusively middle-class or aristocratic territory. Many of Snow's characters are from the upper classes —the system has been only partially democratized; nevertheless, the lower-class man, with sufficient energy and ability, can now occupy the key positions, join the clubs, and receive the honors which would formerly have been denied him because of his origins.

The change which Snow describes was not abrupt, since even Shaw could write of its beginnings. But an important illustration of the strength of this social change came immediately after the Second World War, when the Labor Government came into power despite Churchill's great personal popularity: an Eton education was helpful for a government career, but no longer indispensable; it was pleasant to have a knight as chairman of a corporation, but not essential. More important were the socialization of medicine and certain industries and a comprehensive social welfare program, factors which, to some degree, changed the life of every Englishman.

These social changes made a great impact on the postwar English novel. The well-to-do and aristocratic university men in the novels of Beerbohm, Forster, Powell, and Waugh were replaced by heroes with humbler origins in the novels of Amis, Wain, Philip Larkin, and Andrew Sinclair. The serious-minded scholarship boy, a stereotype in the earlier university novels, now very often was the protagonist; the profligate, gentlemanly, party-going scholar of the prewar novels had now become the stereotyped minor character. An early example of this new type of university novel is Philip Larkin's *Jill,* published in 1946. The protagonist of the novel finds that his working-class origins are a social detriment: he is never accepted by the elegant Oxford set he wishes to join. Nevertheless, he rejects the hard-study-and-no-social-life solution arrived at by a fellow working-class student. Though there is still enough snobbery at Oxford to prevent him from having the friends he wants, the hero refuses to become the scholarship-boy stereotype of the earlier university novels. By the time Andrew Sinclair published his university novel, *My Friend Judas* (1959), even this situation had changed to some extent: intelligence and creativity seem more important than social origins in Sinclair's Cambridge.

The hero of Kingsley Amis' *Lucky Jim* (1954), an instructor at a provincial university, with no self-consciousness about his own lower-middle-class background, mocks the snobbery of his middle-class associates. The protagonist of John Wain's novel *Hurry on Down* (1953) is less concerned with his class background than with the fact that his university education, designed to train middle-class gentlemen, has not really prepared him for the world he encounters when he leaves the university. In these novels, rather than being cowed by the social structure, the protagonists have enough self-confidence to satirize and to criticize it.

A parallel movement in English fiction has been the transition from the middle-class country-house novel of the prewar era to a renewed interest in the working-class novel. This type of novel, rarely as politically committed as the American working-class novel of the 1930s, strives instead to present a realistic picture of working-class life, usually as the writers themselves experienced it.

Alan Sillitoe's *Saturday Night and Sunday Morning* is partly based on personal experience, and his later novel, *Key to the Door,* is even more autobiographical. David Storey's experiences as a professional rugby player who attempts to escape his working-class background form the basis of his novel *This Sporting Life.* Storey used the money from his rugby playing to support himself in London while he studied art. His two years as an art student, with weekends spent in the West Riding as a rugby player, made a deep impression on him. His father, a coal miner, lived by the code, "physical work is good, mental work is evil," and objected to his son's study of art. Storey came to see the north of England as masculine and the south as artistic and feminine, with his weekly journey from south to north and back again linking the two. He feels that this dichotomy is present in his novels: *This Sporting Life* is northern and masculine, *Flight into Camden* southern and feminine. *Radcliffe,* a later novel, has both elements in it. As Storey has written, "That journey therefore has in the end come to represent a universal theme: almost an archetypal experience." [54] A similar attitude towards art in a coal-mining community was discovered by Clancy Sigal, an American whose documentary novel, *Weekend in Dinlock,* is based on his experiences as a guest of a coal miner who was struggling to leave mining and become a painter. Though some of these novels superficially resemble Lawrence's, Lawrence was more concerned with the inner struggles of his heroes; in the novels of Storey and Sigal the emphasis is on the hero's struggle with his environment and community. The novels themselves are closer to Bennett and Zola than to Lawrence.

The hero of John Braine's *Room at the Top* must choose between love and ambition: he can marry the daughter of an industrialist and end his poverty, but he is in love with another woman. Ambition wins out, and in a sequel to his first novel

[54] David Storey, in *Writers on Themselves* (London: The British Broadcasting Corporation, 1964), p. 101.

Braine portrays his hero's unhappy marriage. The lower-class hero of Stan Barstow's *A Kind of Loving* also is unhappily married. After what had been, for the protagonist, a casual affair, he finds he must marry the girl whom he has made pregnant. Unable to live with her and his shrewish mother-in-law, he tries to leave his wife, but the pressure of the working-class community in which he lives forces him to return. Arthur Seaton, the hero of Sillitoe's *Saturday Night and Sunday Morning*, feels that he is a rebel: he drinks, fights, and cuckolds one of his fellow factory workers. In the end, however, he recognizes that his rebellion is only a phase and prepares for a marriage which will turn him into a moral working-class husband.

Along with these novels of working-class life, there has been an increase in fiction which deals with the lower middle class. A recent novel by Angus Wilson, *Late Call* (1964), describes a lower-middle-class family in one of the English new towns. Previous to this, Wilson's novels were written about middle-class and upper-middle-class people. Keith Waterhouse's *Jubb* is also set in a new town. Another of Waterhouse's novels, *Billy Liar*, deals with a young undertaker's assistant who longs to leave his provincial town and become a comedy writer in London. This is the job that the hero of Wain's *Hurry on Down* ends with, after being a chauffeur and hospital orderly, among other things. Amis' *That Uncertain Feeling* is about a provincial librarian, and Larkin's *A Girl in Winter* deals with a bookshop assistant. There has been a parallel movement in the English drama: the plays of Osborne, Wesker, Kops, Pinter, and Shelagh Delaney portray characters of lower-middle-class or working-class origin.

These novels, of course, are in the tradition of the novels dealing with lower-class life which were written by Zola, George Moore, Wells, and Bennett. There is an important difference, however, between these and the newer novels. While Zola and Moore were of, and wrote for, the middle and aristocratic classes, Wells and Bennett had experienced lower-class life, though writing mainly for a middle-class audience. By the 1950s, the English novelist could expect that at least a portion of his audience would be from the lower classes.

Raymond Williams, in his study *The Long Revolution,* has given the statistics which reflect this change. The publication of books in Great Britain had almost doubled from the time of Bennett to the 1950s: the increase was from 12,690 titles in 1924 to 22,143 in 1958; the increase in the British population was much smaller, from 44,027,000 in 1921 to 52,676,000 in 1961. Library book issues increased sharply after the Second World War: from 312 million in 1948–1949 to 431 million in 1957–1958. According to Williams, "Taking all kinds of book distribution into account, a figure of about 15 books read annually per head of population is about the present stage, or 20 per head of the adult population." Moreover, says Williams, "It is probable that in the 1950s, for the first time, we had a majority book-reading public (as compared with a majority Sunday-newspaper public by 1910 and a majority daily-newspaper public by the 1914–1918 war)." [55] Williams' speculation that there was a majority book-reading public in the 1950s is strengthened by a survey which Arthur Marwick, another English historian, cites. In the 1950s, says Marwick, "Book production was higher in Britain than in any other country. In 1950 a poll was conducted into personal reading habits. Fifty-five per cent of those interviewed claimed at the time of the poll to be reading a book. The reading matter was 'mostly fiction.' " [56]

If it has been established, then, that the British reading public was large enough in the 1950s to include even readers from the lower classes, it still remains to be determined whether the books which were being read were these new novels of lower-class life.

---

[55] All of the information on reading and book publication is taken from Raymond Williams, *The Long Revolution,* pp. 170–71. The population figures are from the British censuses of 1920 and 1960.

[56] Arthur Marwick, *The Explosion of British Society, 1914–62,* p. 121.

To judge by the British best-seller lists, they were. Kingsley Amis' *Lucky Jim* had gone into 20 editions in 1958, and had been translated into nine foreign languages.[57] Another of Amis' novels, *Take a Girl Like You,* was in second place on the London *Sunday Times* best-seller list in October, 1960; a month before, Sillitoe's *Saturday Night and Sunday Morning* had been first on the same list.[58] As P. N. Furbank has pointed out, the book sales for many of these novels increase after they have been made into films. "The real formula for success," says Furbank, "is publication as a paper-back immediately after a successful film version—as may be seen from the case of John Braine's *Room at the Top,* which sold half a million paper-back copies in seven months." [59]

In addition to *Room at the Top,* many other novels of lower-middle-class or of lower-class life have been made into successful films. The list includes Braine's *Life at the Top* (1965), Amis' *Lucky Jim* (1957) and *That Uncertain Feeling* (1962; film title: *Only Two Can Play*), Sillitoe's *Saturday Night and Sunday Morning* (1960) and *The Loneliness of the Long-distance Runner* (1962), Waterhouse's *Billy Liar* (1963), Storey's *This Sporting Life* (1963), and Barstow's *A Kind of Loving* (1962). In addition to these novels, a number of plays which deal with lower-class life were made into films: Osborne's *Look Back in Anger* (1959) and *The Entertainer* (1960), Wesker's *The Kitchen* (1961), Pinter's *The Caretaker* (1964), and Delaney's *A Taste of Honey* (1961). It was mainly the fiction and drama which dealt with lower-class life which was adapted into films; most of Snow's novels deal with middle-class life, and though three were made into plays (*The Affair,* 1961; *The New Men,* 1962; *The Masters,* 1963), none of his books has ever been

[57] Kenneth Allsop, *The Angry Decade,* p. 43.
[58] *Sun Times,* Oct. 30, 1960, p. 27, and Aug. 21, 1960, p. 24.
[59] P. N. Furbank, "The Twentieth-century Best-seller," in *The Modern Age,* edited by Boris Ford, p. 432.

adapted into a film. On the other hand, the novels of lower-class life which were made into films (the novels of Braine, Sillitoe, *et al.*) were not made into plays. Obviously, London theatergoing is still a middle-class habit, while movies are accessible to people of any class as well as to audiences outside of London. It seems to be true, or at least producers of films and plays seem to feel, that novels of lower-class life are more commercially successful as films than as plays. This may be additional proof that the novels dealing with the lower classes are enjoyed by people of the classes which they describe, even if only as films, and not in their original form.

For the novelist, the knowledge that his work would be subjected to the scrutiny of readers who were intimately acquainted with the environment he wrote about helped to assure a documentary realism in his works; moreover, these novels were without any condescension toward, or sentimentalization of, the lower classes. A good deal of care was taken to preserve the accuracy of the regional dialects of the characters, especially in the novels of Amis, Sillitoe, Barstow, and Storey and in the plays of Pinter. Most novelists wrote about the environments they themselves had lived in: Sillitoe's and Storey's fiction deals mainly with the working classes, while Amis and Wain (who both attended Oxford) write about lower-middle-class and professional people. Virtually all of the novelists of the 1950s who have been discussed so far are extremely concerned in their fiction with society and contemporary English social change. Most of these novelists are very much opposed to the smug middle-class insularity which, they feel, characterized a good deal of the British fiction written earlier in the century—the writing which F. R. Leavis would contemptuously call "Bloomsbury." The current interest in class changes has been interpreted by some communist critics, especially those writing in East European countries, as a conscious movement towards socialist realism and Marxism.[60]

---

[60] See, for example, V. Evashova, *Zeitschrift für Anglistik und Amerikanistik,* 8:409 (1960).

This may be true to some extent, especially in the case of Doris Lessing and Alan Sillitoe.[61] For most of the other novelists in this group, what resemblance there is to socialist realism is probably unconscious, and, in light of their great concern with the lower classes, a remarkable lack of political commitment, communist or other, exists in this group.

A number of critics have commented on this lack of commitment,[62] and, as will be seen later, Kingsley Amis' Fabian pamphlet *Socialism and the Intellectuals* is really an apology for his lack of interest in politics, while Angus Wilson, a Marxist in the 1930s, now considers himself only a liberal humanist.[63] To some extent this moderation is a result of the postwar division of a good part of the world into communist and noncommunist camps; actually, however, there are even deeper reasons for this political moderation. For one thing, some of the reforms which socialists had agitated for in the 1930s had been brought about by the 1950s; yet the result was hardly the socialist utopia which had been hoped for. Many of the novelists who support the British welfare state are nonetheless quite satirical about it in their fiction: there is still so much social progress to be made, and social reforms bring their own problems. Furthermore, there was a feeling of disillusionment with communism, among British intellectuals, which dated from the days of the Hitler-Stalin nonaggression pact of 1939. No socialistic ideals, it seemed, could prevail over *Realpolitik* or nationalism. In addition, after World War Two there was a feeling of suspicion towards any sort of mass social system, communistic or fascistic. The grand schemes

[61] Doris Lessing's article "The Small Personal Voice," in *Declaration*, edited by Tom Maschler, shows a strong Marxist commitment, though Lessing claims that her fiction is not socialist realism (p. 21). Sillitoe's novel *Key to the Door* also shows some sympathy for Marxism.

[62] "Uncommitted Talents," *TLS*, August 29, 1952, p. iii; Robert Conquest, "Commitment and the Writer," *International Literary Annual 1*, edited by John Wain, p. 13; and John Mander, *The Writer and Commitment, passim*.

[63] *Socialism and the Intellectuals* (London: The Fabian Society, 1957); for Wilson's views on Marxism, see his *The Wild Garden*, p. 17.

of Marx and Hitler had led to a bloody revolution, a world war, and totalitarianism. Hitler's war was totally unjustifiable, and even formerly enthusiastic communists were beginning to have difficulties, twenty-eight years later, in justifying the 1917 revolution. For these reasons, Marxists became liberals and former revolutionaries preached pacifism. A result of these feelings was the lack of commitment among the writers of the 1950s which Robert Conquest describes:

Mr. Philip Larkin wrote: "If I found a novel or poem . . . gripping, original, honest and so on I should be much too grateful to take up a quarrel with its author over motives or material. . . ." Mr. Thom Gunn wrote: "Any good writer is 'committed.' He is committed to his subject and he is committed to himself. But his subject is finally going to be one that Chaucer or Stendhal wrote about and it is not very important whether his approach is political or not. . . ." [64]

Conquest sees an exception to the general rule of noncommitment in John Osborne, but what he says is true for most of the novelists of the period: "It is conceded on all sides of the argument that English writers are not at present very concerned with politics." [65]

The political position of most of these novelists could best be described as a grudging acceptance of the welfare state, imperfect, but the least of many alternative evils. There was no attempt, in fiction or in politics, to return to any form of individualism. As Pamela Hansford Johnson wrote, Snow, Lessing, Cooper, Powell, Wilson, and Amis "repudiate any attempt to abstract man from society." [66] The individualistic hero was too reminiscent of Nietzsche and Wagner. The romantic hero and even romanticism in general were, for some of these writers,

[64] Conquest, *International Literary Annual 1*, pp. 13–14.
[65] *Ibid.*, p. 13.
[66] Pamela Hansford Johnson, *NS*, 56:172 (Aug. 9, 1958).

the precursors of Nazism. They felt that members of the late romantic movements, the symbolists, the decadents, and the experimentalists after them, were connected with Nazism and totalitarianism. As William Cooper wrote,

Incidentally it is worth pointing out that intellectuals who have reached the pitch of decadence in which they are riven by anxiety, suspicion, disgust and despair make the ripest meat for authoritarianism and then totalitarianism. Put it another way—if we have to fight against having Belsens and Dachaus, how much help are we going to get from people who have already settled for existence itself being absurdity, nausea, or nothingness? [67]

Few English novelists of the 1950s (aside from C. P. Snow, as will be seen in a later chapter) would go as far as Cooper. But to a lesser degree this feeling accompanied a distaste for romanticism on aesthetic grounds, and strengthened an impulse among these writers to reject romanticism and all of the subsequent movements derived from it. One of Kingsley Amis' poems is called "Against Romanticism," and Iris Murdoch has begun an article on aesthetics by saying, "It has for some time now been the fashion to say that we are in a morass, and to attempt to get out of the morass by attacking Romanticism; and I am going to do this too." [68] Another writer of the 1950s, Emyr Humphreys, feels that Joyce is a descendant of the English romantic writers: "Joyce belonged to that great stream of English Romantic writing which gushed forth with the publication of the *Lyrical Ballads* in 1798." The end of both the Joyce period and the romantic period, says Humphreys, came after the Second World War.[69]

Parallel to this aesthetic rejection of romanticism is a phi-

[67] William Cooper, in *International Literary Annual 2*, edited by John Wain, p. 33.
[68] "Against Romanticism," a poem in Amis' collection, *A Case of Samples*, p. 30; Iris Murdoch, *Yale Review*, 49:247 (Dec., 1959).
[69] Emyr Humphreys, *List*, 49:557 (Apr. 2, 1953).

losophical rejection of movements and ideologies associated with romanticism. Movements which stress the value of the individual over social values were on a decline in postwar England. Voluntarism, which was associated with Nietzsche, Wagner, and ultimately Hitler, was almost universally rejected. A possible exception was the voluntaristic ideology presented by Colin Wilson in *The Outsider;* but this enjoyed only a short period of popularity in 1956–1957; soon thereafter Wilson's reputation declined.

For the nonreligious intellectual of the 1950s, the main philosophical choice seemed to be between existentialism and logical positivism. As can be seen in the paragraph by William Cooper quoted above, there was some feeling against existentialism in England at this time; one of the few exceptions to this rule is Iris Murdoch. Logical positivism, on the other hand, had strong English roots. To some extent the movement itself is based on Hume's insistence on empirical evidence in determining rational meanings, as well as Bertrand Russell's logical analysis of propositions. In the 1930s and 1940s, two well-known logical positivist philosophers, Ludwig Wittgenstein and A. J. Ayer, taught at Cambridge and Oxford, respectively. Their thought, along with the less technical empiricism of G. E. Moore, influenced a number of the novelists of this period, especially those who had attended Oxford or Cambridge while, or just after, these philosophers taught there.

Some of these novelists incorporated logical positivism into their fiction thematically: In Gabriel Fielding's *In the Time of Greenbloom,* the title character has taken Wittgenstein as his prophet. Kingsley Amis, as will be shown later, was more interested in the linguistic aspects of logical positivism. Kenneth Tynan, the critic, speaking for his generation of English writers, has said:

All of us owe a great debt to semantic philosophy for having taught us to talk sense, and to distinguish always between empirical, analytic, metaphysical, attitude, and value statements. We have been trained to verify what we say, and we know that statements in the last three categories cannot be verified at all.[70]

Derek Stanford, in writing about the younger novelists and poets in 1957, felt they were influenced by Wittgenstein and Ayer, though he said that "Moore's great interest in moral problems is not reflected in recent writing." [71] Stanford says of Amis and Wain, "Both authors reflect in their way aspects of logical positivism, but in Wain's and Amis's case, it is that philosophy translated into lower-middle-class farce as opposed to the world of Oxford-study, West-end-London-drawing-room talk in which the Beaumont Street set flourished." [72]

For some novelists, the logical positivist mood made it possible to put forward progressivist ideas, or ideas which were positivistic in a Comtean sense. Emyr Humphreys, for example, opposes Joyce's antiprogressive, cyclical philosophy:

Eager to reject the facile progressivism of the nineteenth century, Joyce found a view of history which rejected the popular idea of progress, and also provided him with the framework of his two great works. This view he found in *La Scienza Nuova* of Giambattista Vico (a little-known Italian philosopher of the eighteenth century). Vico had a cyclical concept of history which did not really admit the possibility of progress.[73]

Humphreys, who wishes to reinstate the idea of progress, feels that "the novelist who limits himself to a cyclical concept of history (the vicous circle, as Joyce characteristically calls it) deprives himself of some of the main weapons in a story-teller's armory." [74]

The strongest statement for progressivism and Comtean positivism has come from C. P. Snow, whose novels and speeches re-

[70] Kenneth Tynan, "Theater and Living," in *Declaration,* edited by Tom Maschler, p. 115.
[71] Derek Stanford, *Contemporary Review,* 191:234–5 (Apr., 1957).
[72] *Ibid.,* p. 237.   [73] Emyr Humphreys, p. 558.   [74] *Ibid.*

flect his view that the chief hope for mankind lies in scientific progress. This point is emphasized in "The Moral Unneutrality of Science," a lecture given before the American Association for the Advancement of Science, and in Snow's *The Two Cultures and the Scientific Revolution.*[75]

There are two streams of thought, then, which connect the logical positivists (or positivists) with the novelists of this period. In the first place, positivism provided an alternative to voluntarism, existentialism, or other antiprogressive, individualistic philosophies to which writers like Cooper and Snow were opposed. Second, advocates of logical analysis and rationalism appealed to many of the younger writers.

Along with these philosophers, the criticism of William Empson was important for the younger novelists. His greatest influence was on those novelists who also wrote poetry, like Wain, Amis, and Larkin (though Larkin might be better described as a poet who also wrote novels). Empson's criticism stresses the close word study of poems, especially of intentional ambiguity in the words a poet uses. Empson's own poetry is logical, discursive, and filled with intentional ambiguity, but he makes little use of symbolism. Walter Allen has described a talk Empson gave on the B.B.C. dealing with poetry:

"The best poems written in English during this century," he says, "are symbolist, and they are very good. But it has gone on long enough; poets are now finding the rules an obstacle, all the more because literary theorists commonly talk as if no other kind of poetry is possible but symbolist poetry." [76]

Against symbolist poetry, says Allen, Empson "sets what he calls 'argufying in poetry,' poetry as argument, as logical discourse, which, as soon as he mentions it, you realize is exactly

[75] "The Moral Unneutrality of Science" was reprinted in *Science,* 133:256 (Jan. 27, 1961), 133:1272 (Apr. 21, 1961).
[76] Walter Allen, *NYTBR,* Sept. 22, 1963, p. 39.

the sort of poetry he himself has always mainly written." [77] Empson's poetry had a great appeal for the younger writers of the 1950s. John Wain, for example, says that when the "Auden line" of poetry was worn out, "the Empson track was the best one to repair." A number of other poets and critics agreed, and "the Empson boom that followed took me, and I think everyone, by surprise." [78] When Wain uses the word "repair" he means that English poetry in general was worn down; actually Wain has a good deal of respect for Empson's poetry, though he feels it is still not widely enough read. As Wain puts it, "many of the reputations which today occupy the poetic limelight are such as would crumble immediately if poetry such as Empson's, with its passion, logic, and formal beauty, were to become widely known." [79] Wain's own poetry has the same cool, logical, "argufying" quality as Empson's; [80] and Empson has similarly influenced a number of other poets of Wain's generation, as William Van O'Connor has noted.[81]

William Empson and F. R. Leavis are probably the two main sources of critical ideas for these novelists. Empson's main contribution was in providing a critical method which did not conflict with the ideas of the logical positivists but supplemented them: Empson himself, while a student at Cambridge, came under the influence of I. A. Richards and the Cambridge logical analysts. The critical method of Leavis, however, did not appeal so much to the Amis-Larkin-Wain group, especially since they had little personal contact with Leavis: while they were students at Oxford, Leavis taught at Cambridge. But Leavis' advocacy of neglected nineteenth-century writers like George Eliot, his quar-

[77] *Ibid.*
[78] John Wain, "Three Contemporary Poets," in his *Preliminary Essays,* p. 159.
[79] *Ibid.,* p. 180.
[80] This similarity has already been pointed out by John Holloway in the *Hudson Review,* 10:428 (Autumn, 1959).
[81] In *The New University Wits,* pp. 10–11, 34, 118.

rel with the Bloomsbury writers, and his emphasis on morality in literature appealed to many members of the 1950s group. Snow, before Leavis' famous attack in 1962, had praised Leavis in some of his book reviews.[82] Many other writers of the period, while disagreeing with Leavis' dogmatic methods, often accepted some of his conclusions.

As Derek Stanford wrote in 1957, "Literary criticism in England, at the moment, combines the 'logical positivist' temper with the technique of William Empson and the 'verbal sensibility' tests of F. R. Leavis." [83] To these influences, the younger critics added an element of their own: a colloquial, down-to-earth tone in their criticism. The criticism of Amis and Wain usually avoids technical discussions and the terminology of the "new critics." Amis and Wain appeal to the intelligent reader with common sense, rather than with abstruse arguments; their criticism, like their fiction, is seldom esoteric. Other novelists of the period who write literary criticism, Snow and Wilson for example, have a similar common-sense critical style. As has already been shown, all of these novelists, in varying degrees, prefer the Edwardian, Victorian, and eighteenth-century writers to the romantics and experimentalists.

There were, as has been mentioned, exceptions to the general trend of anti-experimentalism. Writers like William Golding, Nigel Dennis, or Lawrence Durrell showed their willingness, in varying degrees, to leave traditional fictional patterns. To some extent this can be explained by their lack of contact with London literary circles: both Dennis and Durrell spent a good part of their lives out of England, and Golding led a relatively isolated life, before he published his first novel, as a schoolteacher in Wiltshire. All three novelists are about the same age (Golding was born in 1911; Durrell and Dennis, in 1912), and so, like

[82] See, for example, *Sun Times,* Jan. 17, 1954, p. 5, and June 17, 1956, p. 4.
[83] Derek Stanford, *Contemporary Review,* 191:236 (Apr., 1957).

Durrell, old enough to have been prewar novelists or to have formed their aesthetic ideas before the war. But these novelists were, numerically if not qualitatively, in the minority. By the early 1950s the dominant critical attitude had become anti-experimental, and very soon afterwards this attitude also predominated among most English novelists.

The general reasons for this trend have already been given; but to write at length about a literary movement without giving sufficient attention to individual writers leads to the critical fallacy in which the reader comes to believe that all of the writers in a movement share the shortcomings or qualities of the group as a whole. For this reason the following chapters are devoted to the three writers—Kingsley Amis, Angus Wilson, and C. P. Snow—who best individually illustrate the reaction against experiment and the traditionalist revival.

CHAPTER TWO

Kingsley Amis

A SERIES of very tenuous connections with a number of other writers led many British journalists, around 1957, to call Kingsley Amis an "Angry Young Man." Amis was often connected with John Osborne, the playwright; the principal reason seems to have been that each had written about a disgruntled young man named Jim. It was generally ignored that Amis' Jim was amusingly, and not angrily, disgruntled; that Amis was, in 1957, thirty-five; and that if he was indeed angry about anything, Amis was showing a mature sense of self-control and keeping the matter entirely to himself.

A reaction set in: literary journalists began to deny that certain members of the "Angry Young Men" belonged in that category; other suggested that the phrase itself was useless. In this flurry it became difficult to define exactly what links connected a writer like Amis with his contemporaries.

The most obvious link is a chronological one. Amis is a member of a group of novelists whose first novels were published between 1952 and 1955; this includes Angus Wilson, Thomas Hinde, John Wain, Iris Murdoch, and William Golding. It is an interesting coincidence that all of these novelists were educated at Oxford. All achieved some measure of success with their first novel; only Angus Wilson had a literary reputation before writing his novel. All of these novelists were careful craftsmen; all showed some interest in the contemporary social and political scene, even if they expressed this interest, as did William Golding, on an allegorical level. In this way they broke with a previous generation of novelists like Ivy Compton-Burnett, L. P. Hartley, Anthony Powell, Angela Thirkell, and Elizabeth Bowen, whose novels were nostalgic about the past. They lacked the concern with style and form which characterized writers like Henry Green or William Sansom.

Amis in particular expresses his distaste for an excess of rhetoric or style in fiction. He objects to the notion which he attributes to Lord David Cecil and the members of the Bloomsbury group that "style is a self-sufficient entity to be separated at will from qualities of subject matter and capable of exhibiting a 'charm' or 'iridescence' of its own." [1] Amis feels that writers who must resort to style do so on account of a weakness, usually a poverty of ideas. [2] He connects writers who emphasized style, like Max Beerbohm or Walter Pater, and experimental novelists like Virginia Woolf. They have, he feels, common faults:

Style, a personal style, a distinguished style, usually turns out in practice to mean a high idiosyncratic noise-level in the writing, with plenty of rumble and wow from imagery, syntax, and diction: Donne, Pater, Virginia Woolf. There is, however, a good deal of nostalgia for style nowadays among people of oldster age-group or literary training; it shows in snorting accusations of gracelessness levelled against some younger novelists and merges into the hankering for "experiment" that still dies hard. [3]

Amis' usual reaction to experimental novels is impatience. In an article describing his own prejudices as a book reviewer,

[1] *Spec,* 203:845 (Nov. 25, 1960).   [2] *Ibid.*
[3] *Spec,* 203:635 (Nov. 6, 1959).

Amis divided the books he was given to review into two groups, the "unambitious" and the "ambitious." The first variety, usually written by women, were books which dealt with social problems and family life; typical faults in these books were "triviality, cowardly reliance on cliché, and indifference to any other effect but that of being agreeable." The second group included poetic and experimental novels, novels of "the grand theme, the contribution to literature, the recording of the fever-chart of our society and the definitive adumbration of our predicament as Europeans." In most of his reviews, Amis says, "it will have become noticeable that I am being much less nasty to the unambitious novelist than to the ambitious." [4] In the same article, Amis compiled a list in which he humorously hoped to ban from literature such things as "All travel books with a novel superimposed," and "All use of allegory, symbol, or other mystification capable of inducing a sober blurb-writer or reviewer to invoke the name of Kafka." [5] The joke was turned against Amis himself when an astute reviewer remembered this article while writing about Amis' *I Like It Here,* a novel superimposed on a travel book.[6]

Amis was quite serious, however, in his distaste for the experimental novel. Here, for example, is what he says in another article:

The idea about experiment being the life-blood of the English novel is one that dies hard. "Experiment," in this context, boils down pretty regularly to "obtruded oddity," whether in construction— multiple viewpoints and such—or in style; it is not felt that adventurousness in subject matter or attitude or tone really counts. Shift from one scene to the next in midsentence, cut down on verbs or definite articles, and you are putting yourself right up in the

---

[4] *Spec,* 193:643–44 (Nov. 19, 1954).   [5] *Ibid.,* p. 644.

[6] Amis' novel was written four years after his review. The "astute reviewer" was Bernard Bergonzi, in *Lon M,* 3:60 (Jan., 1964).

forefront, at any rate in the eyes of those who were reared on Joyce and Virginia Woolf and take a jaundiced view of more recent developments.[7]

Amis feels that it is old-fashioned to praise the experimental novelists; their day is over, and their style has been replaced by a more direct and conventional style—similar to the one which Amis uses himself. The intellectual of the fifties, he feels, finds Joyce and Proust "a waste of time";[8] elsewhere he complains that Lytton Strachey and Virginia Woolf are given too much attention in a book of literary criticism.[9] Amis is unhappy with a novel called *The Great Alphonse* which he considers neo-Joycean; "isn't it getting a bit late in the day," he asks, "for a seventy-page remake of the *Ulysses* nighttown scene and the question-and-answer sequence rolled into one?"[10] Amis finds that the author of this novel, Lawrence Levine, has been influenced too much by Dylan Thomas as well as by Joyce.

Amis sees the same faults in Thomas' poetry as in experimental prose: too much evidence of "style," wordiness, an absence of syntax. He likes some of Thomas' fiction, but not the poetry of "ranting, canting Thomas the Rhymer."[11] As a number of critics have mentioned, Amis' character Gareth Probert, a Welsh poet who is portrayed in *That Uncertain Feeling,* is based on Thomas. Amis treats Probert satirically, and, in presenting a play of Probert's, parodies Thomas' verse.[12]

In 1951 Thomas gave a talk at the University College of Swansea, where Amis was teaching, and the two met. Recalling this meeting, Amis said of Thomas, "Although obviously with-

[7] *Spec,* 200:565 (May 2, 1958). [8] *Spec,* 195:459 (Oct. 7, 1955).
[9] *Spec,* 197:68 (July 13, 1956). [10] *Obs,* July 17, 1960, p. 28.
[11] *Spec,* 195:227 (Aug. 12, 1955).
[12] The play is described in chapter 9 of *That Uncertain Feeling.* Two of the critics who call the play a parody of Thomas are Sam Hynes, in *Commonweal,* 64:51 (Apr. 13, 1956), and Richard Chase, in *Com,* 22:266, (Sept., 1956).

out all charlatanry, he did here and there sound or behave like a charlatan." [13] A poem of Amis' called "A Poet's Epitaph," while not addressed directly to Thomas, provides a summary of Amis' feelings about poets who are "drunk with words":

> They call you "drunk with words"; but when we drink
> And fetch it up, we sluice it down the sink.
> You should have stuck to spewing beer, not ink.[14]

It is not unusual for Amis to mention his literary prejudices in his poems. He feels that quite a number of writers have been overrated by teachers of literature, and he protests against the teachers as well as the writers. Very often one of Amis' literary judgments which appears in a review will have a counterpart in a poem.

One example is *Beowulf;* the last stanza of Amis' poem "Beowulf" contains a protest against those who admire the poem as well as against the poem itself:

> Someone has told us this man was a hero.
> Must we then reproduce his paradigms,
> Trace out his rambling regress to his forbears
> (An instance of Old English harking-back)? [15]

In an article called "Anglo-Saxon Platitudes" Amis says that most Old English poetry is boring, and includes Beowulf, which has a "poverty of human interest." [16] In this article he also says that he finds *The Faerie Queene* and *Paradise Lost* "remote and frigid."

Amis is impatient with any literary work which must be

[13] *Spec,* 199:737 (Nov. 29, 1957).
[14] The poem (quoted here in its entirety) is from Amis' collection, *A Case of Samples,* p. 53.
[15] *Ibid.,* p. 14.
[16] *Spec,* 198:445 (Apr. 5, 1957). This remark must be considered, however, in the context of what Richard Chase calls Amis' "middlebrow" attitude. See Richard Chase, "Middlebrow England: The Novels of Kingsley Amis," *Com,* 22:263 (Sept., 1956).

forced on undergraduates in order to gain acceptance; he is much more appreciative of books which are read spontaneously, without the urgings of scholars. It is only because of such urging that we bother with boring, overrated books; "most scholars," he says, "are men of foggy aesthetic sense, the ideal audience for their own propaganda." [17] The other side of this argument will be seen later, in Amis' defense of science fiction and of Ian Fleming's novels.

All of this does not mean that Amis throws out everything earlier than contemporary literature. Amis is a great admirer of eighteenth-century literature, and this is his special field as a teacher of literature.[18] The humor and tone of Amis' first novel, *Lucky Jim,* are somewhat reminiscent of the eighteenth-century picaresque novel, and one critic finds a "Shandean" quality in Amis' fiction.[19]

Amis has said that he feels a close affinity with Henry Fielding, and finds that there has been a Fielding revival in England since the Second World War.[20] Garnet Bowen, the hero of Amis' third novel, *I Like It Here,* echoes Amis' critical statements:

Bowen thought about Fielding. Perhaps it was worth dying in your forties if two hundred years later you were the only non-contemporary novelist who could be read with unaffected and wholehearted interest, the only one who never had to be apologised for or excused on the grounds of changing taste.[21]

The critical touchstone which Bowen uses is Amis' as well: seeing whether a book will be read voluntarily by a contemporary audience.

A good deal of the humor and satire in his fiction goes back

[17] *Spec,* 198:445 (Apr. 5, 1957).
[18] This is mentioned by William Van O'Connor in his study *The New University Wits,* p. 85.
[19] David Lodge, *Critical Quarterly,* 5:349–50 (Winter, 1963).
[20] On the affinity with Fielding, *Twentieth Century,* 170:50 (July, 1961); on the Fielding revival, *NYTBR,* July 7, 1957, p. 1.
[21] *I Like It Here,* p. 185.

to Fielding, as Amis himself has pointed out.[22] Another eighteenth-century writer, Samuel Richardson, influenced Amis in formulating the plot of *Take a Girl Like You*. His heroine, Jenny Bunn, is a modern Clarissa who spends her time alternately defending her virginity and providing an opportunity for the next assault. In this, and in the many debates on sexual morality which he includes in the novel, Amis resembles Richardson; this similarity has already been pointed out by Bernard Bergonzi and by David Lodge.[23]

Other novels of Amis also have an eighteenth-century flavor. The plot of *That Uncertain Feeling* is reminiscent of Richardson's *Pamela* and of Fielding's parodies of Richardson. The hero of *That Uncertain Feeling* is a librarian, John Lewis, who is urged by his wife to apply for a promotion. Lewis must compete for the position against a number of applicants; the final decision will be made by the local town council. The wife of a councilman, having taken a fancy to Lewis, offers to help him get the job. Lewis yields his virtue, but at the end of the novel, tries to salvage his integrity: though he has an affair with the lady, he refuses the promotion and takes an inferior job. Lewis, like Pamela, must choose between virtue and worldly goods, and both of them have trouble making up their minds because they are sexually attracted to the people who tempt them. In both *Pamela* and *That Uncertain Feeling* the protagonists make the conventionally moral choice in the end, though their experiences leave them somewhat tarnished.

Since Amis is much more attracted to eighteenth-century literature than to the romantic writers, it is not surprising that one of the few romantics he does like is Byron,[24] whose wit has an eighteenth-century flavor. Amis' ideas about romanticism are summed up in his poem, "Against Romanticism." Here he says

[22] *NYTBR*, July 7, 1957, p. 1.
[23] Bergonzi, p. 61; Lodge, *Critical Quarterly*, 5:346 (Winter, 1963).
[24] *O'Connor*, pp. 79–80.

(metaphorically) that the causes for the changes after the eighteenth century were based on "an ingrown taste for anarchy"; the eighteenth century is compared to a "temperate zone" and the romantic period to an anarchic forest. Amis' poem concludes with the hope that there is another "temperate zone" at the end of the forest.[25]

Amis likes the Victorians more than the romantics. In an article called "Communication and the Victorian Poet" he praises the Victorian poets for their rapport with their reading public.[26] Like the Victorian novelists, Amis is concerned with morality and social problems. Though he thinks that Fielding is the great influence on his generation of novelists, he admits that Dickens might also be an influence to a lesser degree.[27] Elsewhere he says that he feels that it is important to "value Mr. Pickwick higher than Raskolnikov." [28]

Amis has an even greater affinity with the novelists of the early twentieth century. Quite a few critics see at least a superficial similarity between Amis' Jim Dixon and the heroes of H. G. Wells.[29] Certainly, in terms of attitude towards class they are somewhat alike.

Amis' fictional style resembles that of the writers of this group, like Wells, Bennett, and Butler. Rejecting the verbal innovations and unchronological sequences of the experimentalists, Amis is closer to these pre-experimental writers. His plots, like theirs, are uncomplicated and chronological, and his style is simple and straightforward. A number of critics feel that Jim Dixon's mild rebelliousness and hatred of sham are entirely contemporary phenomena, but to some extent they are similar to Ernest Pontifex's attitudes in Butler's *The Way of all Flesh*. Though different in

[25] From "Against Romanticism," *A Case of Samples*, pp. 30–31.
[26] *Essays in Criticism*, 4:386 (Oct., 1954).
[27] *NYTBR*, July 7, 1957, p. 1.   [28] *Spec*, 196:830 (June 15, 1956).
[29] Bergonzi, p. 56; Paul West, *The Modern Novel* (London: Hutchinson University Library, 1963), p. 129; and G. S. Fraser, *The Modern Writer and His World*, p. 177.

form, Amis' novel *One Fat Englishman* resembles Butler's *Erewhon* in intention and method: both are sustained satires of a contemporary culture. Amis is familiar with Butler's fiction, and has written an afterword to an edition of *Erewhon*.[30]

Amis liked *Erewhon* for its wit and satirical qualities, and among the next generation of English novelists, Waugh and Huxley appeal to him for similar reasons. He is, however, not at all sympathetic to their ideas of class and society, as has been noted by Richard Chase: "Although Amis sometimes sounds like Huxley and Waugh, he was not, like them, born into the comfortable middle class, and his comedy is not confined, as theirs was, to a mordant satire of the intellectual life and the cultural and social predicaments of that class." [31] Amis himself has said that he feels that Huxley's "brilliance" is "marred by poverty of emotion and incident and by a sort of baroque inlay of erudition." Waugh's humor, he continues, "wonderfully sure and inventive though it is," fails because it is "streaked with cruelty" and weakened by snobbery.[32] This was written in 1957, but by 1961 Amis had mitigated his view of Waugh to some extent:

Evelyn Waugh makes fun of things I feel strongly about, but then I made the discovery that we agree about certain basic things. He makes the sort of characters I dislike behave in a way I like, but if one imagines the whole thing switched around then it becomes acceptable. I laugh at Evelyn Waugh. I don't think I could find a Nazi novel funny.[33]

Amis likes Anthony Powell's novels without necessarily approving of Powell's upper-middle-class settings—a situation similar to his qualified approval of Waugh. Though both novelists are considered popular and entertaining, Amis finds a seriousness in their humor. In England, he writes, "we have either pop-

---

[30] Samuel Butler, *Erewhon*, with an afterword by Kingsley Amis, p. 233.
[31] Chase, p. 264.   [32] *NYTBR*, July 7, 1957, p. 1.
[33] "My Kind of Comedy," *Twentieth Century*, 170:48–49 (July, 1961).

ular entertainers who when scrutinized cease to entertain, or serious novelists, like Mr. Evelyn Waugh and Mr. Anthony Powell, who entertain as well." [34] Amis has said that Powell is one of the writers with whom he feels a close affinity,[35] and he praised Powell highly in a review of two Powell novels in the *Spectator:*

We can think ourselves lucky to have a group of novels which, even more successfully than their author's early work, combine wit and sadness and farce and charm, which, without a hint of keening or gesticulation, are entirely serious. I would rather read Mr. Powell than any English novelist now writing.[36]

Though he has more praise for Powell than for Waugh, Amis' technique owes relatively little to Powell, whose humor is subtle and esoteric. Waugh's comedy, on the other hand, makes Amis laugh, and this is the effect Amis strives for in his own humorous fiction.

Christopher Isherwood, like the writers discussed above, is one whom Amis might call both serious and entertaining. Amis admires Isherwood's prewar writing which was simple and without literary pretenses: "He offered clarity, common sense, easygoing humor and detachment as distinct from the more insistently literary or prophetic qualities of some of his elders." [37] In praising Isherwood Amis again shows his distaste for anything which might be construed as a literary affectation; he likes the later, more eccentric Isherwood novels less.

Like many of his contemporaries, Amis admires Ivy Compton-Burnett. He refuses to be part of an Ivy Compton-Burnett "cult," however; William Van O'Connor points out that Amis disagrees with many of the ideas concerning Compton-Burnett put forward

[34] *Spec,* 191:595 (Nov. 20, 1953).
[35] "My Kind of Comedy," *Twentieth Century,* 170:50 (July, 1961), p. 50.
[36] *Spec,* 194:620 (May 13, 1955).
[37] *Spec,* 208:309 (Mar. 9, 1962).

by her principal admirer, Robert Liddell.[38] In spite of this, and in spite of a number of reservations about her techniques, Amis has said that Compton-Burnett is a writer he enjoys and admires; even more, she is "our most original living novelist." [39]

Generally, among writers who gained prominence before the Second World War, Amis does not care much for those who are in any way "serious." D. H. Lawrence, for example, is a "serious" writer, and Amis has only grudging admiration for his fiction and little admiration at all for his criticism.[40] This does not hold true for Amis' attitude towards the postwar writers. Amis' opinion of his contemporaries is partly colored by the attitudes of the "Movement," a group with which he is often associated.

The "Movement," like many other literary movements, is in part a creation of literary journalists. Philip Larkin, one of those closely associated with the group, has said that "the name at any rate took its origin in a piece of sheer journalism in the *Spectator*." [41] Nevertheless, the term has some usefulness. The "Movement" is a group of poets which arose after the war; many of those included in the group studied at Oxford and then taught at provincial (in some cases, foreign) universities. Those often associated with the "Movement" are Larkin, Amis, John Wain, Thom Gunn, Donald Davie, D. J. Enright, Elizabeth Jennings, John Holloway, and Robert Conquest. All of these poets appeared in two anthologies (which later were called the "Movement" anthologies),[42] and there are a number of other connections between the various members.[43]

[38] O'Connor, p. 78.   [39] *Twentieth Century*, 158:175 (Aug., 1955).
[40] See, for example, *Spec*, 196:156 (Feb. 3, 1956), for a review of Lawrence's *Selected Literary Criticism;* and O'Connor, p. 80, for a more detailed discussion of Amis' attitude toward Lawrence.
[41] Quoted by O'Connor, p. 6.
[42] The anthologies are *Poetry Now,* edited by G. S. Fraser (London: Faber and Faber, 1956), and *New Lines,* edited by Robert Conquest (London: Macmillan and Company, 1956).
[43] For a more detailed discussion of the "Movement" see the introductions to the two anthologies cited above and also O'Connor, pp. 3–15.

The principal influences on the group were William Empson and the Logical Positivists; Empson and A. J. Ayer were both at Oxford while many members of the group were students there. The influence of F. R. Leavis, who was at Cambridge, was smaller.

The poets of the movement rejected the symbolism and allusion that had characterized the poetry of Eliot and his followers. Instead, the "Movement" followed Empson both in his theories and in the poems he had written to illustrate his theories; the verse of the younger poets was terse, flat, and paradoxical. It showed a concern with language as a means of communication and a distrust of metaphysics inherited from the Logical Positivists. Most of the poetry of the "Movement" was technically precise and craftsmanlike, if rarely startling or memorable.

A number of the writers in the "Movement" were novelists as well as poets, and some of the "Movement" ideas carried into their novels. The most important novelists in the group are Amis, Larkin, and Wain; the first two were friendly at Oxford, and both got to know Wain, who arrived at Oxford after them, before they graduated.[44] Amis met Robert Conquest a few years later, and the two collaborated on a series of science-fiction anthologies.[45]

In common with other "Movement" novelists, Amis' fiction is not allusive or symbolic and often shows a careful use of words. Most "Movement" novels are, like the poetry, technically adept and unstartling. Amis is perhaps a more memorable novelist than other members of the group on account of his humor, which most of the others lack, along with any other really distinctive characteristics.

Though most of the prewar novelists whom Amis liked were humorous novelists, he does not make the same demands on his contemporaries. He has a great deal of admiration for Larkin, to

[44] O'Connor, pp. 13–14.
[45] The anthologies are called *Spectrum,* and four volumes have appeared in this series, in 1961, 1962, 1963, and 1965. Amis and Conquest have also collaborated on a novel, *The Egyptologists.*

whom he dedicated *Lucky Jim.* Though he resented being constantly linked with John Wain as an "Angry Young Man," he respects Wain as a novelist.[46] Amis also admires Iris Murdoch; along with Henry Fielding and Anthony Powell, he mentions her as one of the three novelists with whom he feels a close affinity.[47] Though she is not a poet, Iris Murdoch is often considered along with the "Movement" novelists because her age is close to theirs and because she was educated, and later taught, at Oxford.[48] Amis' admiration for Larkin as a poet is great, but Larkin stopped writing fiction after his second novel, and so Iris Murdoch is probably his favorite novelist in this group. Amis found her first novel, *Under the Net,* "thoroughly accomplished," and he has called her "a distinguished novelist of a rare kind." [49]

In dealing with the older postwar novelists, Amis has more reservations. Reviewing William Golding's *Pincher Martin* Amis wrote, "I hope Mr. Golding will forgive me if I ask him to turn his gifts of originality, of intransigence, and above all of passion, to the world where we have to live." [50] He writes with a similar mixture of praise and criticism in reviewing Angus Wilson's *Anglo-Saxon Attitudes:* the book "is clearly a failure, but it is the sort of failure which makes one impatient to read its successor." [51]

The dislike of symbolism and experiment which Amis showed in reference to English fiction remains the same when he deals with literature outside of England. In America, for example, he does not like the older writers whose fiction has a distinguishable style but prefers the younger writers whose style is more subdued. Hemingway and Faulkner, he says, are not too much

    [46] See, for example, Amis' comments on Wain in *NYTBR,* July 7, 1957, p. 1.
    [47] *Twentieth Century,* 170:50 (July, 1961).
    [48] O'Connor (p. 3) considers her as one of the members of the "Movement."
    [49] *Spec,* 192:722 (June 11, 1954).
    [50] *Spec,* 197:656 (Nov. 9, 1956).
    [51] *Spec,* 196:765 (June 1, 1956).

appreciated in England, because of, among other things, their lack of satire:

I can certainly testify that it is the more satirical of American writers who strike the readiest and fullest response in England. . . . The work of Hemingway and Faulkner—and this must not be read as implying any denigration—appears alien, strongly and essentially non-European, and I connect this with their characteristic indifference to humor and satire.[52]

Amis then goes on, in the same article, to list those American writers who have gained wide acceptance in England:

The other side of the picture emerges if the novels and stories of such writers as Louis Auchincloss, Jerome Weidman, and John Cheever are carefully studied, and if the work of Mary McCarthy and Peter de Vries is read at all. . . . Miss McCarthy in fact currently stands higher in English esteem than any other American writer of her generation.[53]

In another article, Amis again says that he admires Auchincloss and Cheever.[54]

There are few contemporary American writers who really can be said to continue the experimental tradition to the degree that Vladimir Nabokov does. Naturally, Amis does not care for him. *Lolita,* he says, is "bad as a work of art . . . and morally bad— though certainly not obscene or pornographic." [55] Nor does Amis like the less controversial *Pnin:* "That this limp, tasteless salad of Joyce, Chaplin, Mary McCarthy, and of course Nabokov (who should know better) has had delighted noises made over it by Edmund Wilson, Randall Jarrell, and Graham Greene is a mystery of dimensions." [56] It should be evident from this comment, as well as from many others, that Amis' criticism is motivated

[52] *NYTBR,* July 7, 1957, p. 1.   [53] *Ibid.,* p. 13.
[54] *Spec,* 194:199 (Feb. 18, 1955).
[55] *Spec,* 203:635 (Nov. 6, 1959).
[56] *Spec,* 199:403 (Sept. 27, 1957).

not only by a dislike for experiment and for style in fiction, but by a cultivated Philistinism as well. Even more than John Wain, who tries to keep his criticism from becoming too technical, Amis' comments usually avoid critical terminology, often contain colloquial phrases, and attempt to appeal to common sense. This is not to say that Amis' criticism is unintelligent or uninformed: the quality of his criticism is high; it is the direction in which the criticism moves which is unusual. Many of his comments seem motivated by iconoclastic impulses, a desire to clear away the rubbish of outworn traditions so that newer forms and values may be considered. Like a good deal of iconoclastic criticism, Amis' comments are at times refreshing and at times hasty and impulsive. His comments about *Beowulf,* for example, fall into the second category. *Beowulf* may well be boring to the common reader and can never have the immediate interest of a contemporary work; nonetheless, for a reader who has absorbed a certain amount of medieval culture, *Beowulf* will be rewarding. Moreover, it will be rewarding in an aesthetic, and not only a scholarly, way. Amis has decided that the price of enjoying *Beowulf* is too high a price to pay; yet to carry this argument to its conclusion would mean that almost every work which is a product of a foreign or older culture is not worth bothering with.

A problem in his criticism is that Amis often does begin to carry this argument to its conclusion. "Filthy Mozart!" says the hero of *Lucky Jim,* and a great chunk of Western Culture falls overboard with a splash. One quickly discovers, however, that Amis is more interested in the splash than anything else. He is too obviously cultured to hate culture that much; one suspects his sincerity.

An even better example of this anti-intellectual pose is given by Kenneth Allsop in *The Angry Decade:*

It is again that symptom of the Fifties, the stubborn disenchantment and insistent lowbrowism, that runs through all Amis's work. Certainly one of the freshest and sharpest critical minds now writing, he can undermine his own authority with a silly piece of bravado such as his introduction to the page review in the *Spectator* of *The Outsider*. "Here they come," he wrote, "tramp, tramp, tramp—all those characters you thought were discredited, *or had never read, or (if you are like me) had never heard of:* Barbusse, Sartre, Camus, Kierkegaard, Nietzsche, Dostoevsky, George Fox, Blake, Sri Ramakrishna, George Gurdjieff, T. E. Hulme. . . ." My italics.[57]

In analyzing the reasons for Amis' anti-intellectualism, Richard Chase points out that the English have for a long time had a successful middlebrow literature, one which has no counterpart in America. "In his breezy way," Chase concludes, "Mr. Amis may be said to carry on the creative task of the English middlebrow." [58]

In place of "highbrow" culture, Amis offers a number of "middlebrow" possibilities. An alternative to Mozart might be jazz. In literature, Amis feels that intellectuals have for too long overlooked science fiction and popular fiction like the James Bond novels of Ian Fleming; whenever intellectuals do consider jazz or science fiction it is in a patronizing manner. In the introduction to his critical study of science fiction, *New Maps of Hell,* Amis insists that his love of science fiction is genuine: "I am not that particularly irritating kind of person, the intellectual who takes a slumming holiday in order to 'place' some 'phenomenon' of 'popular culture'; one recalls with aversion those attempts to 'place' jazz by academic musicians who thought Duke Ellington's band was a kind of minstrel troupe." [59]

Jazz and science fiction, Amis says, have a good deal in common and he compares the two in *New Maps of Hell:*

The two modes themselves, indeed, show marked similarities. Both emerged as self-contained entities some time in the second or third

[57] Kenneth Allsop, *The Angry Decade,* p. 55. The statement "my italics" is Allsop's.
[58] Richard Chase, *Com,* 22:268 (Sept., 1956).
[59] *New Maps of Hell, A Survey of Science Fiction,* p. 10.

decade of the century, and both, far more precisely, underwent rapid internal change around 1940. Both have strong connections with what I might call mass culture without being, as I hope to show in the case of science fiction, mass media in themselves.[60]

If there are links between science fiction and jazz, there are also links between the James Bond novels and science fiction; Amis has included an appendix on science fiction in his study of Ian Fleming's adventure stories.[61]

Amis' promotion of these modes of mass culture is not based on a complete rejection of traditional culture. Though he likes to advertise middlebrow ideas, the advertisements themselves appear in highbrow places. *New Maps of Hell* is a reworked version of Amis' lectures given as part of the Christian Gauss Seminars in Criticism at Princeton University in 1959. Many of Amis' critical articles on jazz and science fiction were written for the *Observer*.[62] Amis' own novels are written so as to gain serious critical attention; his poetry is written for a very limited audience indeed.

Amis has assumed the role of purveyor of mass culture, or at least those segments of mass culture worth bothering with, to the intellectuals who may find mass culture beneath them. He says as much in the following statement: "The prejudice of supposedly educated people towards this type of fiction is fantastic. If you pick up a good science fiction magazine the range of interests appealed to and I.Q.'s employed is pretty amazing. It's time more people caught on. We've been telling them about it for some time now." [63] The prejudice Amis speaks of certainly

[60] *Ibid.,* pp. 16–17.   [61] *The James Bond Dossier,* p. 133.

[62] Jazz criticism may be found in *Obs,* Apr. 13, 1958; July 20, 1958; Aug. 17, 1958; and Sept. 21, 1958. An article on science fiction appears in *Obs,* Nov. 29, 1959, p. 8. Reviews of science fiction novels appear in *Obs,* Dec. 13, 1959; Mar. 20, 1960; Apr. 10, 1960; May 15, 1960; Aug. 21, 1960; Oct. 16, 1960; and Dec. 4, 1960. Articles subsequent to these are listed in the bibliography.

[63] Amis made this comment in a taped interview which was recorded at Cambridge and later used as an introduction to a science-fiction anthology he edited with Robert Conquest, *Spectrum 4,* p. 17.

exists, and a good deal of it, as he says, is probably undeserved.

Amis does not come to mass culture like Orwell, to make analyses, but because he is genuinely attracted to it. He makes this very clear in the foreword to *New Maps of Hell*.[64] He has written little science fiction, but what he did write gave him a feeling of "tremendous liberation." [65] Many of the writers whom Amis likes, like Wells and Butler, have written books which are the predecessors of today's science fiction novels. Amis makes this point often in *New Maps of Hell,* and discusses the place of works like Shakespeare's *The Tempest* and Swift's *Gulliver's Travels* in the history of science fiction.[66] "Swift, if he were writing today," Amis has said, "would have to take us out to the planets. . . ." [67] If science fiction has its roots in conventional literature, it also suggests a refreshing alternative to conventional literature:

Often, I think that part—and I mean part—of the attraction of science fiction lies in the fact that it provides a field which, while not actually repugnant to sense and decency, allows us to doff that mental and moral best behavior with which we feel we have to treat George Eliot and James and Faulkner, and frolic like badly brought-up children among the mobile jellyfishes and unstable atomic piles.[68]

Amis makes a distinction between science fiction, which "maintains a respect for fact or presumptive fact," and fantasy, which "makes a point of flouting these." [69] He does not care at all, he says, for fantasy. Though he does not go into them, it is easy enough to guess the reasons for this dislike. Amis' love of the eighteenth century is reflected in his rationalism, which appears in contemporary terms in the antimetaphysical aspects of logical positivism. Science fiction is both logical and positivistic; fantasy is neither. Amis has no patience with the irrational and metaphysical.

[64] *New Maps of Hell,* pp. 9–10. [65] *Spectrum 4,* p. 20.
[66] *New Maps of Hell,* pp. 30–31. [67] *Spectrum 4,* p. 13.
[68] *New Maps of Hell,* p. 133. [69] *Ibid.,* p. 22.

To some extent Amis' positivism is an offshoot of the Wellsian positivism which appears in many twentieth-century writers; C. P. Snow's concern with science is a second example. Another aspect of this positivism appears in Ian Fleming's novels: James Bond's love of mechanical gimmicks and beautiful machines. Fleming's feelings about machines are almost as intense as those he shows for human beings: a beautiful automobile is described as lovingly as a woman; the explosion or destruction of machines has the violence of death. As Amis points out, there is a link between science fiction and Ian Fleming's novels; [70] but positivism is also a link between Fleming and Amis himself.

Amis is, of course, much more sophisticated and subtle than Fleming in dealing with positivism. His version is almost a parody of Fleming's anthropomorphized machines:

With a shrug and a jerk of the head, Joe moved to the nearby shelter and pulled more chairs out of it, arranging them round the concrete walk by the pool. He did this in the manner of a sadistic animal trainer. If anything looked like starting to go wrong for an instant there would be an outbreak of violence. This policy, Roger had noticed, marked all Joe's dealings with the world of objects.[71]

This scene prepares the reader for a later one in which the same character breaks up his automobile. "This is my car and I can do what I like with it," he says. "Right now I want to beat it up some." [72] And so he does, first by kicking it, and when this does not achieve the result quickly enough he finishes the job with an iron bar.

Amis' own positivism rarely is expressed in the neo-Wellsian admiration for machines of Fleming or of the science fiction novelists. It occurs instead in his rationalism and in his anti-metaphysical attitude which run parallel to the ideas of the logical positivists. As David Lodge says, "Amis' epistemology, as it

[70] *The James Bond Dossier,* pp. 133–35.
[71] *One Fat Englishman,* p. 8.   [72] *Ibid.,* p. 149.

manifests itself in his novels, is profoundly anti-metaphysical, determinedly positivist, nearly solipsist." [73] A good comment on his rationalism comes from Amis himself, in a review he wrote of Colin Wilson's *The Outsider:* "I must say I find Mr. Wilson's book a disturbing addition to the prevailing anti-rational mode, feeling as I do that one is better off with too much reason than with none at all." [74] Amis' logical positivism emerges in another statement in the same review:

Admittedly, to ask oneself "How am I to live?" is to ask something real, though even here it could be argued that the continual taking of moral decisions, a fairly common activity, needs no encrustation of internal catechising to make it valid. But it would be hard to attach any meaning, except as an expression of lunacy or amnesia, to "Who am I?" [75]

Here Amis, using the method of the logical positivist, analyzes the question "Who am I?" It is a meaningless question—a logical positivist might call it a metaphysical statement—and therefore nonsense. K. W. Grandsden, in an article on contemporary fiction, also finds a tendency in Amis toward logical positivism.[76]

Because of this affinity, and because he is a poet as well as a novelist, Amis' fiction shows a great concern with words and use of language. Bernard Bergonzi finds evidence of this in a number of Amis' novels:

In particular, the extremely careful verbal finish of Amis's verse reminds one of the minute attention to words that distinguishes his fiction. John Gross has justly remarked that many of Amis's comic effects originate in his linguistic finesse rather than in the cruder comedy of situation: it is a process which culminates in the character of Julian Ormerod in *Take a Girl Like You,* a figure whose fictional reality is very largely established by his extraordinary vo-

[73] David Lodge, *Critical Quarterly,* 5:346 (Winter, 1963).
[74] *Spec,* 196:831 (June 15, 1956).   [75] *Ibid.*
[76] K. W. Grandsden, "Thoughts on Contemporary Fiction," *A Review of English Literature,* 1:7 (Apr., 1960).

58   *Kingsley Amis*

cabulary. In Wallace Stevens's phrase, he is "a man made out of words," a type that has, perhaps, a recurring appeal for Amis, for one sees something similar in the compulsive verbalizer, Harry Bannion, in *I Like It Here,* a character who, like Ormerod, clearly bears the mark of his creator's esteem.[77]

This concern with language becomes most evident in Amis' novel, *One Fat Englishman.* The hero, an Englishman on a visit to the United States, is a great collector of Americanisms as well as a dispenser of information on English pronunciation. (Here he is on the English pronunciation of St. John: "Sinjurn . . . no. Sinjun. Rhymes with Honest Injun. That's the way to remember it." [78]) Amis' hero, Roger Micheldene, encounters a number of Americans who are interested in amateur linguistics. One of them, Strode Atkins, disagrees with Micheldene in the pronunciation of a few words; in defense of his own pronunciation, Atkins claims to come from one of the "two valleys in West Virginia in which pure eighteenth-century English is spoken." [79] Irving Macher, a young novelist, supplies a blend of college slang and "hip" talk. This, for example is his synopsis of *The Merchant's Tale:* "that story by Chaucer where there's this blinkie oldster with the hot wife." [80] One character, Ernst Bang, is a professional linguist: he is a Germanic philologist, most of whose dialogue is given over to comments on the linguistic idiosyncrasies in the speech of his fellow characters. In the middle of an urgent conversation in which he is trying to determine who his wife's lover might be he interrupts himself: *"Do* and *don't* for British *have* and *haven't.* It's as if Americans regarded having as an activity whereas Englishmen regard it as a state, a condition. I connect this with the frequent American preference for *this* where British usage would favor *that.* . . ." [81] The ultimate joke comes when

[77] Bernard Bergonzi, *Lon M,* 3:51 (Jan., 1964).
[78] *One Fat Englishman,* p. 132.   [79] *Ibid.,* p. 29.
[80] *Ibid.,* pp. 35–36.   [81] *Ibid.,* p. 163. (Amis' italics.)

the philologist concludes his scholarly monologue. "Language," he says, "is before anything else the great social instrument"; he has, of course, completely forgotten about his wife. As James Ginden has correctly pointed out, in the later novels "Amis' humor has become increasingly less farcical and more verbal and imagistic." [82]

Amis' humor is mainly satirical. Martin Green even feels his comedy is "much more thoroughly moral than either Shaw's or Waugh's." [83] Amis himself certainly stresses the value of satire and feels that satirical writing is currently enjoying a revival:

We are in for a golden age of satire, in my opinion, and if this is so we will be fortunate indeed. Satire offers a social and moral contribution. A culture without satire is a culture without self-criticism and thus, ultimately, without humanity. A society such as ours, in which the forms of power are changing and multiplying, needs above all the restraining influences of savage laughter. Even if that influence at times seems negligible, the satirist's laughter is valid as a gesture—a gesture on the side of reason.[84]

Amis defines modern satire as "fiction that attacks vice and folly as manifested in the individual." [85] His own satire usually follows this definition, though one of his weaknesses as a satirist is an uncertainty in his novels as to what "vice and folly" really are, and who possesses them. In *Take a Girl Like You* Amis satirizes both Patrick's lechery and Jenny's persistence in preserving her virginity. This double satire occurs again in *One Fat Englishman*. Roger Micheldene mocks American customs, many of which are valid targets for satire. But Roger is himself such a snob, bore, and hypocrite that it soon emerges that Amis is satirizing both Americans and anti-American Englishmen. The satire in

[82] James Ginden, *Postwar British Fiction* (Berkeley: University of California Press, 1963), p. 43.

[83] Martin Green, "British Comedy and the British Sense of Humor: Shaw, Waugh, and Amis," *Texas Quarterly*, 4:226 (no. 3, 1961).

[84] *NYTBR*, July 7, 1957, p. 1.   [85] *Ibid.*

Lucky Jim is much more powerful because it is not divided in this way: Jim Dixon mocks the hypocrisy of his colleagues in the university and refuses to be subverted by it. Here the satire is more powerful because the things being satirized are more boldly defined.

There is a bit of ambiguity even in *Lucky Jim,* however, which two of the other novels, *That Uncertain Feeling* and *Take a Girl Like You,* share. In all three books, very wealthy characters appear who are not satirized, or satirized less than the other characters.[86] Bernard Bergonzi notices this in two of the novels, *Lucky Jim* and *Take a Girl Like You:* "the personal elegance of Julian Ormerod is an immediate sign that he is a splendid chap: Ormerod, like Gore-Urquhart in *Lucky Jim,* suggests that there is something not only different, but rather special, about the very rich." [87] Vernon Gruffydd-Williams is the rich man in *That Uncertain Feeling;* William Van O'Connor says of him and of his wife, "Amis' inclination is to treat his characters satirically, and almost the only ones who escape this are Jean and Vernon Gruffydd-Williams." [88]

It is difficult to reconcile this trend in Amis' novels with the left-wing views Amis holds and the "class animus" which many critics have attributed to him. To some extent the confusion can be blamed on Amis' own political ambivalence, but it is also true that his political feelings have often been misunderstood and misrepresented.

Part of the confusion came from the "Angry Young Man" appellation: John Osborne was outspokenly left-wing in his political views, and his opinions were attributed to the others in the group, including Amis. There seemed to be sufficient reason to assume

---

[86] This anomaly appears in a number of novelists of the period. Mr. Braceweight in John Wain's *Hurry on Down* and Mr. Brown in John Braine's *Room at the Top,* both very wealthy men, also share a certain amount of immunity from satire. Yet all of these writers, Amis included, tend, politically, towards the left.

[87] Bergonzi, p. 57.   [88] O'Connor, p. 93.

that Amis was far to the left; he made no secret of the fact that he voted for the Labour Party and, at about the same time that the "Angry Young Man" publicity began, he wrote a pamphlet for the Fabian Society called *Socialism and the Intellectuals*.

In reality, Amis was only very hesitantly committed to the left. His allegiance to the Labour Party was weak; Labour, to Amis, was only the lesser of two evils. Before the 1959 election he wrote, "My vote will be anti-Tory, not pro-Labour." [89] As for his pamphlet, despite the fact that it was published by the Fabian society, it had very little to say in favor of socialism. Rather, it is Amis' explanation of his lack of political commitment. Though he agrees generally with most of the policies of the Labour Party, he has refused to become active in it; indeed, he feels that the intellectual has very little to contribute to the Labour Party. "Even the intellectual who takes up some sort of political career, attains some power or influence in that field," Amis said, "stands a good chance of being wrong on any given issue, a rather better chance than the ordinary Labour party or trade union man." [90] The last paragraph of the pamphlet summarizes Amis' own feelings about politics:

It will come as no surprise if I confess in conclusion that I feel very little inclination to go and knock at the door of the local Labour party headquarters. My only reason for doing so, apart from mere vulgar curiosity, would be a sense of guilt. And this is not enough. How agreeable it must be to have a motive for being politically active.[91]

According to William Van O'Connor, *"Socialism and the Intellectuals* roused a furor in liberal journals, most of whom found it an abdication from responsibility." [92]

Amis' feeling cannot be described as a writer's simple refusal

[89] *Spec,* 203:431 (Oct. 2, 1959).
[90] *Socialism and the Intellectuals,* p. 12. [91] *Ibid.,* p. 13.
[92] O'Connor, p. 98.

to become involved in politics; on some issues he takes a stand to the right of the traditional liberal position. Education is one example: Amis feels that a general expansion of British university education is not a good idea. "More," he says in regard to university education, "will mean worse." [93] Similarly, one might expect Amis to adopt a typically liberal antipatriotism. He confesses, however, in an article called "What's Left for Patriotism?" that he is, to some degree, patriotic; this certainly is quite evident in his two novels which are set outside of England, *I Like It Here* and *One Fat Englishman*.

There seems little reason, then, to lump Amis together with writers like Osborne, who show a strong commitment to the left. Amis is seldom partisan, and on particular issues his opinion may vary across the political spectrum. It seems true, as Angus Wilson remarks, that there is a "defensive conservatism beneath the radical surface of his work." [94] It is this mixture of conservatism and liberalism which helps to account for the seemingly irreconcilable elements in Amis' novels: the anti-Americanism as well as attacks on anti-Americanism in *One Fat Englishman,* or Amis' satirical attacks against class together with his admiration for the wealthy in other novels.

This sort of ambivalence occurs elsewhere in Amis' attitudes and ideas. Since he is a poet, a popular novelist, an anthologist of science fiction, and a literary journalist, he feels more sharply than most writers do the differences between his various audiences. Naturally he will try to appear more intellectual to his poetic audiences than to the readers of his anthologies of science fiction. If this were all, he would merely be adopting a series of literary poses; but at times his honesty causes him to reverse the roles, and overcompensate. At this point he may write a slangy book review with an anti-intellectual bias or write a very scholarly article on science fiction. Certain things are quite clear:

[93] *Enc,* 15:6 (July, 1960).
[94] Angus Wilson, *Obs,* Mar. 29, 1964, p. 23.

Amis does not care for the experimental writers, a super-abundance of style, or anything that smacks of romanticism. He likes nonallusive, nonsymbolic poetry, straightforward narrative prose, science fiction, jazz, and Henry Fielding. As for terms like "Angry Young Man," or "liberal," in Amis' case they obscure the issue more than anything else.

CHAPTER THREE

Angus Wilson

A N G U S   W I L S ON is one of the most devoted exponents of traditionalism in fiction on the contemporary English scene. His
knowledge of naturalism comes from one of naturalism's sources:
his study of Zola appeared before his first novel.[1] He has written
many shorter pieces on the English Victorian novelists, especially
on Dickens, who is his favorite. Though his subject matter is
contemporary, his style is Victorian; in this way he seems similar
to writers like C. P. Snow, who can write about the development
of the atomic bomb using words and phrases which echo Trollope. Like Snow, Wilson has attacked the experimental writers,
particularly Virginia Woolf, while attempting to reestablish the
values of the great Victorian novelists. Like Snow again, he has
often paid tribute to the novels of younger traditional writers,
like Amis and Wain, who shared his aesthetic point of view.

The analogy to Snow, however, should not be drawn too far;
though Wilson has supported writers with outlooks similar to his
own, he has never been vehement in attacking contemporaries
whose novels are not traditional. Wilson's attacks on the experi-

---

[1] *Émile Zola: An Introductory Study of his Novels* (1952). *Hemlock
and After,* Wilson's first novel, was published later in 1952.

mental novelists in the early fifties were usually moderate, and at times he followed these attacks with a qualification of his original position in the later fifties. Frequently, he asserts his belief in the value of the traditional novel, leaving a path open, however, for those who do not agree with him to go their own way. A comment like this one is typical:

Most of the English novelists (perhaps all) who have arrived since the war have reflected the predominant, politically detached, social concerns of the community. This has led to a revival of traditional, nineteenth-century forms. It has told against experiments in technique and against exploration of personal sensitivity. I belong to this reaction myself and I believe that it has been a valuable one that has revitalized and restored the novel form. Orthodoxy of the social novel, however, would be as deplorable as the orthodoxy of Bloomsbury. I should be happy to see more than Mr. William Golding swimming against the tide with success.[2]

This was written in 1958; in the early part of the decade, when the traditional novel was still not too well established, Wilson's tone is a bit harsher; but by 1954, when he feels the battle has already been won, it becomes moderate. "The interior monologue, sensitivity as the artist's touchstone, are both now out of favor," he noted in the mid-fifties, and "external observation, social setting, character set firmly in narrative and scene have once again returned." [3] Rather than exulting in the victory of the traditional over the experimental novel, Wilson hoped that advocates of the anti-experimental forms would not succeed in completely suppressing the experimental novel. A few years later he began to feel that just this was happening, and in 1961 he wrote an article blaming C. P. Snow and F. R. Leavis for helping to introduce a literary climate in which all but traditional novels were unwelcome.[4] In the beginning of the article Wilson admitted that he too must assume some of the responsibility for

[2] *Lon M,* 5:44 (Apr., 1958).   [3] *Lon M,* 1:60 (Oct., 1954).
[4] *NYTBR,* July 2, 1961, p. 1.

the new literary climate, and recalled some early attacks on Virginia Woolf which he later regretted.[5]

Unlike many of the writers of the fifties, Wilson's principal *bête noire* was not Joyce, but Woolf. Wilson sometimes writes in mild disparagement of Joyce; [6] but at other times he praises Joyce while attacking Virginia Woolf:

In an essay in *The Common Reader* entitled "Modern Fiction" Mrs. Woolf, writing of the first fragments of *Ulysses* to be published, welcomes the experiment, but speaks of its failure "because of the comparative poverty of the writer's mind." Yet it is surely because of Joyce's real faith in the intellect that he was able to allow full scope to his contact with humanity and to distil from Leopold and Molly Bloom the essence of the tragedy of modern life, from which Virginia Woolf had always to protect herself.[7]

Among the other things which Wilson didn't like in Woolf's novels were "her failure to extend her sympathies outside a narrow class range," her ironic attitude toward the self-educated and socially ambitious, her failure to resolve the problem of evil in the world, and her inability to succeed in her more experimental works, like *Night and Day* and *The Years*.[8] Wilson complains about the excess of sensibility and shapelessness of *The Waves:*

And so, as more and more sensibility is poured into the insufficient, the muslin mould, one sees the juice run away into nothing, and the pulpy fruit is left to us, bright and glittering, but heavy and shapeless like the long interior monologues with which she is compelled to convey the subtle feelings of her characters.[9]

[5] *Ibid.*   [6] *List*, 43:577 (Mar. 30, 1950).
[7] *List*, 44:280 (Aug. 24, 1950).   [8] *Ibid.*, pp. 279–80.
[9] *Ibid.*, p. 280. In a letter to me, Wilson repeated that his views have changed radically since these early articles. "Above all I feel that I underestimated Virginia Woolf as a writer," he said, "and, though her influence in England is spent, she is an important figure for the modern novel generally. Also I have a high regard for the novels of Beckett."
In a second letter he wrote, "I think that my position has been greatly modified, even strongly changed by my own development as a novelist—my feeling that the traditional form was inhibiting me from

This is the attack for which Wilson felt he had to apologize eleven years later; not a particularly vehement or unfair attack. Nor was Wilson's primary contribution to the revival of traditional forms in the novel made by attacking the experimentalists and the members of the Bloomsbury school; this, as Wilson himself points out, was done by Leavis and Snow. Actually, Wilson's attacks on Bloomsbury are tempered by the respect he feels for Bloomsbury's liberal and humanistic values; [10] and though his novels contain a good deal of sharp satire, Wilson is seldom very biting in his criticism. Instead of attacking the experimentalists, Wilson's usual method is to praise the novelists of the nineteenth century; this he has done to a greater extent than any other novelist of the fifties.

The English novelists to whom Wilson is most often compared are Dickens, George Eliot, Henry James, Jane Austen, and Arnold Bennett; and these are the novelists whom Wilson praises most often in his criticism. Walter Allen, for example, says the following about Wilson's relationship to the Victorian novelists: "Wilson is the most ambitious novelist in British English who has appeared since the war; more than any other, he

---

saying all that I wanted to say. To some extent I tried to move out of it in *The Old Men at the Zoo,* and I do more so in my new novel *Laughing Mirrors*—although I shall probably always remain deeply imbued with certain qualities derived from the nineteenth-century novel.

"Then again my attitude has been much altered by some years of teaching and close discussion at the University of East Anglia. Already in my work on Zola and Dickens I have emphasized the degree to which their black (often farcical black) poetry is what makes them greater—certainly not their realism. I have found less and less to satisfy me in the realism of Trollope or Bennett. Perhaps the most striking change has been my conviction that the class sympathies I disliked in Virginia Woolf are superficial and unimportant. I have learned to estimate *Mrs. Dalloway, The Waves,* and *Between the Acts* as among the finest novels in the twentieth century, although, perhaps, by their superb achievement barring that particular poetic road to later English novelists. As for Joyce, my admiration has increased as I have come to appreciate the plays and novels of Beckett."

[10] This point has been made by Jay Halio in his study, *Angus Wilson,* p. 110.

has attempted to bring back into fiction the amplitude and plenitude of the Victorians, so much so, indeed, that at times he seems in conscious competition with one or another of them." [11] Paul West, in his history of the modern novel, echoes this, but, including the post-Victorians among Wilson's predecessors, says that Wilson is in the tradition "running from Trollope to Hugh Walpole." [12]

Wilson probably would not deny the truth of these remarks. "I had always been," he has written, "and still am, addicted to the great Victorian novelists, especially to Charles Dickens." [13] He said that he hopes to do a book of literary essays on nineteenth-century writers,[14] and he has already written a good deal of uncollected criticism on the subject. He has great admiration for the "adult" quality of Victorian fiction:

This "adult" quality of the English novel, this worldliness in the most serious sense of that word, was an essential feature of the greatest Victorian fiction. Jane Austen, Thackeray, George Eliot, Trollope, all could command the serious attention of men and women of affairs, of people who had tasted responsibility in government, law, industry, social service and so on.[15]

It is interesting to see that Wilson includes Jane Austen, who died two years before Victoria was born, in a list of Victorian authors. The inclusion is perhaps justified because Jane Austen has a good deal in common with the other writers on Wilson's list, but it also points out that Austen is one of the few pre-Victorian novelists who interests Wilson.

Other writers may have influenced him more, but it is from Jane Austen that Wilson gets his feeling for the English country-

---

[11] Walter Allen, *Tradition and Dream*, p. 271.
[12] Paul West, *The Modern Novel* I, p. 134.
[13] Angus Wilson, *The Wild Garden*, p. 22.
[14] "Angus Wilson" (interview), *Paris Review*, Number 17 (Autumn–Winter, 1957), p. 105.
[15] *TLS*, Aug. 15, 1958, Special Section, p. viii.

side: "It has not been the rather perfunctory cockney sentimentalism about the countryside of Dickens, who has otherwise influenced me so much, but the much more cherished and deeply felt attachment of Jane Austen that has shaped my responses." [16] Wilson has argued that Jane Austen's love of the country is not based on a snobbish admiration of the landed gentry, but rather on a spiritual feeling that the country provided a calm alternative to frantic city life as well as "a way of acquiring the maximum amount of time and ease in which to prepare oneself for the next world," much as Cowper did at Mrs. Unwin's and as Dr. Johnson did at Mrs. Thrale's country home.[17] It is unnecessary, here, to debate the justice of this claim; rather, it is important to note that the spiritual feeling which Wilson finds in Jane Austen's love of the country is one he shares himself. In *Hemlock and After,* Wilson's first novel, the hero manages to stand up to evil when it menaces him in the country; but when he is in the city it is much more difficult. The novel centers on the hero's efforts to establish a country home for writers; though the scheme is menaced by evil from the country, in the form of a procuress who opposes the scheme, its first real setback comes when a group of homosexuals from London shock the guests at the home's dedication. This opposition is repeated in other novels; *The Old Men at the Zoo* describes the struggles of a zoo director to provide a natural preserve for wild animals, and *Late Call* tells of the debate in a country town whose citizens are uncertain whether to build on a piece of property or to leave it in its natural state as a park.

This opposition of country and urban values, with its metaphorical connotations, is important enough to Wilson to be discussed at length in his Ewing Lectures, given at the University of California in 1960; indeed the title of these lectures in their published form, *The Wild Garden,* refers to this opposition. It

[16] Wilson, *The Wild Garden,* p. 91.
[17] Angus Wilson, *List,* 68:1080 (Dec. 27, 1962).

may seem that this opposition could much more easily be traced to the romantic and preromantic poets than to Jane Austen; but this is not really the case. The romantic poets were most interested in the effects of the countryside on the individual person, while Wilson shares with Jane Austen a desire to investigate the city-country opposition as it affects groups and communities of people. It is not only a feeling for the country, but the integration of this feeling into the social novel, which Wilson inherits from Jane Austen.

"Jane Austen," Wilson has said, "possesses and haunts me for many hours every week," and after he finishes reading Austen's books, he says he is able to "see the novels from outside as total works, as significant invented tales." But with Dickens, he says it is otherwise: "The inside feeling obstinately refuses to give place to an outside view." [18]

Dickens first "exerted a strong hold" over Wilson when he "was a somewhat sophisticated boy of eleven." His love for Dickens has not diminished since then: "The intense haunting of my imagination by scenes and characters from Dickens' novels has continued and developed into my middle age." [19] Wilson, a humanist without religious commitment, is not put off by Dickens' more religious point of view: "Dickens' dilemma —that of a simple New Testament Christian who found little evidence of the Kingdom around him—is in great degree that of the modern humanist who sees man lagging behind his achievements." [20] Wilson admired Dickens' dialogue and his ability to create a vivid scene, and regretted that F. R. Leavis did not include Dickens in his list of authors in the great tradition.[21]

Wilson has also seen a connection between Dickens' fiction and his own novels: "I never remember a time when Dickens was not at once the novelist I most admired and most enjoyed; no other writer has been so great a stimulus to my own approach

[18] *Critical Quarterly,* 2:101–2 (Summer, 1960).   [19] *Ibid.,* p. 101.
[20] *Ibid.,* p. 108.   [21] *Ibid.,* pp. 102, 104.

to writing fiction." [22] Elsewhere he has expressed amazement that a critic should call him an experimental writer: "I've deliberately tried to get back to the Dickens tradition." [23]

With these admissions, it is hardly surprising that a number of critics should have made a comparison between Wilson and Dickens; Walter Allen, G. S. Fraser, John Mander, F. R. Karl, Jay Halio, and a reviewer for the *Times Literary Supplement,* among others, have found similarities between the two novelists.[24]

There is also a strain in Wilson's writing which goes back to George Eliot, though the Dickensian element may at times eclipse it. As Wilson said in an interview with Frank Kermode, his writing contains "a great deal of . . . the George Eliot approach." But mixed in with it is "a great lump of a kind of Dickensianism, and this is what distinguishes me from that sort of George Eliot writing: that I have got this—how can I say it —this grand guignol side." [25] By "grand guignol" Wilson says he means sadistic impulses which he feels in himself, and which at times come through in his books; these elements are more prevalent in Dickens than in George Eliot.[26]

If this is true, *Hemlock and After* is extremely strong in Dickensian elements: a central scene deals with the hero's discovery of sadistic impulses within himself; many characters, like the procuress Mrs. Curry, seem to go back to Dickens; and, according to Wilson, the novel has a Dickensian ending.[27]

---

[22] *Enc,* 6:75 (Apr., 1956).
[23] *Paris Review,* No. 17 (Autumn–Winter, 1957), p. 101.
[24] Allen, *Tradition and Dream,* p. 272; Fraser, *The Modern Writer and his World,* p. 152; Mander, *The Writer and Commitment,* p. 117; Karl, *A Reader's Guide to the Contemporary English Novel,* p. 246; Halio, *Angus Wilson,* p. 105; *TLS,* Sept. 9, 1960, Special Section, p. vii.
[25] Frank Kermode, *Partisan Review,* 30:70 (Spring, 1963).
[26] *Ibid.*
[27] Walter Allen finds that Mrs. Curry reminds him of a Dickens character (*The Novel Today,* p. 30); Wilson's comment comes from the *Paris Review* interview cited above, p. 94.

Wilson's second novel, *Anglo-Saxon Attitudes,* resembles Dickens to some extent, but is even more similar to George Eliot's fiction: with its great number of characters and preoccupation with moral questions, it is very much like *Middlemarch.* Wilson feels that despite its weaknesses, "there is a quality about *Middlemarch* which permits it alone of great English novels to pass all but a very few contemporary tests." [28] If this statement is extreme, it attests to both Wilson's admiration for George Eliot and his confidence that his audience would not split hairs over extremism in this direction.

Walter Allen has written that another novel of Wilson's, *The Middle Age of Mrs. Eliot,* is principally influenced by George Eliot; [29] in addition, an obvious source is Henry James, whose minute investigations into social details Wilson follows in this novel. Perhaps as a clue to the source-hunting reader, Wilson, early in the novel, lists the books his heroine and her brother liked to read: "There was nothing for it but to seek the escape she and David had found in the past. *Emma, The Mill on the Floss, The Small House at Allington, The Portrait of a Lady* lay together with the hand luggage." [30] The heroine, Meg Eliot, finally begins to read *Daisy Miller.* In this way, Wilson pays homage to a number of those writers who influenced him in the composition of his novel, just as the heroine's name may be a tribute to George Eliot.

Wilson paid a different sort of tribute to another one of his literary predecessors, Émile Zola, by doing a critical study of him. One of the reasons Wilson may have written this book is that he felt that Zola was being neglected while so many other nineteenth-century novelists were being revived.[31] Another purpose Wilson had was to give a new definition to Zola's naturalism, a definition which could show that naturalism and imaginative

[28] *TLS,* Aug. 15, 1958, Special Section, p. viii.
[29] *Tradition and Dream,* p. 273.
[30] *The Middle Age of Mrs. Eliot,* p. 37.   [31] *Émile Zola,* p. 24.

writing were not necessarily incompatible: "The purpose of my book about Zola, who notoriously depended upon exact fact for the stimulation of his imagination, was to show that what mattered was the nature of his imagination, not the facts that stimulated it." [32] In order to show how this relationship of fact and imagination operated, Wilson's criticism takes a very biographical approach, an approach rarely encountered in modern criticism. He moves chronologically through Zola's life and shows how particular incidents influenced the development of the books Zola was writing at the time. By comparing incidents from the author's life with finished work in which these incidents figure, Wilson hopes to show the imaginative genius of the author, for whenever a biographical occurrence emerges in a piece of fiction in an altered or an embellished form, the results can only be ascribed to the novelist's imagination. Using Zola's notebook and details of his life, Wilson shows that Zola's fiction is much more imaginative than is usually assumed.

Wilson's interpretation of Zola's naturalism underplays the scientific notions Zola himself was fond of, and stresses the creative aspects of his work:

His long apprenticeship to the romantic writers and his youthful efforts to succeed as a poet bequeathed to his novels a lyricism of imagination, which his advancing technical powers eventually fused into the body of his work, so that in his greatest novels there is a complete unity of personal fantasy and social observation that forces his readers to accept his view of the world as the objectively real one.[33]

Naturalism or realism without an imaginative strain, Wilson feels, is sterile. If he had to choose between fantasy and realism in his own work, he has said, "I should consider the 'real' as the less essential." [34]

[32] *The Wild Garden*, p. 138. [33] *Émile Zola*, p. 8.
[34] *The Wild Garden*, p. 137.

Wilson's study of Zola resulted not only in a more sympathetic understanding of naturalism as Zola used it, but in an aesthetic foundation for Wilson's own novels as well. It is with some justice that Jay Halio writes, "In a sense, from Zola's notebooks Wilson's novels also were born." [35] Wilson's analysis of his own writing, *The Wild Garden,* is written using the same biographical technique employed in the study of Zola. Wilson feels, moreover, that his own writing has a similar blending of imaginative and naturalistic elements.

Wilson also learned about handling controversial sexual themes from Zola. Zola helped to show that sexual themes could be used for artistic, and not prurient reasons. Wilson points out Zola's use of promiscuity as a symbol of social corruption:

. . . his convictions of the evil foundations of society, the product of the equivocal social position of his family and his own resulting personal isolation, had found a particular symbol in sexual promiscuity. It was portrayed as the central cause of failure, corruption, decay and futility for all classes of society in his novels.[36]

Though Zola was condemned for his treatment of sexual subjects in his own time, his acceptance or rejection today usually is not on this basis.[37] In *Hemlock and After,* Wilson introduces homosexual themes with a frankness that was perhaps encouraged by Zola's eventual vindication. While Wilson never makes homosexuality itself a symbol of evil—a number of homosexuals are favorably portrayed in this and other novels—male prostitutes and panderers are used as symbols of a corrupt society. In *Hemlock and After,* published soon after the Zola study, the themes of homosexuality and evil frequently converge; this is less true in Wilson's later novels like *The Middle Age of Mrs. Eliot* and *Late Call,* where the homosexual characters are all given a rather sympathetic portrayal.

[35] *Angus Wilson*, p. 10.   [36] *Émile Zola*, p. 8.
[37] An appendix in Wilson's book on Zola studies the reception Zola has received from English and American readers; Wilson makes a similar point there (*ibid.*, p. 130).

Zola, Wilson feels, gave him ideas about the basic form of fiction, but he also learned from Proust: "Zola has certainly influenced me a great deal in the form and shape of my novels. From Proust I get the feeling about paradox and the truth of improbability—especially the latter." [38] By "improbability" Wilson means that strange events do occur in real life, and the inclusion of such events in fiction may actually lend verisimilitude to the plot. The principal sort of improbability which Wilson refers to is the juxtaposition of people who seem to have very little in common and the revelation that, contrary to expectation, strong links can be forged between them. Wilson believes that "the strangest and most unlikely lives are in fact interdependent." [39] This idea is one of Wilson's justifications for the huge number of characters in *Anglo-Saxon Attitudes:* eventually even the most minor characters are shown to have ties with the important characters.

The three writers who most greatly influenced his fiction, Wilson feels, are Proust, Zola, and Dickens.[40] The choice of these writers, along with Jane Austen, George Eliot, and Henry James, shows the depth of Wilson's roots in the traditional novel. Another group which interests Wilson is the one which flourished in England around the turn of the century, and which includes Butler, Galsworthy, and Bennett. Wilson is not so fond of this group as he is of the Victorian writers, and he objects to them because of their share in the destruction of Victorian traditions; not that he is a narrow lover of Victoriana, but he feels that the "anti-Victorian progressivism" of this group was no better than the "Victorian progressivism" it was replacing.[41]

Wilson has mixed feelings about Butler's books ("uneven, brilliant, and boring"), and he resents Butler as an anti-Victorian: "The greatest father-hater, and in his own tenacious, ob-

[38] *Paris Review,* no. 17 (Autumn–Winter, 1957), p. 98.
[39] *Ibid.,* p. 95.
[40] *Ibid.,* p. 98.
[41] *Atlantic Monthly,* 200:190 (Nov., 1957).

sessive way the most skilled demolisher of the Victorian Bastille, was Samuel Butler." [42]

Galsworthy does not fare much better. Wilson liked some of Galsworthy's fiction when he read it as a boy, but this affection did not last: "I first read *The Forsyte Saga* at the age of fifteen with great respect and pleasure. I re-read it in my late twenties with less respect but still great pleasure. I must confess that I re-read it last week with no respect and precious little pleasure." [43] Wilson finds a lack of conflict in Galsworthy's fiction, and an inability of the author to keep his material under control; this second flaw "reveals alike his lack of values and the cold heart beneath his sentimentalism." [44]

Arnold Bennett, on the other hand, interests Wilson both as a novelist and as the victim of Virginia Woolf's famous attack, "Mr. Bennett and Mrs. Brown." Bennett, Wilson feels, is beginning to emerge from the eclipse he suffered after Woolf's attack, and he welcomes the revival; it is the duty of a younger generation, says Wilson, to reinstate the writers their fathers rejected.[45] Virginia Woolf's protest that Bennett's characters, based mainly on external observation, were not real seems weak to Wilson; Mrs. Woolf's own characters, he says, are no more convincing than Bennett's: "It is not easy now to feel that Mrs. Dalloway is any more 'real' than Constance or Sophia Baines. They are only attempts at conviction touching upon different emotions in the readers, and very convincing all three are if the appropriate emotions are ready to respond." [46] Wilson praises Bennett for investigating provincial English society, but he feels that though Bennett's novels have marks of greatness, they never become really great.[47]

Wilson's feelings about the generation of novelists which came after Bennett are similar to those he had about Galsworthy, whom he liked in his youth and then grew impatient with. Writers like Huxley and Waugh impressed the young Angus

[42] *Ibid.*, p. 192   [43] *NS,* 51:187 (Mar. 3, 1956).   [44] *Ibid.*
[45] *Lon M,* 1:59 (Oct., 1954).   [46] *Ibid.*, p. 60.   [47] *Ibid.*, p. 61.

Wilson with their smartness, but later seemed a little empty.

Huxley, says Wilson, was the god of his adolescence, the center of his intellectual pretensions; Wilson admired him because he could be satirical about an intellectual world to which Wilson still aspired. By the time Wilson came to Oxford, however, his admiration for Huxley had ended. Left-wing ideas had made Wilson hostile to Huxley's "anti-democratic views"; some sexual experiences removed the glamor from Huxley's "outspokenness"; and he had found enough culture for himself no longer to be dazzled by Huxley's "proliferation of 'culture names.' " [48]

Nevertheless, Huxley had made an impression. When Wilson wrote his first short story, "Raspberry Jam," "I added to what came from the heat of my own fancy a character designed to give an element of wit and worldliness. I was proud of my creation. It was only afterwards that I realized that the addition was pure pastiche of Mr. Scogan or Mr. Cardan." [49] Wilson says he has heard John Wain make an admission similar to his own about Huxley's early influence, and he also detects strains of Huxley in the work of Kingsley Amis.[50] Consciously, Wilson feels, he is in reaction against Huxley, but he admits that what one reads in his adolescence can have a deep unconscious effect.[51]

As a young man, Wilson also liked Evelyn Waugh, but his admiration for Waugh did not diminish like that he had had for Aldous Huxley; in 1960 Wilson said he ranked Waugh "above all contemporary novelists." [52] A satirist himself, Wilson likes Waugh's satire except when it becomes too biting. As might be expected, however, he does not care at all for Waugh's reactionary political views.

[48] *Enc,* 5:73 (July, 1955).   [49] *Lon M,* 2:54 (Aug., 1955).
[50] *Enc,* 5:74 (July, 1955).
[51] Interview in *Paris Review,* no. 17 (Autumn–Winter, 1957), pp. 97–98.
[52] *Enc,* 14:79 (Jan., 1960).

Ivy Compton-Burnett is a reactionary of a different sort. Her works show that she admires the Victorian novelists perhaps more than any other English writer today, and she is one of the few who use Victorian settings as well as style. Though her novels "are deeply entrenched in the great tradition of the English novel," Wilson feels she is a great experimentalist: "She has rigorously adapted form and language to accord with her aims, which is surely the only serious experiment to be considered." [53] He finds her one of the outstanding writers on the contemporary scene, "one of our really considerable novelists." [54]

Though he likes Ivy Compton-Burnett's fiction, Wilson is impatient with younger writers who refuse to use contemporary settings. The post-Second World War novels of Elizabeth Bowen, Nancy Mitford, and Angela Thirkell, he felt, were weakened by their nostalgic themes. Graham Greene and Jocelyn Brooke wrote novels filled with "the guilt that writers felt about society in the 1930's." The best of these writers, Elizabeth Bowen, wrote well; but her group was still "a school of death, nostalgic, wistful, even at its most loving only expressing the sort of courage with which the aristocrats faced the inevitable guillotine." [55]

Wilson parodied these nostalgic writers in a short book called *For Whom the Cloche Tolls: A Scrap-Book of the Twenties,* published in 1953; soon afterwards he was happy to note the rise of a new group of novelists who no longer depended on childhood memories for the subject matter of their novels: "This claim, at least, may be made for the post-war English novel in the hands of Mr. Powell, Mrs. Lessing, Mr. Cooper or C. P. Snow, that the novel has now a firm structure of contemporary society, an ethic set solidly in contemporary England." [56] Wilson's own novels resemble the books written by the members of

[53] *Lon M,* 2:64 (July, 1955).   [54] *Obs,* Sept. 17, 1961, p. 30.
[55] *American Mercury,* 73:48–49 (Dec., 1951).
[56] *TLS,* Aug. 15, 1958, p. viii.

this group, since they combine a traditional style with contemporary settings. He does not, however, praise them without qualifications.

C. P. Snow, for example, has written a number of articles in which he expressed his admiration for Wilson's fiction,[57] but Wilson's praise of Snow has been more cautious: "I share his belief in modern English society and his preferences for plots and stories, but I am very unhappy with the suggestion that this is the only way in which novels can be written." [58] Elsewhere Wilson says, "I don't believe, as Snow does . . . in the didactic novel." [59]

William Cooper, another one of the novelists whom Wilson praised for writing novels with contemporary themes,[60] is in Wilson's opinion "a brilliant and accomplished novelist." [61] Cooper, who was urged to begin writing by C. P. Snow, is praised by Wilson in an early review for a "well-written and well-planned realistic novel"; in a later review, however, he found "a certain slickness, a touch of 'smart alecky' which destroyed the real vein of personal poetry" which was latent in Cooper's novels.[62]

In general, Wilson is not displeased with many of his younger contemporaries. He is happy that "the great middle-class strangle-hold upon the English play" has been broken by writers like Arnold Wesker and Shelagh Delaney.[63] He likes Amis and Wain, and sometimes singles out one of their books, like Wain's

---

[57] Examples occur in Snow's article "The English Realistic Novel, 1957," *Moderna Sprak* [Stockholm], 51:265 (1957); and in Snow's review of Wilson's *Such Darling Dodos* in *Sun Times,* July 23, 1950, p. 3.

[58] *NYTBR,* July 2, 1961, p. 12.

[59] Frank Kermode, *Partisan Review,* 30:69 (Spring, 1963).

[60] A later novel of Cooper's, however, *Disquiet and Peace,* is set around 1906.

[61] *Obs,* February 8, 1959, p. 19.

[62] *List,* 43:577 (Mar. 30, 1950); *Enc,* 7:83 (Aug., 1956).

[63] *Partisan Review,* 26:632 (Fall, 1959).

autobiography, *Sprightly Running,* for special praise; he finds that he has a good deal in common with Wain.[64]

Wilson's love of the Victorian writers, then, can be seen both in his praise of these writers themselves and in his taste for neo-Victorians like Ivy Compton-Burnett. Most of the novelists whom he likes have the "adult quality" and the "moral seriousness" often associated with Victorian fiction. All of Wilson's own fiction, with the exception of *For Whom the Cloche Tolls,* has this moral, adult, serious quality. Most of Wilson's short stories center on either an important moral decision or a moral revelation: someone's true colors are revealed. Both of these themes can be illustrated with "A Visit in Bad Taste," the short story of Wilson's which is his favorite.[65] The story begins with a couple, whose views are established as "liberal," facing an important decision: shall the wife's brother, who has just emerged from prison, be permitted to stay with them? When the couple decides that he must go, the extent of their liberalism is delineated.

Wilson's novels usually have an important moral issue at their centers, with lesser moral problems occurring in the subplots. As he has said himself, "my own novels are essentially traditional in form and my preoccupation is strongly—too strongly for many critics—a social and moral one." [66]

Wilson's emphasis on tradition and morality, as well as his taste for novelists like George Eliot and Henry James, might make it seem as though he were a follower of F. R. Leavis. As has already been mentioned, this is not the case. While Wilson does agree with many of Leavis's critical judgments and uses a number of his critical terms, he is repelled by Leavis's dogmatism and severity:

[64] *Obs,* Sept. 16, 1962, p. 22.
[65] This story is collected in *The Wrong Set;* Wilson remarks in *The Wild Garden,* p. 42, that it is his favorite.
[66] *NYTBR,* July 2, 1961, p. 1.

No one in England, except perhaps T. S. Eliot, has done more to rescue literary criticism from the vapors and anemia of bellelettrism and dilettantism than Leavis. His fight has been long and uphill, but it must be squarely said that, in the course of fighting, his natural vigor, bluntness and tenacity have hardened too often into aggression and moral violence.[67]

Wilson objects to Leavis' strong style, which "has too often become an excuse for proffering personal sensibilities as ethical absolutes." [68] He is afraid that the effect of Leavis' criticism on his younger followers is to make them too hasty in their literary judgments:

I have found among the youth attending lectures today too many who, in their pleased certainty with rejecting this or that famous author for not being in "the great tradition," have made literature into no more than a pin-pricking critical exercise. Primarily a moral educationalist, Leavis has thought to exalt English literature by making it the touchstone of moral values for the young. Great literature is much more than this, and the truth needs to be reasserted.[69]

Those followers of Leavis who do look at a book outside of the context of "the great tradition" frequently judge it on the basis of whether it adds to the health of society. Wilson, who was trained as a historian, feels that this attitude is based on a false historical premise: that contemporary society is less healthy than societies which preceded it. This is not so, says Wilson, "society is not more sick now than it has ever been, only sick in a different way." [70]

To Wilson, Leavis' system of criticism has its logical end in an orthodox and strictly limited formula for writing only "healthy" novels which will limit the genuine artist in the same way that socialist realism does; the critic will end by destroying that which it is his job to preserve:

[67] *Ibid.*   [68] *Ibid.*   [69] *Ibid.*, p. 12.   [70] *Ibid.*

If "literary opinion" or influential critics or even the educated reader impose upon the novelist the measure of some social myth, some dogmatic view of moral health, then eventually we may be sure that this supposedly life-enhancing myth will destroy the true life in the work of art. And the professional life-loving critics will then have satisfactorily rendered useless the only real gift that the novelist can make to the world.[71]

This is a just and courageous charge. The English novel of the nineteen fifties has been, if anything, too "healthy": too careful, too timid, too unwilling to step outside of neatly delineated boundaries. The system designed to frustrate a potential Marquis de Sade has helped to eliminate the possibility of a Gide or a Faulkner; it may be one of the reasons why Samuel Beckett makes his home in France.

Other writers, some as traditional as Wilson, share his views. John Wain, for example, though he spares Leavis himself, has a complaint similar to Wilson's in an article dealing with some of the contributors to *Scrutiny*.[72] Wain says that once a judgment is established in *Scrutiny* it becomes a "fact"; "if you doubt that 'fact,' you merely identify yourself with the corrupt modern culture that *Scrutiny* exists to fight."

Wilson agrees with Leavis, up to a point, about the descriptive aspects of morality in literature: a concern with morality can be useful to the novelist. But he eliminates from this formula the prescriptive elements which may imply that the best novels all have a moral theme, that novels still to be written should have moral themes, or that any particular moral approach, "healthy" or otherwise, is a superior one.

Moral ambiguity is, of course, an important tool of the serious novelist. Characters who can easily be typed, whose personalities are entirely good or evil, do not seem real—to use E. M. Forster's term, are flat. Where a prescriptive moral formula

---

[71] *Ibid.*   [72] Wain, *Obs,* Oct. 27, 1963, p. 25.

which advocates "health" is employed, the opportunities for round characters are diminished.

In his own writing, Wilson does not use only round characters. A number of his minor characters, most notably Mrs. Curry in *Hemlock and After,* are entirely evil and at the same time quite Dickensian. As Wilson said about Mrs. Curry in an interview, she is "a kind of embodiment of evil." [73] On the other hand, Wilson's other characters are almost never entirely good or moral; his heroes all have flaws.

Wilson explains that there are two types of evil characters in his novels; the first kind are the flat characters of Mrs. Curry's type, people who are committed to evil; the second kind are people who are not aware of the moral implications of their actions, who "accept a *pattern* of behavior and morality instead of self-awareness." [74] Ingeborg, Gerald Middleton's wife in *Anglo-Saxon Attitudes,* is an example of this type. The heroes in Wilson's novels are always morally self-aware; if they do evil, they know it while they are doing it or soon thereafter.

This presentation of evil on three moral planes—intrinsic evil, unconscious evil, and conscious, reluctant evil—is quite effective: the serpent, Eve, and Adam are presented in similar terms. Instead of using morality within a theological framework, however, Wilson has used liberalism and humanism as a basis for the moral code of his heroes.

Wilson is far too intelligent a writer to present the liberal humanism of his major characters in simple or dogmatic terms; indeed, this would be a capitulation to his sin of doing evil through lack of moral self-awareness. His characters prefer the opposite end of the spectrum: a self-awareness so analytical and introspective that it ends in paralysis of the will and inaction. Attempting to live decently and morally, intellectually un-

---

[73] Interview in *Paris Review,* no. 17 (Autumn–Winter, 1957), p. 99.
[74] *Ibid.* The italics are Wilson's.

able to accept religious ethics, Wilson's heroes govern their lives with a set of impeccable humanistic precepts. The inevitable conflicts occur. The most carefully considered moral actions give pain to others, and Wilson's protagonists withdraw to a world of moral inactivity. Bernard Sands's solution in *Hemlock and After* is the most extreme withdrawal, death; David, Meg Eliot's brother in *The Middle Age of Mrs. Eliot,* leads a life of monastic quietism. Only Gerald Middleton manages to struggle back into the world of moral decisions; but most of his life has already been wasted in years of inaction and torpor.

When a typical fictional hero achieves a spiritual rebirth he often attains this rebirth by means of faith in religious or other doctrines. The religious hero can understand his situation even when confronted with moral irrationality when he realizes that God's ways need not be comprehensible to man. This solution is not possible for the humanistic hero. His creed is man-made and rational; when it becomes irrational it fails. This is the key to the pessimistic tone which pervades so many of Wilson's novels: the difficult process of moral self-education leads the intelligent humanist to the gloomy truth that there is no ultimate salvation in humanistic terms. Wilson refuses to sentimentalize, and rarely does he permit even a partial solution to this problem; the usual alternatives are withdrawal, a breakdown, or death.

Wilson's pessimism at times makes him treat his characters with hatred and contempt. He finds many of his less sympathetic characters physically repulsive and their relationships disgusting; he mocks their affectations, their clothing, even their interior decoration. As C. B. Cox has pointed out in his study of Wilson's humanism,[75] this disgust hardly seems consistent in one who calls himself a humanist.[76] Cox argues that Wilson's disgust

[75] C. B. Cox, "Angus Wilson: Studies in Depression," in *The Free Spirit.*
[76] Wilson has often maintained his own position as a humanist. In *Critical Quarterly,* 2:106 (Summer, 1960), for example, he said he was "a humanist without transcendental beliefs."

for human beings "is not only hardly suitable for a humanist, but also seriously affects Wilson's values." [77] The only answer to Cox's charge is that Wilson is not a humanist on account of his idealistic admiration for humanity; he is a somewhat embittered humanist who has chosen humanism because he can find nothing better. As with many satirists, his disgust grows out of the fragments of shattered optimism; his thought of what man could be leads to his disgust with man now.

The satirist who springs to mind for a comparison is Swift; and like Swift, Wilson at times makes the reader feel that the disgusting is cultivated for its own sake. Even more depressing is Wilson's idea of evil. In the three categories of evil listed earlier, only the highest one, the one of the morally self-aware man, permits action which may negate evil. Yet as has been pointed out, the usual price of self-awareness is moral paralysis, which again destroys the possibility of the good moral action. Here Wilson's Calvinist background emerges in his portrayal of a world full of sinners, with only a handful of the elect extant; and these few elect are so filled with self-doubt that they cannot recognize each other or, for that matter, themselves.

This sort of depressing picture diminishes the moral force as well as the verisimilitude of Wilson's fictional world. The bitterest hell is the one with a memory of paradise; the most tragic fall is from high estate where the chance for salvation is narrowly missed. Wilson's hell is depressing more than anything else; the absence of salvation or the possibility of salvation produces resignation and not tragedy.

The obvious answer to this charge is that the world, to the clear-sighted man, does appear this way; we live in an unheroic age, where the banal has undermined all tragedy. But this answer (the cliché of our times, and one which Wilson would probably hesitate to use) is ultimately inadequate. It is unhistori-

[77] Cox, p. 117.

cal and rejects everyday experiences of moral actions and happiness. Wilson's gloom is essentially personal and not based on a post-atom bomb *Weltanschauung.* The one novel in which a cataclysmic event is presented, *The Old Men at the Zoo,* proves this: the Third World War is presented in an impersonal manner; there is little fear that humanity, or even a portion of humanity, will be wiped out; the war lasts a short time and life quickly becomes normal afterwards. More important, the war as seen through the eyes of Simon Carter, Wilson's narrator, is more a series of personal inconveniences than anything else.[78] The greatest of these inconveniences is hunger, which finally leads to the moral center of the book: Simon, a naturalist so engrossed in the study of badgers that he grew to prefer badger-watching to social contacts with other people, is driven by hunger to trap the badgers and eat their flesh. The war, of course, is the indirect cause of what for Simon is the ultimate act of debasement and evil; nonetheless Simon's sin is personal, and comes after he has made a moral choice.

A different nonpersonal reason can be found for Wilson's pessimism. As Wilson has said, "like most people of my generation in their forties, I have been influenced at a deep level by the ideas of Freud and Marx." [79] Like so many others in the thirties, Wilson assumed that Marx's thought would provide a panacea for social injustices, while Freud's ideas would bring an eventual end to inner disturbances. As Wilson says in *The Wild Garden,* this gave him a cosy sense of optimism that was finally destroyed by the impending Second World War.[80] With this disillusionment came a lack of trust for any ideology which provided the foundation for Wilson's pessimism. He is sharp, for example, with some of the newer playwrights like Kops, Wesker, and Doris Lessing, whose plays contain a Marxist message. He is

[78] Cox (p. 156), makes a similar point.
[79] *Critical Quarterly,* 2:103 (Summer, 1960).
[80] *The Wild Garden,* p. 17.

afraid that their messages may be as unsophisticated as the "naively Marxist" plays of the prewar years.[81]

Wilson is less disturbed by naive Marxism in the younger generation than he is by a growing wave of conservatism. A number of his plots, and many of his subplots, deal with liberal-conservative conflicts; very often these conflicts are between parents and children, or between people of different generations. Characters with similar points of view appear throughout Wilson's fiction, and it will be useful to summarize these catagories before going any further.

Wilson's liberals may be divided into three groups. The first consists of lower-middle-class people who were politically active in the thirties, supported hunger marches and peace strikes, and may even have been Marxists; now, in middle age, they hold some of their old beliefs but are not too active politically. The Harkers, in "Such Darling Dodos," are an example of this group. A closely related group contains upper-middle-class liberals; most of Wilson's heroes, like Bernard Sands, are in this category. They are often fairly wealthy and always very cultured; they frequently abstain from political activities and demonstrations (Sands, for example, will not speak at anti-nuclear warfare rallies) because their liberalism is complex enough to need a more sophisticated outlet; participation in mass demonstrations might misrepresent certain aspects of their liberalism. A third and less important group is the new left, usually made up of students whose attitudes are a revival of the left-wing opinion of the thirties.

The conservatives also fall into three categories. First are the old conservatives: they opposed the liberals of the thirties and are delighted to see that young people, for the first time since the war, are finding it fashionable to be conservative again. Tony, an old conservative in "Such Darling Dodos," happily

[81] *Partisan Review*, 26:632–33 (Fall, 1959).

discovers that Michael and Harriet Eccleston, a young couple, and she the daughter of a liberal, are not liberals at all. They are typical of Wilson's young conservatives, who are snobbish, hire French-speaking servants, send their children to public schools, and revive the Anglo-Catholicism abandoned by their fathers. A third, and again not too important, group is made up of young neofascists. They are an unkempt bunch who spout an English version of Nietzschean voluntarism; their major appearance is as a group of Colin Wilson types in "A Bit Off the Map."

Angus Wilson's short stories and novels describe conflicts between various members of these groups; almost every possible combination is presented. In *Late Call,* for example, Harold, a lower-middle-class liberal secondary school headmaster, finds it difficult to relate to his children. This is not very surprising: his son Mark participates in ban-the-bomb demonstrations and accuses his father of having sold out in his liberal views, while his daughter Judy is a snob who wants to be sent to private school and tries to cultivate friends from socially prominent families. There are many examples of conservative children who are a disappointment to their liberal parents; Gerald Middleton and Bernard Sands both have this problem. Occasionally the opposite situation is presented: Norman, a young fellow traveler, shocks a conservative relative with his views; she immediately wires his parents that he has taken up with "the wrong set," which provides the title for this story.

As Wilson explains, many of the political types he introduces come from his own experience. His own family life gave him insights into the old conservatives, "the various older generations of a section of the British middle class actively in decline." [82] As he reveals in *The Wild Garden,* the "old sporting gentleman" stereotype who appears very often in Wilson's fiction is based on his father; he drinks, gambles, cannot repay money he bor-

[82] *The Wild Garden,* p. 44.

rows, tells tall stories of his experiences in the First World War, and tries to win approval with a "gentleman of the old school" manner.[83] He is saved from total ruin only by a patient and long-suffering wife. Harold's father in *Late Call* is an example of this type; other examples appear in "Rex Imperator," "What Do Hippos Eat?", and a number of other stories. Other conservative types are drawn from the various people Wilson met in his youth, when his family lived in middle-class hotels in Kensington.

These people provided Wilson with material for his first stories, the "drunk majors" and members of the "philistine bourgeoisie," for whom Wilson had "emotional sympathy, but no intellectual regard." [84] The next group he wrote about was the next group he encountered in his own life, "the cultured upper middle class supporters of Left Wing causes, the well-to-do-Socialists of the 'thirties." [85] Wilson first met these people in his adolescence:

When my mother died in my fifteenth year I sought and in some degree found substitutes for her affections among the mothers of my friends. These families, unconnected but not wholly dissimilar, differed from my own by being more cultivated, richer, more elegant and, above all, more liberal politically. It was they who, altered indeed out of all recognition, became the center of my attack upon the deficiencies of a liberal socialism to which I still give my own moral and cultural allegiance. This attack reflects my slow and gradual realization of the many evasions, the failures of imagination and the coldnesses of heart, that marred the ideals of the families of my adoption.[86]

Jay Halio identifies one of these families as the Pickering Walkers, to whom Wilson dedicated *Such Darling Dodos;* this

---

[83] Jay Halio calls this stereotype "the Raffish Old Sport" in his discussion of stereotyped figures in Wilson's fiction (*Angus Wilson,* p. 13). Wilson describes his father in *The Wild Garden,* pp. 13–14.

[84] *The Wild Garden,* p. 45.   [85] *Ibid.*   [86] *Ibid.,* pp. 46–47.

family, and similar families, Halio says, provided Wilson with the models for Bernard and Ella Sands and the Padleys, a liberal couple in Wilson's play *The Mulberry Bush.*[87] The eventual failure of these families to live up to their liberal ideals is one of the most recurring problems encountered in Wilson's fiction.

Many other themes, like those already mentioned, are taken from life by Wilson. His method, like Zola's, is to take incidents, characters, themes, and background details from life and blend them into his fiction. This, of course, could be said of any novelist; but the difference with Wilson is a matter of degree: in his fiction not only is a great amount taken from life, but many of those details which are important to Wilson recur from novel to novel. In his best-known novel, *Anglo-Saxon Attitudes,* for example, the Middleton family is related to the liberal families described earlier. Gerald Middleton, a historian and the head of this family, has betrayed one of the basic tenets of his profession: he has failed to investigate an important archeological discovery, which he suspects may be a fraud, because of his closeness to those who would be damaged by the exposure of the fraud. Middleton himself had two originals in real life, according to Wilson.[88] Middleton's field is medieval history, which is what Wilson studied at Oxford; his work at the British Museum brought him into contact with many scholars, some of whom he used as a basis for characters in the novel. Cuspatt, a minor character, is a museum expert; another minor character, a charlady, is based on a woman who kept the cloakroom in the British Museum.[89] According to Jay Halio, "a remark overheard in the Museum canteen about the dating of the Sutton Hoo burial ship suggested the theme of professional responsibility in *Anglo-Saxon Attitudes*"; [90] the archeological discovery in the novel has a good deal in common with the Sutton Hoo burial ship, in terms both of the nature of the discovery and of the events sur-

---

[87] *Angus Wilson*, p. 4. [88] *The Wild Garden*, p. 30.
[89] Jay Halio, *Angus Wilson*, p. 9. [90] *Ibid.*

rounding the discovery. The inspiration for the fraud may also owe something to the discovery made around 1953 by Dr. J. S. Weiner and an Oxford colleague that the Piltdown Man was a hoax. Weiner's discovery came after Dr. Kenneth Oakley of the British Museum applied a chemical dating test to the remains of the Piltdown Man; Oakley also helped to unmask the fraud. Here again Wilson's work at the British Museum may have provided him with fictional material.

Many other themes, more important elsewhere in Wilson's fiction, appear briefly in *Anglo-Saxon Attitudes*. The "old sporting gentleman" mentioned earlier makes a perfunctory appearance and borrows ten pounds from his landlord.[91] The theme of cruelty to animals, central in *The Old Men at the Zoo,* is introduced when Larrie sadistically kills a baby owl. A dotty spinster, Rose Lorimer, has prototypes in the stories "Raspberry Jam," "A Little Companion," and elsewhere. Homosexual characters often appear in Wilson's novels as the brother or the son of a central character; this is true in *Late Call, The Middle Age of Mrs. Eliot,* and *Anglo-Saxon Attitudes*. Gerald Middleton, at the end of the novel, decides to fly to Mexico; air travel as a means of escape also occurs at the end of two other novels.[92] *Anglo-Saxon Attitudes* opens with a description of a depressing Christmas party; two stories, "Christmas Day in the Workhouse" and "A Flat Country Christmas," have this theme.

Similar lists can easily be made for Wilson's other novels. Analysis of these novels would show even more elements taken from life, since, according to Wilson, *Anglo-Saxon Attitudes* is based less on "experience" and more on "reading and knowledge" than any of his other fiction.[93]

In addition to Wilson's admiration for Zola's method, there

---

[91] *Anglo-Saxon Attitudes,* p. 55.
[92] The others novels are *Hemlock and After* and *The Middle Age of Mrs. Eliot.* Wilson makes this point himself in *The Wild Garden,* p. 94.
[93] *The Wild Garden,* p. 131.

is another important reason why so much of his own experience is incorporated into Wilson's fiction. Wilson began writing, he says, after a nervous breakdown; "this defeat finally forced me to rearrange my experience of life in imaginative terms, to try to make sense by making fictional patterns." [94] This early writing, suggested by an analyst as a form of psychotherapy (he also suggested collecting wild flowers), did not bring any worthwhile results. "It was only two years later, when the war was well over and my illness seemed at an end, that I sat down, as they say in faith-healing testimonies, and 'just wrote a story one Sunday.' " [95]

Nevertheless, some of Wilson's statements about his writing do make it seem as though putting his experiences on paper contributes to some sort of a catharsis, like this comment in *The Wild Garden:*

With my last volume of short stories, *A Bit Off the Map,* and the novels that have followed it, the need to regroup the events of my childhood and adolescence seems to have been worked out; the themes of my nervous crisis—the unthroning of innocence, man's two hells—also reached their climax in *Mrs. Eliot* and have given way to other themes less apparently connected with my life, or at present still too close to me to yield to my analysis.[96]

One factor, then, in Wilson's introduction of personal themes is to have these themes "worked out"; but this is not to belittle Wilson's artistry in blending and arranging his personal experiences, nor his craftsmanship in presenting a finished work.

Wilson's interest in psychoanalysis, the self-analytic nature of his fictional methods, and the knowledge of Freud which he acquired in the thirties might lead one to expect a Freudian bias in his fiction. Actually, this is only partially true. A good deal of Wilson's writing is concerned with understanding the psychological makeup of his characters. John Mander finds that most of Wilson's short stories can be divided into three groups: "the

[94] *Ibid.,* p. 20.   [95] *Ibid.,* pp. 20–21.   [96] *Ibid.,* pp. 47–48.

'psychological' stories, the 'social' stories, and those in which the psychological and social analysis are successfully combined." [97] In this survey, he finds that the psychological stories predominate. A number of the psychological stories, he says, "fit together a little *too* snugly"; they remind him of "the analyst's casebook." The human existence Wilson portrays, says Mander, is reduced to a causal pattern. Furthermore, psychology is not really Wilson's aim in these stories: "This is not to deny that few writers have digested Freud so thoroughly, and made such use of his insights, as Mr. Angus Wilson. But psychological analysis of this sort does not appear to be Mr. Wilson's main intention in these stories. It is society itself he is concerned to analyze." [98] Mander concludes that these two aims conflict, that Wilson's stories are weakened by an ideological incompatibility.[99]

Neither the social-psychological conflict nor the influence of Freud on Wilson is as strong as Mander suggests. Wilson does, as Mander says, have a deep knowledge of Freud; yet he is unwilling, in his characterizations, to use purely Freudian means of analysis. This can be demonstrated by citing the description of Ingeborg Middleton's neurosis in *Anglo-Saxon Attitudes:*

So much, thought Gerald, for 1928. And so it had gone on for four years. Freudians would probably have imputed some exceedingly unpleasant suppressed motives to Inge's behavior. For himself, he found it easier to believe that her actions were those of a spoilt girl who had turned to a woman who was slightly cracked. . . . She was, in fact, unbalanced. Mentally and emotionally unbalanced he had decided in those years to consider his wife, which was probably the same as what the Freudians would have said.[100]

Gerald Middleton's hesitancy to use Freudian terms in analyzing his wife's ailment echoes a similar attitude in Wilson. To some

---

[97] Mander, "The Short Stories of Angus Wilson," in *The Writer and Commitment,* p. 116.
[98] *Ibid.,* p. 117.   [99] *Ibid.,* p. 118.
[100] *Anglo-Saxon Attitudes,* p. 136.

extent it is a reversion to a pre-Freudian novelistic type of psychology, using character types and motivation somewhat as Dickens did. This is most true with Wilson's minor characters. With more important characters Wilson is Freudian to a degree, but also uses non-Freudian analysis (as in the example above). In addition he has a psychological theory of his own based on childhood vision and fantasy.[101] Childhood vision is important for the writer both as a source of his own imaginative inspiration and as a method of presenting the psychological background of one of the writer's characters. At times, Wilson's theory of childhood vision seems very close to Freud, as when neurosis is explained as a form of infantile regression: this may occur when the childhood fantasy is not successfully incorporated into adult life. Wilson's main interest is in the fantasy itself, however, and he feels that a lack of such fantasy in fiction may result in dryness and sterility.[102]

While he is in many ways a follower of Freud, Wilson seems to have a certain reluctance against committing himself entirely to a Freudian point of view. His feeling about Freud is somewhat parallel to his feeling about Marx: great interest in the thirties coupled with some disillusionment afterwards, leading to a moderation, rather than a repudiation, of his original position.

Because of this lack of absolute enthusiasm for Freud as well as his use of non-Freudian psychological techniques, Wilson is rarely a writer, as Mander suggested, of "casebook" stories. It is true, however, that characters Wilson himself seems to dislike are insufficiently analyzed; this is a situation where his stories could use more of the "casebook." Characters who are conserva-

---

[101] Wilson discusses this in *The Wild Garden*, pp. 141–50 *et passim;* a good explanation of Wilson's theory is in Halio's *Angus Wilson*, pp. 93–103.

[102] Two of Wilson's short stories reflect his interest in childhood fantasy, "Raspberry Jam" and "Necessity's Child." Wilson illustrates his theories using these stories as examples in *The Wild Garden*, pp. 141–46.

tive or fascistic in Wilson's fiction rarely have an unconscious; their nastiness is taken for granted and seldom is analyzed. This weakness in Wilson's characterization has been pointed out by A. O. J. Cockshut in a critical article.[103] To some extent this fault may be attributed to a Dickensian flatness which Wilson uses in characterizing his less important characters.

Another fault which is connected with Wilson's traditionalism is his weakness in using symbolism. Wilson's only sustained attempt at using symbols occurs in his fourth novel, *The Old Men at the Zoo;* the novel he wrote after this one, *Late Call,* is a reversion to his usual less symbolic style.

In *The Old Men at the Zoo* Wilson makes frequent equations between human beings and animals, and attempts to make some of these equations symbolic. Wilson's sense of satire and irony undermines this effort, however, and the result is often not symbolism but caricature. During a bombing attack of London, for example, an imperialistic, Victoriana-loving director of the zoo is blown into the air by an explosion and lands on top of a bronze lion on the lion house. C. B. Cox says of this scene, "The symbolism is obvious. This scene is full of horror but, as usual, Wilson cannot resist making the situation absurd." [104] The symbolism here is used for nothing more than a joke, and is weakened by its obviousness; Wilson undercuts many of his other efforts at symbolism in this manner.

Wilson's love for the Victorian novelists at times causes him to become too imitative of them; Walter Allen makes this point about one of the characters in *Anglo-Saxon Attitudes:*

Mrs. Salad, the cockney char, could only have been created, one thinks on first meeting her, by Dickens. She might be Mrs. Gamp's half-sister, and Wilson puts phrases into her mouth that would not have shamed Dickens. But Mrs. Gamp is so brilliantly idiosyncratic a creation, so utterly *sui generis,* that a second Mrs. Gamp, or even

[103] Cockshut, *Essays in Criticism,* 9:50 (1959).   [104] Cox, p. 156.

a half-sister to her, is unthinkable. Mrs. Salad emerges as a remarkable piece of pastiche. As soon as this is realized the sense of her reality departs. She comes out of literature, the mimicry of literature, rather than out of observation of life.[105]

When Wilson borrows a technique, instead of a character, the result is at times equally unfortunate. *The Middle Age of Mrs. Eliot* is Wilson's most Jamesian novel, and in it he uses James's technique of a minute examination of details and a very slow pace. This slow pace, at times barely tolerable in James, becomes boring in Wilson's novel.

Despite these faults, Wilson, especially in his first two novels, is a fine writer. James Ginden, who has surveyed the entire period, calls him "the best contemporary English novelist." [106] If some of his weaknesses can be attributed to his traditional style, so can many of his strengths. In Wilson's case it seems futile to speculate whether his style would be any better or worse if it were not traditional.

[105] *Tradition and Dream*, p. 272.
[106] James Ginden, *Postwar British Fiction*, p. 164.

CHAPTER FOUR

C. P. Snow
as Literary Critic

ONE EVENING in 1948 C. P. Snow encountered Leonard Russell, the book editor of the London *Sunday Times*, in a corner of the billiard room at the Savile Club. Snow "brooded unfavorably on the moment-by-moment story, the Virginia Woolf novel of sensitivity, and plotted its overthrow," and Russell was sympathetic. On another evening Snow handed Russell a paper titled "Credo," expressing similar sentiments. A short time later, after reading the paper, Russell sent a telegram to Snow offering him a regular column reviewing fiction for the *Sunday Times*. Snow accepted.[1]

For the next four years, from the beginning of 1949 to the end of 1952, Snow's reviews appeared about every other week in the *Sunday Times*. Cautiously at first, and then more directly, Snow began to attack the experimental novel.[2] In 1950, writing

---

[1] *Sunday Times* [London], Mar. 6, 1960, p. 18. The *Sunday Times*, which is published in London, is not to be confused with the *Times* [London] *Literary Supplement,* or the London *Times.*

[2] Snow has a number of names which he uses for the experimental

about "moment-by-moment fiction," Snow called it "arid and mindless." [3] In 1953 he published a more detailed attack:

Looking back, we can see what an odd affair the "experimental" novel was. To begin with, the "experiment" stayed remarkably constant for thirty years. Miss Dorothy Richardson was a great pioneer, so were Virginia Woolf and Joyce: but between *Pointed Roofs* in 1915 and its successors, largely American, in 1945, there was no significant development. In fact there could not be; because this method, the essence of which was to represent brute experience through the moments of sensation, effectively cut out precisely those aspects of the novel where a living tradition can be handed on. Reflection had to be sacrificed; so did moral awareness; so did the investigatory intelligence. That was altogether too big a price to pay, and hence the "experimental" novel . . . died from starvation, because its intake of human stuff was so low.[4]

Snow compared himself with one who cries that the emperor has no clothes,[5] and he began to oppose the experimental movement in various publications both in and outside of England.[6]

Snow's objections fell into a number of categories: he felt that the experimental novel, which was "as dead as cold potatoes," [7] created a gap between writer and reader; that it confused the younger novelists; that it was antiscientific, old-fashioned, and politically regressive; that it was not really experimental; and that it resembled abstract painting.[8] Snow opposed

a syndrome of attitudes in literature, nearly all quite modern, apparently unconnected, which spring from the same root—the ro-

---

novel: "moment-by-moment novel," "novel of sensibility," "stream of consciousness novel," "Alexandrian novel," and "symbolic novel."
[3] *Sun Times,* July 23, 1950, p. 3.
[4] *Sun Times,* December 27, 1953, p. 3
[5] *NYTBR,* Jan. 30, 1955, p. 28.
[6] *Spec,* 186:82 (Jan. 19, 1951); *NYTBR,* Jan. 30, 1955, p. 1; *Moderna Sprak* [Stockholm], 51:265 (1957).
[7] *NYTBR,* Jan. 30, 1955, p. 28.
[8] These ideas are expressed, *passim,* in the articles cited above.

mantic conception of the artist, the alienation of the intellectual, the aesthetic of the anti-novel, the abdication of the generalizing intellect, the hatred of the scientific-industrial revolution, the prizing of verbal innovation, the desire to contract out of society.[9]

James Joyce and Virginia Woolf were the novelists Snow attacked most frequently. Joyce was mentioned in the first book of Snow's ever published, a detective novel called *Death Under Sail* (1932). Here his principal character reflected on "the extraordinary prudery of the Irish Catholic," and found it "responsible equally for the censorship in Boston (Mass.), gang warfare in America, [and] Mr. James Joyce. . . ." [10] Twenty-two years later Snow said that if not for an anti-experimental trend, "serious novel-writing would have frittered itself to death in a welter of mindless subjectivism (the final warning was *Finnegans Wake*), a welter which was almost meaningless in semantic terms, and certainly meaningless in human terms." [11] Joyce abandoned "the reflective intelligence" and "narrowed the range of the novel," and Snow also complained about "Joyce's onanistic reveries." [12] Snow frequently linked the work of Joyce and that of Virginia Woolf: "I began to write in quite deliberate reaction . . . against the kind of purely aesthetic novel represented, say, by Joyce and Virginia Woolf. It seemed to me then, as it seems now, that that kind of aestheticism has little meaning and no future." [13]

At times his list is expanded to include many of the experimental novelists, imagist poets, and their precursors and descendants, such as Dorothy Richardson, Dujardin, Yeats, Eliot, Pound, Hulme, Wyndham Lewis, Gide, Kafka, Faulkner, and Beckett, as well as Joyce and Virginia Woolf.

One of the most serious charges that Snow levels against this

[9] *TLS,* Aug. 15, 1958, p. iii.   [10] *Death Under Sail,* p. 63.
[11] *Sun Times,* Dec. 26, 1954, p. 5.
[12] *Kenyon Review,* 23:11, 14 (Winter, 1961).
[13] Interview, *REL,* 3:105 (July, 1962).

group it that they were social reactionaries. In the *Times Literary Supplement* he discussed a number of these writers and a syndrome of attitudes which they possessed:

This syndrome is seen at its most complete in writers like T. E. Hulme, Joyce, or Pound. It has been visible in a considerable sector of advanced literature all through the first half of the century. It is a social and psychological phenomenon of some interest, and I hope to deal with it a little more fully some time, in particular to explore the connection which seems to be close, though not in individual practitioners inevitable, between this sector of advanced literature and extreme social reaction—not conservatism, but extreme social reaction. This is a connection which is now clear, though, through a curious deficiency in social insight, we were slow to see it.[14]

The implication is clear: there is some sort of a political link between Joyce and Pound. While it may be futile to deny that Pound was a social reactionary, there can be no denying that Joyce was, if anything, apolitical. This sort of accusation is all the more irresponsible because Snow never mentions that Joyce and Virginia Woolf, the two writers he most opposes for stylistic reasons, were in fact not politically reactionary. The only truly reactionary *novelist* in the group is Wyndham Lewis, and Snow never attacks him as a writer; instead he praises Lewis for an attack on abstract art.[15] Indeed, this is often Snow's method: he mentions the political ideas of Eliot, Yeats, Pound, and Hulme without criticizing their art; deplores the novelistic styles of Joyce, Virginia Woolf, or Dorothy Richardson while saying little about their politics; and then pretends that each group is guilty of the other's faults.[16]

Snow's argument begs the question whether it is intellectually ethical to criticize a work of art because of the writer's political

[14] *TLS,* Aug. 15, 1958, p. iii.   [15] *NYTBR,* Jan. 30, 1955, p. 28.
[16] Snow does this again in *The Two Cultures* (Cambridge: Cambridge University Press, 1964), pp. 7–8.

opinions. Furthermore, Snow is inconsistent in his application of this political criterion. Dostoevsky, in Snow's own words,

was virulently anti-Semitic: he prayed for war: he was against any kind of emancipation at any time; he was a fanatical supporter of the autocracy, and an equally fanatical opponent of any improvement in the lives of common people (on the grounds that they loved their suffering and were ennobled by it). He was in fact the supreme reactionary: other writers since have aspired to this condition, but no one has had his force of nature and his psychological complexity.[17]

Yet Snow constantly praises Dostoevsky as one of the greatest novelists of all time; two paragraphs above the one just quoted he says, "Dostoevsky is to this day one of the novelists I most admire." One wonders, if Dostoevsky is forgiven, why aren't the writers of the early twentieth century? Snow's attack seems somewhat ill-considered.

A number of critics—among them Herbert Read, Lionel Trilling, and Angus Wilson—have felt that there was some injustice in Snow's attack on various modern writers. Read's defense of Yeats, Eliot, and Pound is sidetracked by a pointless discussion of usury; [18] but Trilling points out that the social ideas of these poets were not transmitted to the younger poets who inherited their aesthetic tradition.[19] Wilson, in the *New York Times Book Review,* bemoaned the fact that Snow "has come to confuse estheticism and concern with formal experiment with a political regressivism, to associate the traditional novel form he likes with sound, progressive social principles." [20]

If they were not social reactionaries outright, Snow felt, most contemporary literary intellectuals were nevertheless apathetic about social questions. "I found," he said, "that the literary

[17] "The Two Cultures: A Second Look," an addition in the 1964 edition of *The Two Cultures,* p. 91.
[18] *Lon M,* 6:41 (no. 8, 1959).   [19] *Com,* 33:472 (June, 1962).
[20] *NYTBR,* July 2, 1961, p. 12.

intellectuals, or at least those who dominated literary sensibility during most of our time from roughly 1914 until fairly recently, had abandoned any serious concern for the progress of their fellow men." [21] This observation is perhaps too broad; certainly novels such as *Ulysses* and *Mrs. Dalloway* are not only free from social unconcern but are extremely preoccupied with human beings and their relationships to their social surroundings. Even if one examines such novels as Camus' *The Plague* or Golding's *Lord of the Flies,* where the characters are removed from their normal social environments, one must recognize the intense concern with society in general which Camus and Golding feel. Most of the novels of Joyce, Woolf, and Richardson do not demonstrate that their authors had abandoned a "serious concern for the progress of their fellow men."

Not only was the aesthetic novel socially harmful, according to Snow, but it harmed novel-writing as well. During the period from 1925 to 1945, aesthetic novelists brought the novel close to death:

The coroners of literature gathered hopefully around. The novels which were receiving the serious attention were the mindless and unreadable novels of sensibility. The coroners said that the novel was dead. The gap between this specialized art and any reading public was getting wider and wider. Plenty of novels, some good, some bad, were reaching the reading public; but they were not the novels literary persons were writing about. Many intelligent readers were just plain baffled. They did not have the patience to follow the course of this esthetic war; but when asked to venerate—or above

---

[21] *Recent Thoughts on the Two Cultures,* p. 5. This comment is taken from the printed version of a speech given by Snow at Birkbeck College of the University of London. In a letter to me (Oct. 31, 1966) Snow has written of the speech, "The oration at Birkbeck was given off the cuff, and it was in the second edition of *The Two Cultures* that I expressed myself in what was to me a more satisfactory manner." For remarks parallel to the ones I quote, see *The Two Cultures,* pp. 7–8.

all, read—wodges of moment-by-moment sensation, they passively went on strike.[22]

Snow seems to feel that it is the job of the author to approximate the level of intelligence of his audience, at least in serious literature. There is also no real evidence that fewer people are reading aesthetic novels today than twenty years ago. If book sales are any indication, it seems that the very opposite is true.[23] Geoffrey Wagner, refuting Snow on this point, has written, "The recent reception of novels by writers like Durrell, Nabokov, or Pasternak suggests, albeit mildly, that the taste for aesthetic fiction has not been wholly eradicated in the Anglo-Saxon-speaking countries yet." [24]

In his articles on the experimental novel, Snow usually discusses groups of novelists and their general faults, seldom finding specific shortcomings in specific novelists. While he has written an article criticizing Henry Green,[25] and another on Ronald Firbank,[26] these writers are certainly not in the vanguard of experimental novelists. Snow has never written a detailed analysis of any of the works of Joyce or Woolf or Richardson. His picture of the experimental novel is a pastiche of its worst qualities, as though all experimental novels were as monotonous as the *Pilgrimage* series, as obscure as *Finnegans Wake,* or as feministic as some of the novels of Virginia Woolf. Such criticism has an obligation to recognize the collective qualities of the group of novels it examines, but Snow sees few good qualities in these books.

As an alternative to the experimental novel Snow advocates

---

[22] *NYTBR,* Jan. 30, 1955, p. 1.
[23] For a discussion of increased sales of *Finnegans Wake,* for example, see Clive Hart, *Structure and Motif in Finnegans Wake,* (Chicago: Northwestern University Press, 1962), p. 23.
[24] *Twentieth Century,* 167:110 (Feb., 1960).
[25] *Spec,* 185:320 (Sept. 22, 1950).   [26] *Spec,* 186:82 (Jan. 19, 1951).

a return to realism, mainly the realism of those Victorian novels which place an emphasis on society and morality.[27] Pamela Hansford Johnson, Snow's wife, has written:

> Mr. C. P. Snow is a neo-realist: or so I should describe him if I had not a distaste for schools and labels. He augments the traditional realism of the English novel—realism in the line of Trollope, Thackeray, George Eliot, Galsworthy, and Bennett—with the technical enrichments this century has brought to the novel; that is, a greater emphasis upon visual presentation and upon the analysis of character from within.[28]

Snow himself has said that he considers the five best novelists of all time to be Tolstoy, Proust, Balzac, Dostoevsky, and Dickens; George Eliot, Trollope, Stendhal, and Turgenev are good, but a bit lower on the scale.[29] Not all of these novelists are of the same generation, but all of them were alive and writing during some part of the reign of Queen Victoria.

Though Dickens may be his favorite English writer, Snow's style has most frequently been compared to George Eliot's or to Trollope's.[30] In his interest in morality and society, Snow especially follows George Eliot, and praises her for this.

> She was, through her father's avocations, and the friends of her youth, drawn closer to the Industrial Revolution than Thackeray or Trollope, sons of the upper middle-class, or Dickens, descended from clerks and domestic servants, could ever be. None of these had the width or depth of social knowledge to have written *Middlemarch*.[31]

[27] Snow does not, however, care for naturalism. He feels that Zola's influence has never been great in England, but makes no mention of Moore or Gissing. See *TLS,* Aug. 13, 1958, p. iii.
[28] *English Association Essays and Studies,* n.s., 3:83 (1950). A similar observation has been made by F. R. Karl in *C. P. Snow: The Politics of Conscience,* p. 4.
[29] "Interview with C. P. Snow," *REL,* 3:103 (July, 1962).
[30] See, for example, Derek Stanford, *Meanjin,* 19:247 (1960); Earl Miner, *Nat,* 190:554 (June 25, 1960).
[31] *Sun Times,* January 17, 1954, p. 5.

Snow has said that any culture whose main output is of novels which do not deal with society is one that he would be suspicious of.[32] Furthermore, "The novel only breathes freely when it has its roots in society." [33] This, of course, not only upholds the ideals of the Victorian novel, but at the same time is an indirect censure of the type of modern fiction in which the hero is isolated from society. William Cooper, a follower of Snow's, praises him for having seen "that the artist who removes himself from society is fitted to speak for no one but himself, and that what he says for himself will, in the present state of affairs, probably sound dated and sterile." [34] This view is extreme: there is no reason why the artist, having removed himself from society, should be any less effective in describing the society he has left; it is just as possible that his social ideas will become more objective from a distance. Snow and Cooper share an opinion that the writer who removes himself from society or is hostile towards society is antisocial; but Lionel Trilling has criticized Snow on this point and has emphasized that these writers are in fact expressing Western's society's need for self-criticism.[35] Such writers, far from being antisocial, are much more beneficial to society than those who blandly accept society as it is.

Another danger inherent in emphasizing the social content of the novel has been pointed out by F. R. Karl. "If literature were to follow the course suggested by Snow, it would become an arm of social criticism; the 'untruths' that literature should tell us would become transformed into social commentary." [36] The converse of this is also true; that is, that the novel which is preoccupied with a sociological point of view is usually of little value as sociology. Geoffrey Wagner examines sociological novels, such as *Blackboard Jungle* and *The Man in the Gray*

[32] Interview, *REL*, 3:105 (July, 1962).
[33] *NYTBR*, Jan. 30, 1955, p. 29.
[34] *Nat*, 184:104 (Feb. 2, 1957).   [35] *Com*, 33:473 (June, 1962).
[36] Karl, p. 154.

Flannel Suit, in an article called "Sociology and Fiction"; [37] he concludes that they are uniformly inferior to their nonfiction counterparts, *Retreat from Learning* and *The Organization Man.* Snow's style, Wagner feels, is close to sociological fiction and even Soviet realism. [38]

One of the difficulties in understanding Snow and his critics on this matter is that they all mean different things by the term "social novel." Snow feels that a novel with a hero isolated from society is antisocial, while Trilling believes no such thing; Wagner makes a distinction between the social and sociological novel, which Snow does not do. [39] It is easy to see, then, how Snow can praise a novel like Henry Morton Robinson's *The Cardinal* "because it conveys a great deal of information," [40] while Wagner thinks this novel is bad for the very same reasons.

A basic distinction should be made between the sociological novel and the social novel. While the sociological novel treats its characters primarily as members of a particular social stratum or vocational group, the social novel is much more concerned with human beings reacting to other human beings. The social novel does, from time to time, embroider sociological details into the general narrative fabric; but the primary focus is not on scientists or aristocrats or executives, but on human beings who also happen to be these things. It is easy to see why the social novel has a far greater universality than does the sociological novel; for while the latter may interest the reader with the details of lives vastly different from his own, these very differences restrict his empathy and his ability to identify with the characters.

Snow's own novels illustrate this point. *The New Men* and *Corridors of Power* are weakened by their excessive sociological

[37] *Twentieth Century,* 167:110 (Feb., 1960).   [38] *Ibid.,* p. 113.
[39] Wagner does not disagree with Trilling's requirements that the novel be related to society. *Ibid.,* p. 113.
[40] *Sun Times,* Mar. 18, 1951, p. 3. Snow has frequently praised novels for giving information. See *Sun Times,* Jan. 13, 1952, p. 3; June 15, 1952, p. 11; Dec. 14, 1952, p. 5.

interest in the details of scientific or political life, at the expense of human affairs. *The Masters,* on the other hand, while it presents a detailed picture of academic life, is still primarily concerned with a human struggle. This gives *The Masters* the universality which is lacking in the other two novels. As Walter Allen has pointed out, this novel presents a microcosmic view of any political action.[41]

The superiority of the social over the sociological novel may be seen in the transient appeal of most sociological novels. While one may readily wish to reread a social novel, once one has gleaned the information presented in a sociological novel there is little left to inspire another reading. Another reason for the transience of the sociological novel it that in its concern with the minutiae and trivia of particular professions or social classes it has little time to deal with more enduring or persistent human problems. Hence the sociological novel is rarely also a philosophical novel. This is true in Snow's novels, as F. R. Karl has pointed out in the concluding paragraph of his book:

What Snow himself has provided is an intelligent view of society, full of many mature judgments and an adult awareness of human nature. What he has failed to provide is the larger sense of the world in which details become symbolic of greater things, in which man not only is involved in doing his job or making an important decision, but is also concerned with the grander questions of his fate in a seemingly meaningless universe.[42]

It is not so much that Snow is to be criticized for not writing philosophical novels; this, after all, must remain his decision as a novelist. But Snow, as a critic, seldom praises any contemporary writer whose style differs greatly from his own, and sees

---

[41] *Reading a Novel,* p. 52. Lionel Trilling made a similar point in his essay "The Novel Alive or Dead," in *A Gathering of Fugitives,* pp. 129–30. Trilling finds *The New Men* less successful than *The Masters,* which presents "a paradigm of the political life."
[42] Karl, p. 155.

little value in a philosophical strain in the contemporary novel. Snow's writing is without philosophical allusions: the materalism of his characters is not supported by references to Locke or Hume, nor is their agnosticism challenged by the ideas of Kant or Berkeley; he speaks of aesthetics without mentioning Aristotle, and he seems unaware of the debt his own thinking owes to Comte. This is perhaps because Snow, as a science student, did not receive the liberal education which was standard fare for so many of his contemporaries.

This may also explain why Snow's writing, again unlike most English writing, has no classical allusions. Aside from an occasional reference to Roland or to *The Saga of Burnt Njal*,[43] most of Snow's allusions are to books of the nineteenth century and later.

Among nineteenth-century English writers, the two Snow praises most are Dickens and George Eliot. Dickens, Snow feels, is the only English writer who can compare with Tolstoy or Dostoevsky, and is a much more profound writer than has been, until recently, acknowledged. Dickens was quite aware of what we call symbols, though he called them emblems; [44] he is "the greatest master of the symbolic-realistic novel"; [45] and he is a relatively unexploited subject for literary scholarship. As Snow wrote in the *Sunday Times,* "I am prepared to bet that, within two generations, Dickens's works will become, after Shakespeare's, the greatest single quarry for textual research." [46]

While considering Dickens a greater novelist, Snow is almost as enthusiastic about George Eliot, who, he feels, has been underestimated since her death. She, more than any writer except Tolstoy, has satisfied a contemporary feeling that "serious art needs a hard moral core." [47] For similar reasons, Snow praises Trollope and most of the preeminent English writers of

[43] *Science and Government*, p. 83.   [44] *NS*, 54:119 (July 27, 1957).
[45] *Sun Times*, Dec. 27, 1953, p. 3.
[46] *Sun Times*, Jan. 17, 1954, p. 5.   [47] *Ibid.*

the Victorian period. Suprisingly, Snow does not mention Jane Austen, though he indicates in a passing reference that he does not care for two of her contemporaries, Ann Radcliffe and M. G. Lewis.[48]

Though Snow says that his favorite writers are two nineteenth-century Russians, Tolstoy and Dostoevsky, and though he feels that he was more influenced by these Russians than by any English novelists,[49] this is not apparent in his fictional style. Snow has said that he likes the Russians very much,[50] and they seem to like him: he is one of the more popular Western writers in the Soviet Union. Recently one of the Russian universities awarded him an honorary degree.[51] Snow and his wife have edited a book of Russian stories,[52] and Snow himself has shown a certain interest in Soviet literature. But though he occasionally praises the Soviet realists for writing about science or politics, Snow includes none of them in the same class as Tolstoy and Dostoevsky.

When he was a young man, Snow's favorite writer was Dostoevsky; as he grew older, however, his taste shifted so that now he prefers Tolstoy.[53] It may seem strange that Snow cares for Dostoevsky at all, especially because of the chauvinistic, existential, and antisocial strains which are sometimes to be found in Dostoevsky's works. Yet Snow does admire him, and excuses Dostoevsky by saying, "Posterity is in the long run forgiving, if a writer is good enough." [54] In spite of this apology (which he makes for no other author), Snow, a little uncomfortable with

[48] *Sun Times,* Oct. 16, 1949, p. 3.
[49] Interview, *REL,* 3:104 (July, 1962).
[50] *Enc,* 18:91 (Feb., 1962).
[51] In March, 1963, Snow was elected an Honorary Doctor of Philological Sciences by the University of Rostov-On-Don. He was nominated for the degree by Mikhail Sholokhov.
[52] *Winter's Tales Number 7.* These stories were edited and introduced, though not translated, by Snow and Pamela Hansford Johnson.
[53] *The Two Cultures, and A Second Look,* p. 90.
[54] *Ibid.,* pp. 91–92.

Dostoevsky, has tried to show that he is outside the main tradition of Russian literature:

> To think that Russian novels were "wild, whistling, incomprehensible," comes from thinking that Russian novelists were like Dostoevsky. This is about like saying that Blake was the typical English writer.
>
> In fact, the Russian tradition in prose fiction has always been more tied to the earth, more animated by broad human sense, than our own: compare Tolstoi, Turgenev, Chekhov, Leskov, Gorki, with Dickens, Henry James, Kipling, Thackeray, D. H. Lawrence. Which side is the less cranky? How steady and sensible this Russian tradition is one can see even in the works of such emigre writers as M. Henri Troyat, writing a generation after leaving his native land.[55]

The adjectives "steady" and "sensible" point up the qualities that Snow finds most pleasing in the Russian literature of the nineteenth century. Tolstoy especially, with his strong interest in history, his ability to write a sustained narrative relatively free of stylistic ornamentation, and his moralistic tone, fulfills Snow's idea of what a novelist ought to do.

Two French novelists, Balzac and Proust, are also included in Snow's "top alpha class" [56] of writers. Snow has less to say about Balzac than about any of the others, but it is easy to see how he fits into the group: the interconnected quality of his novels, the broad view he takes of the society with which he was contemporary, and his position as the first realist and practitioner of Comte's theories [57] all endear him to Snow.

It is also easy to understand Snow's liking for Proust. Snow feels that most contemporary writers have had to choose between two alternatives: to follow Joyce, and write stream-of-conscious-

---

[55] *Sun Times,* Nov. 30, 1952, p. 5.
[56] Interview, *REL,* 3:104–5 (July, 1962).
[57] For a discussion of the link between Comte and Balzac, and of Balzac as the first practitioner of realism, see William York Tindall, *Forces in Modern British Literature,* p. 121.

ness novels, or to follow Proust. Obviously, Snow places himself in the second camp; he also feels that most contemporary English writers agree with him on this point.[58] The stream-of-consciousness method, Snow feels, forced writers like Joyce to abandon the "reflective intelligence," while Proust's method did not. In this way Joyce "narrowed the range of the novel," while Proust widened it.[59] Snow goes on to attempt to show the poverty of the stream-of-consciousness technique by examining what would have happened if Proust had used it:

The great Proustian parties involve most of the problems that a novelist of politics is faced with, as he sets his scene. The social setting has to be made actual; and in this model of the social world, as in any political model, the number of persons has to be considerable. To communicate all this required every weapon that Proust possessed, including his tireless commenting intelligence. Can you imagine it being done by any conceivable method of moment-by-moment flux? Just to ask that question is to remind oneself how little can be done in terms of moment-by-moment flux.[60]

The stream-of-consciousness technique, however, did not reach full flower until *Ulysses* was published in 1922; since Proust died in that year, it is rather futile to speculate what the result would have been if he had tried to use this technique. Furthermore, it is axiomatic that a novelist suits his technique to his general aesthetic scheme; Snow's question is no more sensible than asking what *Ulysses* would be like if it were written in a Proustian style.

Proust is the most modern writer on Snow's list of the greatest novelists; Balzac is the earliest. As has already been pointed out, the lives and the writing careers of all the novelists Snow

[58] *TLS*, Aug. 15, 1958, special section, p. iii.
[59] *Kenyon Review*, 23:10–11 (Winter, 1961).
[60] *Ibid.*, p. 16. When Snow uses the term "moment-by-moment flux" he means the stream-of-consciousness. See note 2, where the various terms Snow uses to denote the stream-of-consciousness are listed.

likes overlap the years in which Victoria reigned in England.[61] There are good reasons why this should be so.

The stream-of-consciousness technique which Snow opposes has its roots in the writers of the 1880s and 1890s such as Dujardin, Moore, Bergson, the James brothers, and others. These, in turn, are linked to the decadent movement of that time, and ultimately to the romantic movement in England and on the continent.[62] In certain aspects (such as the idea of the hero who is both superior to and removed from society), the stream-of-consciousness writers are often indebted to the romantic movement.

After the romantic movement had been superseded by the decadents, a strong countermovement arose, especially in Victorian England, against the antisocial tendencies of the decadents. This movement stressed moral and social values against the doctrine of art for art's sake, and included many of the novelists in the group Snow prefers. These Victorian writers felt that art for art's sake was synonymous with the abandonment of all social responsibility by the individual, and that it overemphasized Darwinian, Nietzschean, and romantic ideas. After the Second World War all of these concepts were connected, in popular thought, with the rise of the Nazi movement. Just how accurate a connection this is, in terms of intellectual history, is unimportant here; but many people did believe in just such a link, and that belief did help to discredit the romantic movement and all that followed it.[63]

[61] Victoria's reign was from 1837 to 1901. Stendhal died in 1842; *The Charterhouse of Parma* had appeared in 1839. Proust's first work was *Les Plaisirs et les jours,* published in 1896. The major portions of the careers of Dickens, George Eliot, Trollope, Turgenev, Tolstoy, and Dostoevsky all fall within these dates.

[62] For links between the stream-of-consciousness writers and the writers of the 1890s, see Tindall, pp. 187 ff. Mario Praz, in *The Romantic Agony* (New York: Oxford University Press, 1951), traces the connections between romanticism and the decadents.

[63] See Jacques Barzun, *Romanticism and the Modern Ego* (Boston: Little Brown and Company, 1943), for a discussion of the tendency to link romanticism and fascism.

When Snow mentions in his Rede Lecture that a scientist asked him whether the writers of 1915 had helped bring about Auschwitz and Snow found that he could not "defend the indefensible," [64] the question deals not only with writers like Pound, who were actually involved with fascism, but implicates any authors who could have been accused of abandoning the individual's responsibility to society.

This feeling is connected with the revival of interest in the Victorian novelists which began after the Second World War in England. A great part of this revival was certainly based upon a sentimental remembrance of the stability and power of the British Empire in the time of Victoria; but a good part of it was also the popular idea that romantic and neoromantic philosophy and literature were directly responsible for the Nazi movement. After the war the Victorian novelists seemed like prophets whose moral warnings had been disregarded, and with their revival came a repudiation of all those who had opposed them.

The idea that romanticism and Nazism are closely linked contains elements of truth, though it is in the last analysis inaccurate. Discussions of the subject are abundant; it is enough to say that the implication that experimental writers in England were in any way responsible for what occurred in Germany is a historical oversimplification.[65]

When Snow wished to disparage the idea that a writer can hold "one of his novels in its totality in his own head" (in a discussion of the merits of chapter titles), he called this idea "false and self-destructive romanticism." [66] It is difficult to understand exactly what Snow means here by romanticism, but in this article, which deals with stream-of-consciousness novels, he gives the term a negative connotation.

Just as Snow praises the steady and sensible aspects of literature, he distrusts the wildness of romanticism. The distrust is

[64] *The Two Cultures*, p. 7.
[65] This has been adequately demonstrated by Barzun, *passim*.
[66] *Kenyon Review*, 23:12–13 (Winter, 1961).

bolstered by the feeling (which is very strong with many writers in England) that the success of a particular work of art, especially a literary work, is intimately connected with its moral qualities. This idea, which is found in both Platonic and Marxist aesthetics, is certainly a very old one. Its present recurrence in England may be attributed to a number of sources: the writings of Matthew Arnold, which had a great influence on subsequent English educational theories; the revival of religious writing, such as that of T. S. Eliot or of Charles Williams; and, most important, the criticism of F. R. Leavis.[67]

Despite Leavis' well-publicized attack on Snow, Snow's position is similar to Leavis' on questions of morality in art. Snow's praise of Tolstoy and George Eliot for their "hard moral core" has already been noted. In a review of current American fiction Snow, deploring sex-obsessed novels, said, "No culture is healthy if clever writers fluctuate uneasily between the unreadable and the obscene." [68] This is a statement which could have been made by a Leavisite, or at least one with which most Leavisites might agree, and it is perhaps because Snow was moving so close to his camp that Leavis made his famous attack on Snow.

As morality became more important in English aesthetic thought, art for art's sake, which took a definitely amoral stand, was discredited. The ideas of Pater and Wilde, which seemed to permit the artist to damn society, were deemed irresponsible by many British writers after the Second World War.

Because of this Snow found it possible to accuse even those writers who were quite obviously not fascists of being irresponsible. When Snow levels this accusation at the experimental novelists, especially Joyce, he is again inexact. Joyce, in his

[67] See Vincent Buckley, *Poetry and Morality: Studies on the Criticism of Matthew Arnold, T. S. Eliot, and F. R. Leavis* (London: Chatto and Windus, 1959).
[68] *Sun Times,* July 9, 1950, p. 3.

early aesthetic theory,[69] speaks of static and kinetic works of art, and condemns the kinetic works, i.e., those which are didactic or pornographic. Any work of art which is truly fascistic would have to be propagandistic, and this Joyce would condemn as a didactic work of art. Snow never recognizes Joyce's more sophisticated version of the theories of Wilde and Pater, and so extends his attack against the experimentalists: but this is the danger inherent in attacking a member of a movement by attacking the movement, and not the individual works of the author.

Just as Snow finds the Victorian novelists who do not hold a romantic or an art-for-art's-sake position most satisfying, the contemporary writers he likes most are those who have kept all traces of symbolism, stream-of-consciousness, and other experimental techniques out of their novels. Snow does not care at all for symbolism, and he condemns even writers who are outside the experimental group, like E. M. Forster and L. P. Hartley, for using this technique: "With the only two senior living English novelists of distinction who have, as it were, underlined their symbols, E. M. Forster and L. P. Hartley, one is—or at least I am—more comfortable elsewhere in their books." [70] But Snow defends the totally nonsymbolic writers of this period, who he feels, were unfairly eclipsed by the experimental novelists.

The two Catholic novelists, Graham Greene and Evelyn Waugh, emerged in the late Twenties, Greene reverting to a tradition of narrative established by R. L. Stevenson and Conrad, Waugh producing a highly individual kind of romantic satire: these two attracted, and have kept, a certain degree of attention. But D. H. Lawrence, a much greater writer than Joyce, has only quite re-

[69] This theory is expounded by Stephen Dedalus towards the end of *A Portrait of the Artist as a Young Man*. It is possible to argue, as some critics have done, that Joyce put this theory forward ironically, though his own writing does not contradict the theory. Snow, however, does not take this point of view, since he never mentions the theory in the first place.

[70] *TLS,* Aug. 15, 1958, p. iii.

cently received serious critical examination: novelists as good as William Gerhardi and James Hanley received no real hearing at all: Joyce Cary—more creatively rich than any I have mentioned except Lawrence—was forced into critical esteem, very much too late and very much too grudging, only by the efforts of up-and-coming writers younger than himself.[71]

Snow similarly has praised the novels of Anthony Powell and of Pamela Hansford Johnson, who is Snow's wife.[72] Ivy Compton-Burnett, he feels, "has many of the gifts, not of a good but of a great novelist." [73] Henry Green, who is closer to the experimental novelists, does not come off quite so well; he is unfavorably compared with William Gerhardi in one article and called "a writer of eccentric distinction" in another.[74]

Most of the younger English novelists have turned away from experimental techniques; Snow has used this fact as a justification of his own aesthetic theories:

There are a dozen or more promising novelists in England—Doris Lessing, William Cooper, Emyr Humphreys, Francis King, Kingsley Amis, J. D. Scott, Brigid Brophy, John Wyllie are some of the best. Not one of these, in his practice, shows any interest in the sensibility novel or the *avant garde* of ten or twenty years ago. Several of them have explicitly and roughly savaged it. None of them wants to shrink away from society; their attitude to their art is much tougher than their immediate predecessors; some of them are going to be heard of.[75]

Snow is especially fond of one of these novelists, William Cooper. Cooper, like Snow, started out as a scientist and under Snow's tutelage began to write novels; Walter Allen has noticed the affinity of their styles.[76] Cooper has written a pamphlet on Snow for the British Council, and one of the characters in his

---

[71] *Moderna Sprak* [Stockholm], 51:267 (1957).   [72] *Ibid.,* p. 268.
[73] *Sun Times,* June 26, 1949, p. 3.
[74] *Spec,* 185:320 (Sept. 22, 1950); *Sun Times,* May 14, 1950, p. 3.
[75] *NYTBR,* Jan. 30, 1955, p. 29.   [76] *Tradition and Dream,* p. 251.

novel *Young People* may be a portrait of Snow.[77] Snow, for his part, dedicated a novel to Cooper and has continually praised his books.[78]

Though he once said that he was out of sympathy with the angry young men, Snow has written very favorable comments on Kingsley Amis, John Wain, and John Braine;[79] he feels that these novelists have advanced the cause of realism and have awakened a new concern with society in their fiction. Angus Wilson is praised for going back to "the panoramic social novels of Zola and Dickens"; Snow gave his book of short stories, *Such Darling Dodos,* a favorable review even before Wilson became well known.[80]

William Cooper has said that Snow is well liked by the newer novelists,[81] and it is certainly true that he has offered them encouragement. Because of the reviewing position he held on the London *Sunday Times* he was able to help popularize many of the newer novelists who were to become prominent in the 1950s. The list of those novelists for whom he wrote favorable reviews in the early 1950s includes Thomas Hinde, Brigid Brophy, Mervyn Jones, Francis King, John Wyllie, Emyr Humphreys, Doris Lessing, and Gwyn Thomas, as well as a number of somewhat older novelists, such as Alexander Baron, P. H. Newby, Olivia Manning, and H. E. Bates.[82]

[77] *C. P. Snow.* On *Young People,* see "Atticus," in *Sun Times,* Feb. 9, 1958, p. 3.
[78] Snow dedicated *Homecoming* to Cooper. For articles by Snow on Cooper, see *Moderna Sprak,* 51:267 (1957), and *Sun Times,* Mar. 5, 1950, p. 3.
[79] On angry young men, see *Life,* 50:136 (April 7, 1961); on Amis, see *Essays and Studies by Members of the English Association,* 14:7 (1961); *Moderna Sprak,* 51:267 (1957); *Sun Times,* Dec. 26, 1954, p. 5, and Jan. 8, 1956 (letter). On Wain and Braine, see *Sun Times,* Dec. 27, 1953, p. 3; *Moderna Sprak,* 51:267 (1957).
[80] Comparison with Zola and Dickens, *Moderna Sprak,* 51:267 (1957); review, *Sun Times,* July 23, 1950, p. 3.
[81] *Nat,* 184:104 (Feb. 2, 1957).
[82] These reviews by Snow all appeared in the *Sunday Times:* Hinde, *Mr. Nicholas,* May 18, 1952, p. 9; Brophy, *Hackenfeller's Ape,* Dec.

In dealing with contemporary literature outside of England, Snow's position has been, again, to favor the realistic novel. He shows a great affinity for the point of view of the contemporary Marxist critic, George Lukács, who feels that the high point of the novel was in the nineteenth century.

In discussing the argument against modernism in Lukács' book *The Meaning of Contemporary Realism,*[83] Snow said "Lukács sees its characteristic features as rejection of narrative objectivity: dissolution of the personality: ahistoricity: static view of the human condition (meaning by this mainly what I have called the social condition)." [84] Antipathy to modernism is not the only common ground for Snow and Lukács; they share an admiration of Balzac, Stendhal, and Tolstoy; a feeling that these novelists were superior to twentieth-century novelists; and a conviction that morality plays an important part in literature, which Lukács derives from Tolstoy, and, to some extent, from the traditional Marxist position.[85] Though Lukács has said that the hero in fiction should not be isolated from society, he does not make exaggerated claims for the modern Socialist realists and criticizes some aspects of Socialist realism; this makes it

---

27, 1953, p. 3; Jones, *No Time to be Young,* Jan. 27, 1952, p. 3; King, *The Dividing Stream,* June 17, 1951, p. 3; Wyllie, *The Goodly Seed,* Dec. 27, 1953, p. 3; Humphreys, *The Voice of a Stranger,* Aug. 28, 1949, p. 3; Humphreys, *Hear and Forgive,* Sept. 21, 1952, p. 5; Lessing, *The Grass Is Singing,* April 8, 1951, p. 3; Lessing, *Martha Quest,* Nov. 2, 1952, p. 5; Thomas, *The World Cannot Hear You,* June 17, 1951, p. 3; Thomas, *Now Lead Us Home,* May 4, 1952, p. 6; Baron, *There's No Home,* Feb. 19, 1950, p. 3; Manning, *School For Love,* Sept. 9, 1951, p. 3; Newby, *The Snow Pasture,* Jan. 16, 1949, p. 3; Bates, *The Jacaranda Tree,* Jan. 16, 1949, p. 3; Bates, *Colonel Julian and Other Stories,* July 1, 1951, p. 3; Bates, *Love for Lydia,* Oct. 5, 1952, p. 5. Most of these novelists write in nonsymbolic, nonexperimental styles; all the reviews are favorable.

[83] Translated from the German (New York: Merlin Press, 1962).

[84] *The Two Cultures, and A Second Look,* p. 95.

[85] Lukács' ideas on nineteenth-century literature are set forth in *Studies in European Realism,* (New York: Grosset and Dunlap, [Universal Library], 1964).

easier for Snow to accept his position. Though they are both advocates of nineteenth-century realism, neither feels that naturalism was a very successful movement, though for different reasons.[86] Like Snow, who makes a connection between the modernists and fascism, Lukács says that the modernists who reject the nineteenth-century thinkers support, whether consciously or unconsciously, Fascist ideology and hence reject humanistic culture.[87] Thus Snow and Lukács agree on many general points, though in choosing their favorites from among the twentieth-century novelists they sometimes differ: Lukács likes Mann, for example, more than Snow who has written, "very little of Dr. Mann's established work has much appeal for me." [88] Usually the areas of disagreement between the two, however, can be explained by Lukács' more traditionally Marxist point of view where Snow is interested only in realism per se. Snow's favorite contemporary European writers, then, are realists who are not primarily committed to any political point of view, like François Mauriac, Georges Simenon, and Alberto Moravia, whom Snow called, "one of the best novelists now writing." [89]

Snow is more critical of those novelists who are less realistic. He feels that Gide was overrated during his lifetime; that Hesse's *Magister Ludi* "does not come to earth often enough for the reader to get patches of rest"; and that Sartre's novels are not "great works of art, but they have other kinds of distinction." [90]

[86] Lukács qualifies his admiration for Zola because he didn't understand the essence of socialism (*ibid.,* p. 95). He is similarly unenthusiastic about German naturalism (*ibid.,* p. 247). Snow feels that while current English writers are turning back to realism, naturalism "has never struck any sort of roots here. I mean naturalism as opposed to realism, naturalism as exemplified by, say, Zola or James T. Farrell" (*TLS,* Aug. 15, 1958, p. iii).

[87] Lukács, *Studies in European Realism,* p. 4.

[88] *Sun Times,* Apr. 20, 1952, p. 3.

[89] In *Sun Times.* On Mauriac, Feb. 11, 1951, p. 3; on Simenon, June 26, 1949, p. 3; on Moravia, July 17, 1949, p. 3, and Mar. 9, 1952, p. 3.

[90] In *Sun Times.* On Gide, July 12, 1953, p. 5; on Hesse, May 15, 1949, p. 3; on Sartre, Aug. 6, 1950, p. 3.

Snow also opposes the French anti-novel, which, he feels is a rehash of the Joyce-Woolf experimental novel.[91]

Snow finds evidence of a trend towards the anti-novel not only in France, but also in the United States; "since 1945," he wrote, "the anti-novel aesthetic has been on the retreat in this country, but has been active both in France and America."[92] Snow is not very comfortable with most American literature; at times he implies that only Americans produced novels dealing with sex and violence, indeed, that this was all that was being written in America:

No great country at the height of its power has ever produced a literature as sad as America's today. Not tragic, for the major notes are not sounding—but sad, bewildered, lost. That is not the whole story, of course; it is easy to overemphasize the dark spots and forget the vigorous human works of art, such as Mr. J. G. Cozzens's.[93]

It may seem strange that in 1950, when he wrote this, Snow could find only this one bright spot on the American scene; yet it is true that Cozzens is the only American writer Snow has ever vigorously endorsed. Snow has called Cozzens "one of the best American novelists alive," and "one of the few novelists now practising whom a grown-up person can read with respect."[94] When Cozzens' novel *By Love Possessed* reached the top of the American best-seller lists Snow wrote, "A fine writer has suddenly become known all over the United States. It is splendid. It is particularly splendid because this great public is being given something hard, intellectually and morally hard, to bite on."[95] Snow's own style and subject matter are not far from Cozzens', and this helps explain what would seem like inordinate praise.[96] Nothing, however, but the extremity of Snow's position

[91] Frank Kermode (interview), *Partisan Review*, 30:76 (Spring, 1963).
[92] *TLS*, Aug. 15, 1958, p. iii.   [93] *Sun Times*, Apr. 2, 1950, p. 3.
[94] *Ibid.*, Dec. 8, 1957, p. 8.   [95] *Ibid.*
[96] Snow has been compared to Cozzens before, by F. R. Karl and Walter Allen. Karl finds that *The Affair* "superficially resembles" *By Love Possessed* (*C. P. Snow*, p. 136). Allen said in *Tradition and Dream*, p.

in opposing even the traces of the stream-of-consciousness movement can explain Snow's comparison of Cozzens with writers who are undoubtedly his superiors: Hemingway, Faulkner, Dos Passos. "Mr. Cozzens," Snow writes, "is much the soundest of his generation of writers (which includes Mr. Hemingway, Mr. Faulkner, and Mr. Dos Passos), and he wears much better." [97] Snow does not care for "Hemingway derelicts," and he has called Faulkner "a genuine, but very limited, artist." [98] Snow does like Fitzgerald, and he has mentioned in passing that he thinks Malamud and Bellow are good writers.[99] Shortly after a blistering attack on Norman Mailer and James Jones, however, he wrote the following: "We hear a good deal of nonsense about talentless American writers, while some of the most gifted do not raise so much as a whisper here. Why is there not more fuss for example about Mr. Auchincloss? Or Mr. Wallace Stegner, one of the deepest, truest, and most likeable writers in America?" [100] Snow's criticism here is too partisan in advocating only anti-experimental ideas, and too quick to censure those novels which fall outside his narrowly set limits. One cannot blame Snow for attempting to uphold a certain aesthetic point of view, but when this position demands that an ephemeral writer like Cozzens be ranked over writers like Faulkner and Hemingway, the position itself must be reexamined.

It is as true for American literature as for literature in general

---

185, that they were similar in their interest in "human ecology"; but Snow is "much more sanguine than Cozzens" while "Cozzens has a much more deterministic view of human nature."

[97] *Sun Times,* Nov. 20, 1949, p. 3.

[98] On Hemingway, *Sun Times,* Dec. 8, 1957, p. 8. On Faulkner, *Sun Times,* Oct. 16, 1949, p. 3.

[99] Snow calls Fitzgerald "a fine writer" in the *Sun Times,* July 31, 1949, p. 3. In *The Two Cultures, and A Second Look,* p. 93, Snow says he admires Malamud; he praises an essay by Bellow in *TLS,* June 9, 1961, p. 351.

[100] The attack on Mailer and Jones, mainly for their obscenity and violence, is in the *Sun Times,* Feb. 3, 1952, p. 3. The reference to Auchincloss and Stegner was in the same publication, May 4, 1952, p. 6.

that Snow often prefers books of the best-seller variety to books that may sell more slowly but are undoubtedly of a higher quality. As we have seen, he has reservations about the novels of Gide, Mann, Hesse, Sartre, Hemingway, and Faulkner, not to mention the English experimental writers; yet he is enthusiastic about books by Daphne Du Maurier, Nevil Shute and Nancy Mitford.[101] He has also praised a number of historical novels, especially those by C. S. Forester and Zoe Oldenbourg, which were best sellers.[102]

One reason for this attitude is that Snow believes that there is a correlation between the value of a work and the number of people who read it. A writer must have "a sizeable audience of an education similar to his own"; this saves him from "solipsism, which is the occupational disease." [103] If a writer does not care about his audience, a widening gap grows between reader and writer; this is dangerous, both for literature and culture.[104] Snow once speculated why a writer like Hervey Allen had an enormous audience, while few people bothered to read the obviously more gifted Denton Welch.

Why, if Welch was so gifted, would nineteen out of twenty of my highly educated and literate acquaintances say that his books had no interest for them? It is not because they are philistines: for they are not philistines. The answer resides in the nature of Welch's gift. It belonged to that stream which came into prose fiction with Miss

[101] On Daphne Du Maurier, *Sun Times,* July 29, 1951, p. 3; on Nevil Shute, *Sun Times,* June 11, 1950, p. 3; on Nancy Mitford, *Sun Times,* July 31, 1949, p. 3.

[102] On C. S. Forester, *Sun Times,* May 28, 1950, p. 3; on Zoe Oldenbourg, *Sun Times,* Jan. 30, 1949, p. 3, and Nov. 14, 1954, p. 5. Snow's taste for the historical novel again brings him close to George Lukács, who has written a study of the form, *The Historical Novel,* translated from the German by Hannah and Stanley Mitchell, (Boston: Beacon Press, 1962; original ed., Moscow, 1937). Of course Lukács, as a Marxist, has reasons different from Snow's for liking the historical novel.

[103] *TLS,* Aug. 15, 1958, special section, p. iii.

[104] This view is set forth in the *Sun Times,* Dec. 28, 1952, p. 7.

Dorothy Richardson and Joyce, and which set out to write of *moment-by-moment* experience, the moments of sight, sound, smell, which to such writers seemed the essential stuff of art.[105]

Snow explains, in this article, that if the influence of the moment-by-moment writers were to increase, "the gap between the artistic novel and any kind of public would soon become uncrossable —and, in my view, prose fiction would wither away."

It seems unfair of Snow to choose a writer like Welch, who died at the age of thirty-one, for this comparison. Moreover, Allen's historical novels are written for a less intelligent audience, and thus a larger audience, than Welch's books; furthermore, Welch, Joyce, and the stream-of-consciousness writers had and have larger audiences than Snow implies.[106] But it is even more important to ask how many readers Hervey Allen has today. Good writers (Gerard Manley Hopkins and Herman Melville are only two examples) may never, until after their deaths, acquire a large audience; they may, like Pepys, write very well when writing only for themselves. If a gap exists between the reader and the writer, it is sometimes on account of the reader's, and not the writer's, mediocrity. The size of the audience for a particular book is seldom a valid critical tool within a few years of the writing of that book. For Snow, who has often been on the best-seller lists himself, this point may lose some of its force.

Another thing Snow likes about best sellers is that they are not difficult to read. He complains that "very few will find *Magister Ludi* easy to read"; of Faulkner's *Intruder in the Dust* he writes, "It is genuinely hard to read the book at all. In any case, Mr. Faulkner would not be particularly readable. . . ."[107] On the other hand, *The Dividing Stream* by Francis King is "lucid,"

---

[105] *Ibid.*   [106] *Spec*, 185:320 (Sept. 22, 1950).
[107] *Magister Ludi, Sun Times*, May 15, 1949, p. 3; *Intruder in the Dust, Sun Times*, Oct. 16, 1949, p. 3.

"remains easy to read," and "presents no difficulties of any kind to the reader." [108] John P. Marquand is "eminently readable"; Nevil Shute's *A Town Like Alice* is "always readable"; Jerome Weidman's *The Price is Right* is "very readable"; W. Somerset Maugham is "the most professional and readable novelist of his generation," though "true to her school and method" Eudora Welty "is impossible to read." Some rather infrequently read authors are readable: Catherine Gaskin, Ann Meredith, and N. C. Hunter are, respectively, "intoxicatingly readable," "always readable," and "most readable." As might have been expected of the experimental movement, "no other tendency in the world has ever produced such totally unreadable results." [109] It may have been gathered by now that the word is one of Snow's favorites.[110]

Other words often recur in Snow's criticism; among the ones most frequently encountered are "warm," "human," and "heavyweight," all terms of approbation: C. W. Grafton's novel *Beyond a Reasonable Doubt,* for example, is "clear-headed, human, and warm." Snow qualifies his admiration for Doris Lessing because "her human responses are strong rather than warm." Sometimes Snow's use of "human" seems to occur in contradictory contexts; in one review Snow says of Cozzens' novels, "warm and human as they are, his books lack impact"; a few months later he writes

[108] *Sun Times,* June 17, 1951, p. 3.
[109] The following citations are all from the *Sun Times.* On Marquand, see Dec. 4, 1949, p. 3; on Shute, June 11, 1950, p. 3; on Weidman, June 25, 1950, p. 3; on Maugham, Apr. 30, 1950, p. 3; on Welty, Sept. 3, 1950, p. 3; on Gaskin, Feb. 25, 1951, p. 3; on Meredith, July 1, 1951, p. 3; on N. C. Hunter, Dec. 30, 1951, p. 3; on the experimental movement, Sept. 3, 1950, p. 3.
[110] In his first 80 reviews for the *Sunday Times* Snow used the word 30 times. The disease seems to be communicable, however. The reviewer for the *Times Literary Supplement* (Sept. 7, 1956, p. 524) said, *"Strangers and Brothers* and *Time of Hope* may well, in time, become unreadable." Bernard Bergonzi said that Snow's prose is, at its worst, "so arid as to be almost unreadable," (*Twentieth Century,* 167:214 Mar., 1960). Edmund Wilson wrote in the *New Yorker,* "My only objection to [Snow's] novels is that I find them almost completely unreadable" (June 2, 1962, p. 118).

that it is easy to forget "the vigorous human works of art, such as Mr. J. G. Cozzens'." At times it is difficult to understand exactly what Snow means by "human": "Dr. Alex Comfort is a strong and individual figure and I believe that he will be a good human influence on the literary scene." "Heavyweight," as Snow uses it, means substantial, describing a person to be reckoned with; so that J. B. Priestley's *Thoughts in the Wilderness* makes it clear "what a heavyweight he is," and George Eliot is "one of the most gifted women who have ever lived, one of nature's heavyweights in both mind and personality." [111]

These words, as they are used, can mean too many things. They make Snow's criticism imprecise: unreadable can mean hard to read, verbally dense, unentertaining, unclear, disorganized, or obscure; by human Snow may mean humane, humanitarian, or humanistic. Heavyweight and warm are similarly ambiguous.

Snow's critical formula is too predictable: any warm, human, readable novel which displays no experimental tendencies is approved of. Using this formula Snow praised many mediocre books and rejected many that were worthwhile; nevertheless Snow's theories were, on the whole, approved of in England.

In 1948 F. R. Leavis had called *Ulysses* "a dead end"; but he had not really followed up his attack on Joyce, and the London literary world was ready for someone to continue this attack.[112] That Snow began, in 1949, to carry on this attack against the experimental writers was not so much due to his understanding of the *Zeitgeist;* it was more that Snow had finally been given a platform from which to speak and that the English

[111] The following citations are all from the *Sun Times*. On Grafton, Jan. 28, 1951, p. 3; on Lessing, Apr. 8, 1951, p. 3; on Cozzens, Nov. 20, 1949, p. 3, and Apr. 2, 1950, p. 3; on Comfort, Jan. 30, 1949, p. 3; on Priestley, Nov. 17, 1957, p. 8; on Eliot, June 17, 1956, p. 4.

[112] Leavis' remarks were in *The Great Tradition* (London: Chatto and Windus, 1948). Leavis' most concentrated attacks were, of course, on Virginia Woolf and the Bloomsbury group, rather than on Joyce.

were ready to listen. Snow's aesthetic ideas had not changed over ten years: *Strangers and Brothers* (1940) is no different, stylistically, from his later novels, *Time of Hope* (1949) or *The Masters* (1951); but postwar Britain had changed. The socialization of various industries, new theories in education and town planning, increasing social mobility, and the growing respectability of sociology as an academic pursuit all combined to make the upper-middle-class *belles-lettres* approach seem outmoded; and experimental novelists, especially such writers as Virginia Woolf, were connected with the *belles-lettres* tradition. Marxist criticism, though by the postwar years toned down to a rather weak pink, still had helped to strengthen the idea that literature must be socially relevant; this idea united the Marxists and ex-Marxists with all those who were eager for the revival of Victorian literature, including sentimental Tories who read the Victorians to remember what life had been like when there really was a British Empire.

In this atmosphere any young English novelist who had ever admired Joyce was forced to choose between the experimental technique and the new realistic style. The choice was complicated by the fact that Joyce was not only a great innovator in English fiction—he was also the chief exploiter of his own innovations. For a young novelist who wanted to use experimental techniques, to surpass Joyce seemed impossible; to equal him would be to imitate him. The only possible answer seemed to be to move in an entirely different direction.

The years 1949 to 1952, when Snow reviewed new fiction for the *Sunday Times,* were critical years. He did not really discover any of the better novelists of the 1950s like Amis, Wain, Golding, or Iris Murdoch; their first novels came in 1953 and 1954, when Snow had given up his regular reviewing column. He did give favorable reviews to novels by Cooper, Doris Lessing, Thomas Hinde, and to a book of short stories by Angus Wilson; [113] but more important than this, he had helped to establish a critical climate which was receptive to the first novels by these writers. It must also be remembered that Snow's criticism and novels gave many of the yet unpublished novelists both a theory and practical examples which presented an alternative to the experimentalists, at the very time that the younger novelists were still working on their manuscripts. That few of them actually imitated Snow is immaterial; the contribution he made was to show that it was possible to reject the experimentalists and to get away with it. In this way Snow became the aesthetic spokesman for one part of the English population, much as he was later to become a spokesman on social and general cultural topics.

[113] Snow's reviews of these novelists appeared in the *Sunday Times* on the following dates: Cooper's *Scenes from Provincial Life,* Mar. 5, 1950, p. 3; Lessing's *This Was the Old Chief's Country,* Apr. 8, 1951, p. 3; Lessing's *Martha Quest,* Nov. 2, 1952, p. 5; Hinde's *Mr. Nicholas,* May 18, 1952, p. 9; Wilson's *Such Darling Dodos,* July 23, 1950, p. 3.

CHAPTER FIVE

C. P. Snow as Novelist

I N 1961 the Royal Society of Literature created a new honor called "Companion of Literature" (C. Litt.), which was to be awarded to living writers "who have brought exceptional distinction to English letters." The *Sunday Times* decided to hold a survey of its readers to find who they thought should receive the awards. The vote was as follows: [1]

1. Winston Churchill	6. Bertrand Russell
2. T. S. Eliot	7. C. P. Snow
3. W. S. Maugham	8. Robert Graves
4. E. M. Forster	9. Aldous Huxley
5. Graham Greene	10. Osbert Sitwell

The only writer on this list to have achieved his reputation well after the Second World War is C. P. Snow. Even in the early 1950s Snow was not too well known; but by the time of this survey he was already considered one of the most distinguished living English writers.

Snow's career as a writer of fiction began in 1932, when he

[1] *Sun Times,* May 7, 1961, p. 33.

published a mystery novel called *Death Under Sail*. This book, which he wrote while he was still doing biochemical research at Cambridge, contains many of the themes and stylistic devices which Snow was to use in later novels. Though Snow was only twenty-seven at the time the novel was written, his protagonist, Ian Capel, is in his fifties; even at this time, Snow liked to use middle-aged men as his characters. The Trollopian chapter headings, which were to become one of Snow's trademarks, are present in this book. The theme of stolen research, which would be important both in *The Search* and *The Affair,* is briefly mentioned. More important than these, however, are suspense and melodrama, which, in one way or another, are present in all of Snow's later fiction.

The classical mystery story achieves suspense most often by presenting a puzzle which is not solved until the end; usually it is the question of the murderer's identity. *Death Under Sail,* no different in this respect, opened the way for Snow's use of this device in his subsequent novels. In some novels—*The Masters* and *Corridors of Power,* for example—the question of who will win an election produces suspense; in other novels—*Strangers and Brothers, Homecomings,* and *The Affair*—suspense is introduced by making the reader wonder about the outcome of a trial. Very often the suspense is supplied only by the question of whether a man at a crucial point in his career will manage to make his way successfully despite a number of obstacles.[2]

Snow himself has noticed the transition of the suspense theme from *Death Under Sail* into his later novels:

My first book was a good old-fashioned murder story (character name of Christopher did it), but I don't intend to write any more murder stories either. Suspense is a valuable convention; you can carry a lot of deeper stuff if the narrative is strong. There is noth-

---

[2] Richard Mayne, *Enc,* 21:76 (Nov., 1963), has pointed out a number of the similarities between *Death Under Sail* and Snow's later novels

ing so suspenseful as an academic committee. I enjoy writing about university life, partly because I was attached to it so long.[3]

English murder stories often have extremely respectable settings and are populated by well-bred characters (or they were in the time of the "Raffles" tradition, before the more violent American stories began to influence the British). Snow's detective story takes place on a yacht, and the murderer's motive is to prevent the victim from revealing certain facts about his health which would disqualify him for an important job, and hence prevent him from attaining a higher social level. Similarly, in Snow's later fiction there is usually a respectable setting, and if one of his heroes is not a member of the respectable classes, he yearns to become one.

After *Death Under Sail,* Snow published *New Lives for Old* (anonymously) and *The Search.* Both these books were concerned with science, though each one in a different way. *New Lives for Old* is set in the future and attempts to anticipate what life might be like in a more technologically advanced society; *The Search* is the story of a young scientist, much like Snow, who makes the decision to leave science. After these books Snow began to write the novels of the *Strangers and Brothers* series, a task he is still engaged in.

The remarkable thing about all of these novels, written over a period of thirty years, is how little stylistic change or development there is from one novel to the next. By 1934, in *The Search,* Snow's style had become set to such an extent as to show almost no important change thirty years later in *Corridors of Power.*

Snow's prose style is level, unadorned, realistic in the manner of many Victorian novelists. Considering his use of chapter titles and his interest in politics, he is most like Trollope. He scrupulously avoids any sort of poetic effects in his prose, and he par-

[3] *New Yorker,* 37:44 (Dec. 16, 1961).

ticularly excludes experimental effects from his novels; as he has often said in his literary criticism, he is totally opposed to the James Joyce-Virginia Woolf experimental techniques.

In effect this means that Snow has eschewed all devices such as allusion, symbolism, the stream of consciousness, complex uses of time (there are rarely even any flashbacks in his books); little attention is given to the sounds of words or the rhythms of sentences; rarely are .there any vivid passages or striking metaphors; and there is no conscious use of allegory or myth. Instead the prose is straightforward and never difficult to understand— "readable," as Snow puts it. In this respect Snow's style is similar to that of many popular writers—H. G. Wells or J. G. Cozzens, for instance—who tried never to baffle their readers.

The prose in Snow's novels is often ponderous; when he wishes to emphasize a point he repeats it. For example:

On the way back her anxiety recurred, but Charles met us in the hall and his smile dispelled it.

"I'm pretty certain that all is well," he said in a low voice.

She kissed him. He stopped her talking there, and we went into the drawing room.

"I'm pretty certain that all is well," he repeated.[4]

In this passage, which is not atypical of Snow's usual technique, Charles March's reassuring phrase is made twice, after the fact that he wished to be reassuring has already been established in the narrative.

Snow's repetitions and unadorned style are seen by some critics as an advantage, Derek Stanford, for example, has written:

---

[4] *The Conscience of the Rich*, p. 183. Unless noted otherwise, all of the novels in the *Strangers and Brothers* series which were published by Scribners in New York were used in that edition. For the two exceptions, *Time of Hope* and *The Masters*, the editions used were published by Macmillan in New York. See the appended bibliography for other editions.

For those who have two feet planted on the earth (which is how C. P. Snow pictures himself), existence is rightly seen as a number of banalities and clichés. To avoid them, with too nice a precision, is to forgo their communicative power. It is, so to speak, to fiddle the books, presenting experience in too choice verbal terms. The aim of naturalism in art is to narrow the gap between art and living; to present the former in the dress of the latter; to reduce, as far as possible, the autonomy of self-conscious literary language.[5]

According to Stanford, Snow consciously uses banalities to present what he presumably considers banal situations. Snow, however, seems to find his subject matter quite interesting; he does not contrast banal passages with vivid ones to show that he is consciously injecting banality. His dialogue, for example, shows little tonal difference from the surrounding narrative; there is no obvious shifting away from banality or repetition.

Stanford further assumes that the successful naturalistic novelist must match his style to his subject matter; in order to write of banal situations, then, he must himself descend to a banal style. Even the most fanatic devotee of naturalism would not care to follow this assumption to its logical conclusion: to write boringly about boredom, illiterately about illiteracy.

Some defenders of Snow do not even agree that the style is banal. William Cooper, for one, has said that while the style may appear simple, it is actually "strong and subtly poetic." [6] In support of this Cooper mentions that in a certain passage Snow uses monosyllabic words over eighty percent of the time, while only two adverbs appear, as though there were poetry in monosyllables, or adverbs were dangerous words to use. But the main point about Snow's style, Cooper feels,

is that it has been developed firstly to give *absolute conviction on the plane of immediate fact,* though it has been developed so

[5] Derek Stanford, *Meanjin,* 19:237 (1960).
[6] William Cooper, *C. P. Snow,* p. 36. A rebuttal of some of Cooper's more extravagant assertions has been given by Bernard Bergonzi in *Twentieth Century,* 167:214 (Mar., 1960).

flexibly that it can also be used for both motive and analytical purposes. It has a compelling tone which arises not only, or even mainly, from knowledge, but from the author's total involvement in what he is doing. To read it is to believe it.[7]

Cooper's phrase "absolute conviction on the plane of immediate fact" seems like an overstatement. Snow's use of a first person narration throughout the *Strangers and Brothers* series, as well as in other novels, greatly diminishes the sense of absolute verisimilitude. Lewis Eliot, the narrator, is by his own admission ambitious and incapable of giving of himself to another person. Despite this, Snow's characters constantly rush to him with their secrets, fill him with their confidences, which of course makes him capable of transmitting them to the reader. This device, often used in a transparent manner, makes Snow's novels lack verisimilitude even when judged from a realistic or a naturalistic point of view. Moreover, to present his fiction on the "plane of immediate fact" Cooper speaks of, Snow would have to vary his language even more than he does to correspond to the shifts in tone and nuance which come with changing moods or speakers.

A more reasonable justification for Snow's prose style has been given by Frank Kermode. In a discussion of the relative merits of Snow and Samuel Beckett, Kermode finds that he prefers the former because Snow, among other things, is "a good deal easier and more pleasant to read." [8]

This comment may help to explain why Snow is so often on the best-seller lists: he is not too difficult for the general reader, he introduces no complicated philosophical problems, he employs no stylistic embellishments. As Derek Stanford has said, Snow's prose is "dear to the lending library reader," and similar to that of the women's magazines.[9]

---

[7] *C. P. Snow,* p. 37. The discussion of monosyllabic words is in a note on page 35, and the reference to adverbs on page 36 of this book. The italics in the quoted passage are Cooper's.

[8] "Beckett, Snow, and Pure Poverty," in his collection, *Puzzles and Epiphanies,* p. 155.

[9] Stanford, p. 236.

Snow's style is not always simple: nor does his vocabulary, as Cooper implies, include mainly monosyllables. At times, after long stretches of ordinary words, Snow uses a rare word. Describing the great social changes of the twenties, Snow writes, "It was a great climacteric of hope, and George embodied it in his flesh and bone." [10] Not only does Snow place a relatively obscure word like "climacteric" next to a homely phrase like "flesh and bone," but the word itself is not used with the greatest precision. By "climacteric" Snow means a time of great hope, a time of improvement; the usual connotation of the word conveys the opposite.[11]

William Cooper, in discussing the words which appear in Snow's prose, has said:

The simple common words, because we use them all the time, often using the same word for different purposes, are the words which have come to acquire separately the most elaborate nexus of allusions; and therefore, strung together they can make the most subtle and pregnant of sentences. Furhermore, because they are simple and common, they do not distract in a "literary" sense: because they are familiar, one feels naked to their meaning.[12]

But many of the words which Snow uses, "pantocrater" or "irenicon" for example, do what Cooper says they don't do: they distract in a literary sense. In a single novel, Snow used such words as "mumpsimus," "subfusc," "pyknik," "inspissated," "mana," "cachinnation," and "valetudinarian." [13] All these words were used in a rather simple context, though they have less obscure synonyms which would be more in keeping with the usual vocabulary Snow uses; all stand out from the text rather glaringly.

[10] *Time of Hope,* p. 112.
[11] In physiology the word means a decline in reproductive activity, i.e., menopause.
[12] Cooper, *C. P. Snow,* pp. 35–36.
[13] "Pantocrater," *Homecomings,* p. 137; "irenicon," *Strangers and Brothers,* p. 150; "mumpsimus," etc., *Corridors of Power,* pp. 182, 230, 322, 329, 269, 296, and 296, respectively.

At times Snow uses words in a confusing manner. In *The New Men* the following passage occurs: "to Martin it was jet-clear that, despite its emollients and joys, individual life was tragic. . . ." [14] Leaving aside the unusual conjunction of the words "emollients" and "joys," one wonders exactly what Snow is trying to convey with the term "jet-clear." Jet means either a hard black substance or a stream of gas or liquid issuing from an orifice. Is Snow talking about the clarity of reflections in polished jet, or the transparency of a gas issuing from a jet? In *The Affair,* Snow described Hanna Puchwein's head as "Hamitic"; *Webster's New International Dictionary* (third edition) defines the Hamites as "a group of African peoples . . . that are Muslims, are highly variable in appearance but mainly Caucasoid. . . ." Even after taking the trouble to look up the word in a dictionary, one cannot be certain what Hanna Puchwein looked like.[15]

In opposing the experimental writers, Snow has frequently come out against "poetic" fiction and verbal innovation; [16] his own fiction, shows, perhaps, too little concern with individual words and concentrates more on the plot. Despite the fact that the use of a strong plot line had never fallen into disuse among popular writers of fiction, Snow was one of the first postexperimental writers to reassert the value of the plot, make his verbal texture subservient to the plot, and justify this shift of emphasis by actively opposing (rather than merely ignoring) those experimental writers who had deemphasized the value of the plot in their works.

Snow has succeeded, both with his criticism and with his fiction, in making the critical climate in England more receptive

---

[14] *The New Men,* p. 301.

[15] For other discussions of Snow's use of obscure words, see *TLS,* Sept. 7, 1956, p. 254, and Apr. 15, 1960, p. 237; also *Spec,* 197:362 (Sept. 14, 1956).

[16] See, for example, Snow's article "Challenge to the Intellect," *TLS,* Aug. 15, 1958, special selection, p. iii; see also Snow's book reviews in the *Sun Times,* from 1949 to 1952.

to his own type of realism. His novels represent a new phenomenon in that they deal with modern technical innovations, such as the development of the atomic bomb; but the language and style he uses in describing these phenomena are derived from the Victorian and Edwardian novelists. As Alfred Kazin has said, Snow's novels "do not, as some of Snow's admirers often glibly suggest, offer a new technique to the English novel." [17]

Because of his concern with technology, some critics have called Snow's prose "scientific." In his book on Snow, for example, F. R. Karl said that "Snow, like Wells, for example, has forsaken 'romantic' prose for 'scientific' prose, just as he forsook so-called modern techniques for the more straightforward narrative of the post-Victorian novel." [18] While Snow has frequently said that it is important for the modern artist to come to terms with the discoveries of contemporary science,[19] there is really little that can be called scientific in his prose style. He is not a follower of Zola and the naturalistic movement which actually attempted to use scientific methods in the writing of fiction, and he has never propounded any theories which incorporate scientific practices into fictional technique. Nor has his imagery particularly reflected modern technology; usually his images center on cosy interior scenes or lighted windows seen from the outside. Snow's vocabulary, likewise, employs few technical terms except when he happens to be describing a scientific operation. Usually Snow's sole use of science is as background matter, since some of the people he writes about happen to be scientists. Indeed it is the profession of scientist, rather than scientific knowledge, which most interests Snow. His novels *The Search* and *The New Men* do not teach the reader very much about science, but attempt rather to show what the men who are dedicated to science are like. In *The New Men* Snow has an opportunity to deal with science in a very direct

---

[17] Alfred Kazin, *Reporter*, 20:38 (Feb. 5, 1959).
[18] F. R. Karl, *C. P. Snow*, p. 17.   [19] *NYTBR*, Jan. 30, 1955, p. 1.

manner, for he is concerned with describing the building of an atomic pile and, eventually, a bomb. Yet there is actually very little nuclear physics in the novel, since the main emphasis is put on the bureaucratic problems involved in the project. In *The Search* one hears all about Arthur Miles's education, social life, and planning for a scientific institute, but his actual research projects (perhaps since few readers would understand them) are only cursorily described. *The Affair,* which deals with a scientific fraud, gives only vague hints at the nature of the fraud and exactly what the purpose of the research was.

This weakness could have been avoided. Angus Wilson's *Anglo-Saxon Attitudes,* a novel contemporary with Snow's, deals with a historical fraud, but here one has a very clear idea of the exact nature of the fraud as well as of the scholarship connected with it; Wilson has even written an appendix, in which various scholarly documents concerned with the fraud are included. Snow has frequently complained that contemporary artists ignore science; as he said in *The Two Cultures,* "It is bizarre how very little of twentieth-century science has been assimilated into twentieth-century art." [20] It is one thing to write about scientists and still another to write about science, and Snow has not really done the second; he has not incorporated very much science into his art. The reader can learn more science from almost any modern science-fiction novel than from Snow.

Snow has accused the experimental writers of belonging to the chief group which, in its art, has ignored modern scientific developments.[21] While it is true that not many characters who are scientists appeared in the novels of the experimental writers, science itself nevertheless made a great impact on their thought and style. The "Ithaca" chapter of Joyce's *Ulysses,* for example, is far more stylistically concerned with science than any of

[20] *The Two Cultures,* p. 16.
[21] *Ibid.,* and *NYTBR,* Jan. 30, 1955, p. 1.

Snow's prose. Many of the theories of time which are employed by various experimental writers are an attempt to incorporate not only the theories of Bergson, but also those of Einstein.

The greatest impact of modern science on the experimental novelists came in an area which Snow ignores entirely: psychology. Some use of Freud's theories was made by Joyce and Mann, writers whom Snow opposes. Less-well-known experimental writers, like May Sinclair, used entire novels to illustrate Freudian statements.[22] For Snow, "science" seems to mean mainly the physical sciences; he has not recognized that the experimental novelists made great use of modern psychology in their novels, and he has virtually ignored the discoveries of Freud, Jung, and other contemporary psychologists in his own novel writing.

In an interview Snow defended his exclusion of material relating to modern psychology in the following manner:

> As a young man I read a good deal of analytical psychology. As a scientist I was suspicious of it, more than I was as a writer. To an extent, that is still true. That is, I believe that though a writer today must know what analytical psychology is about, he is unwise if he lets it enter explicitly into his work. I have a fairly deep scientific feeling—I don't think it is more than a feeling—that probably the proper concepts of analytical psychology have not yet been reached. Which means that if you use the present concepts it is going to look very odd and amateurish when the real concepts are discovered.[23]

In this manner Snow rejects a great portion of modern science; the exact reasons for his "fairly deep scientific feeling" are not

[22] May Sinclair's *Mary Olivier* is directly influenced by Freud. Characters suffer from the Oedipus complex or from repression in a manner not entirely dissimilar to that of patients in psychological case histories. For more on Freud's influence on May Sinclair and other experimental writers, see chapter 8 of William York Tindall's *Forces in Modern Literature*. For a detailed study of Freud's influence on Joyce and Mann, see Frederic J. Hoffman, *Freudianism and the Literary Mind*, especially chapters 5 and 8.

[23] Interview, *REL*, 3:100 (July, 1962).

given. While it is impossible to defend analytical psychology in as few words as Snow has dismissed it, it may be pointed out that, even if it were determined at some future time that "the proper concepts of analytical psychology have not yet been reached," this is still not enough reason to dismiss the entire discipline. Modern psychology may still be in its infancy, but it is the best knowledge we have in this area. Snow, however, prefers to use a more intuitive, pre-Freudian psychological approach:

I would suspect that for the representation of personality in art, certainly in a novel, the ordinary terms we use among ourselves of things like will and conscience and so on, are closer approximations to what people are like than the present representations of analytical psychology. So therefore, for myself, I deliberately damp it down in all my work, though you will find traces here and there. And I think I am not sorry. It was a deliberate choice and if I was starting again I should make the same choice.[24]

What Snow has done, actually, is to reject the idea of the psychological unconscious. His fictional use of psychological motivation is similar to the method of the Victorian novelists; that is, a particular character will pursue only goals which he consciously recognizes as goals. Occasionally some of Snow's characters do act in a seemingly irrational way, as when Martineau in *Strangers and Brothers* leaves a respectable law practice and turns into a religious crank, or when C. J. B. Palairet, a scientist with an impeccable reputation, is revealed to have forged certain scientific data before he died, in *The Affair*. But Snow makes no attempt to explain this irrational behavior, so out of keeping with all the character's previous actions, in psychological terms. A similar lack of psychological explanation is evident when Snow writes about mental illness, as in the case of Sheila Eliot and Roy Calvert; no real analysis is ever made of their

[24] *Ibid.*, p. 101.

drives or the reasons for their behavior; one is told that they are sick, and this must serve in place of more acute insights into their maladies. As Stephen Wall has written, "Even Eliot's own emotional development cannot be fully shared because his first wife's neurosis is reported rather than recreated. Roy Calvert is a similar case." [25]

It might seem as though, for all his opposition to the experimental writers, Snow might admire their development of the stream-of-consciousness technique because of its ability to display the psychic makeup of a character. Actually, he does the opposite: "I mentioned before that the novel in English has never been strong in causal psychological insight. It is also short of introspective insight, which is closely connected but not quite the same thing. The stream of consciousness inhibits these insights, introspective insight with special finality." [26] Snow defines introspective insight here as the quality with which a character sees himself "with total intimacy and at the same moment as though one were someone else." He concludes that "immersed in the stream of consciousness one can never achieve the second part of this illumination." [27]

This is one example of Snow's inconsistency in attacking the experimental movement. He first condemns it for rejecting modern science; rejecting an entire discipline of modern science himself, he feels that the experimental movement is to be blamed for not rejecting it with him.

One of the chief merits of the stream-of-consciousness method is that, whatever its faults may be, it recognizes the extreme complexity of the motivations which combine to form human behavior. Snow's idea of human behavior is simpler and somewhat deterministic. In a letter he wrote to his publisher in 1938, he said his object was to answer the question, "How much of what we *are* is due to accidents of our class and time, and how

[25] Stephen Wall, *Lon M*, 4:70 (Apr., 1964).
[26] *Kenyon Review*, 23:13 (Winter, 1961).   [27] *Ibid.*

much is due to something innate and unalterable within our-selves?" [28]

As in some forms of Calvinistic theology, the exact amount of determinism in Snow's thinking is difficult to measure. It seems as if his characters are free agents because he puts less stress on the environmental aspects of life ("class and time") than he does on the will and personality; nevertheless the will and per-sonality themselves seem to be predetermined. Thus nothing can alleviate the fits of depression of Sheila Eliot or of Roy Calvert, and Sheila takes her own life, while Calvert volunteers for a suicidal mission in the war. These suicidal acts, because Sheila and Calvert were somehow driven to them, because the two seemed to have no escape from their own personalities, are less the acts of free agents than the predestined fates of people with a certain sort of personality.

This deterministic strain is perhaps easier to detect in the case of Lewis Eliot. Lewis, of course, is born to succeed; one knows he will succeed because of the nonchronological order in which the novels were published. Reading *Time of Hope* (1949), in which Lewis Eliot is struggling to establish himself as a lawyer, one already knows from *Strangers and Brothers* (1940) that Eliot will succeed in his career, or from *The Light and the Dark* (1947) that Eliot became a good enough law-yer to be able to win a fellowship in law at Cambridge. If, on the other hand, one decides to read the novels according to their internal chronology and begins with *Time of Hope,* he still gets hints that Eliot will succeed. This passage, for example, occurs while Lewis is still trying to make up his mind about risking a legacy in order to study for the bar:

In one's "own best interests"—this was the first time I heard that ominous phrase, which I later heard roll sonorously and self-righ-teously round college meetings, round committees in Whitehall,

[28] Quoted by Cooper in *C. P. Snow,* p. 30. The italics are Snow's.

round the most eminent of boards, and which meant inevitably that some unfortunate person was going to be dished.[29]

No matter how the reader approaches the *Strangers and Brothers* series, it is impossible for him not to know that some measure of worldly success is going to come to Lewis Eliot, even while he is reading about Lewis' earliest struggles. Similarly, Sheila's suicide, which is described in *Homecomings* (1956), has already been alluded to in other novels.[30]

This foreknowledge strengthens the deterministic strain which is present in the novels as a result of Snow's easily detected attitudes towards his characters. Because of this determinism, when the anticipated event finally does occur, it seems right, just, congruent with reality. But this congruence may be too easily attained, because the sense of justice which accompanies the event does not grow out of real psychological necessity; ultimately, therefore, it lacks force. The reader accepts the truth of a certain situation because he knew, after all, that it was to happen. This can be a powerful tool if it is combined with psychological insight; but Snow uses it without any deep analyses of his characters.

This sort of analysis is virtually impossible for any of the peripheral characters in the novels because they must be perceived through the eyes of Lewis Eliot, and any real delving into their thoughts would destroy the illusion of the first-person means of narration. At times this very thing seems to happen; Lewis knows the thoughts of characters which have never actually been expressed by them.[31] Usually, however, this is not a very successful compromise, and it does not permit Snow to get very far beneath the surface of his characters.

[29] *Time of Hope*, p. 132.
[30] Sheila's suicide took place in 1939; the action of *The Light and the Dark* ends in 1943; *The New Men* takes place during and after the Second World War. Both novels were published before *Homecomings*.
[31] There are many places where this occurs in Snow's novels. One example is in *The Affair* (p. 299) when Eliot knows what Mrs. Nightingale is thinking though she has really said nothing to give away her thoughts.

Most of the insights into the personalities of the peripheral characters come from Eliot himself. When he does make enough shrewd insights, he begins to seem omniscient; when he fails to make them, the books lack psychological understanding; this is a problem inherent in the first-person means of narration.

For some writers this has not really been a problem, since many first-person narratives have traditionally used the combination of irony and a naïve narrator; quite a few *Bildungsromanen* employ this technique. With a naïve narrator, two things are possible: psychological growth on the part of the narrator as the novel progresses, and a psychological situation in the novel which is better understood by the reader than by the narrator (irony). Whatever loss there may be in psychological understanding of peripheral characters, in such a novel, is compensated for by watching the psychological growth of the hero.

This does not really happen in the *Strangers and Brothers* series: while Lewis Eliot becomes more important and assumes more responsible positions throughout the series, he changes very little psychologically. From the earliest novels, Snow uses him to explain the actions of other characters in such a way as to make him always know more about what is happening than the reader does; thus the possibility of irony is precluded.

It is also important to notice the fictional time in a first-person narrative. The time can be almost simultaneous with the action (as in a narrative based on a journal or diary), or the novel can be written from a time long after the events took place. Snow uses the second technique, as can be seen from the passage quoted above ("this was the first time I heard that ominous phrase, which I later heard roll sonorously and self-righteously round college meetings . . ."). Snow's point of view is after the action of a particular novel, and even beyond that, as though all the events which the series will describe had already taken place. Because Lewis Eliot recounts his story from this late fictional time, he cannot really be naïve, for he already has the knowledge which he gains throughout the progress of the books; no real psychological development in him can be shown. Even the young Lewis Eliot seems like the sober, judicious, middle-aged man; as F. R. Karl has said, "Eliot's childhood is not enough that of a child; it is too much an adult's view of childhood. There is too little childish reality, too much adult interpretation of what a child is like." [32] This quality is apparent not only in Lewis Eliot's narration of events concerning himself but in all of his narration. There is no distinct separation between the author and his narrator; everything must be taken from Eliot's point of view. Characters who do not conform to his opinions or who do not share his ambitions are either unsympathetically treated, like R. S. Robinson and G. S. Clark, or not very well understood, like Calvert and Sheila Eliot.

A number of critics have found this one of the central weaknesses in Snow's series. As Kathleen Nott, for example, points out,

the characters seldom have real insides or real and convincing passions: and one wonders whether the narrative device which Lewis Eliot provides, is, not so much a convenient god's eye view, as a way of dodging the problems of subjectivity, a reversal that is of our whole artistic development, towards a more primitive or juvenile concern with "humours" or the kind of personage one meets in a morality-play.[33]

Many other critics have come to similar conclusions about the weakness of Snow's first-person narrative, among them Bernard Bergonzi, Jay Halio, Graham Martin, and Stephen Wall.[34] All these critics have found that Snow never manages to overcome the problems which are introduced by his particular approach to the technique of the first-person narrator.

[32] F. R. Karl, *C. P. Snow*, p. 44.
[33] Kathleen Nott, *Enc*, 18:95 (Feb., 1962).
[34] Bergonzi, *Twentieth Century*, 167:216–17 (Mar., 1960); Halio, *Northwest Review* (Winter, 1962), p. 97; Martin, "Novelists of Three Decades," in *The Modern Age*, ed. by Boris Ford; Stephen Wall, *Lon M*, 4:71 (Apr., 1964).

Seeing the peripheral characters through Lewis Eliot's eyes raises still another difficulty, hinted at by Kathleen Nott above: Eliot very often sees people as types, as collections of attributes, or even similar perhaps to E. M. Forster's "flat characters." Mrs. Beauchamp in *Homecomings,* for example, is the prototype of the inquisitive landlady. Mrs. Henneker, in *Corridors of Power,* seems to appear only so that she can bore Lewis Eliot at dinner parties with talk about the biography of her dead husband which she is writing. Herbert Rose, a colleague of Eliot's who appears in many of the novels, is cold, efficient, and overbearingly polite; aside from that we learn little about him. When any of these characters appear, they behave in a predictable manner: it is impossible to imagine Hector Rose without an effusive remark. In the same way, Lester Ince is a stereotype of the jazzy younger generation; M. H. L. Gay is the typical absent-minded professor; Lord Boscastle stands for the snobbish English aristocrat. It is with a real sense of astonishment that the reader discovers any human characteristics at all in these stereotypes, as when Lord Boscastle displays deep grief at the death of his son.

Snow does a better job in giving life to his more important characters: the central figures in his novels rarely emerge as stereotypes. Here, however, there is a different problem: very often the dialogue Snow has written for these characters begins to sound very much like that of Lewis Eliot, or even of Snow himself. When Roger Quaife addresses Parliament in *Corridors of Power,*[35] his rhetoric is indistinguishable from Snow's in his Rede Lecture. Snow's intellectuals rarely say anything about their intellectual interests: his academic characters seldom discuss their academic pursuits. An entire novel, *The Light and the Dark,* is devoted to Roy Calvert, who is presented as one of the world's leading specialists on an ancient dualistic religion.

[35] See p. 206.

Yet one learns very little about his work—though he spends hours on it daily—from Calvert's dialogue. As has already been mentioned, scientists in Snow's novels rarely discuss the work they are doing: it is as though all academic persons have an unwritten ban on shoptalk. On the other hand, characters who are involved in politics or management do talk about their interests, and even the academic characters love talking about their managerial or bureaucratic functions. Snow's academic characters are presented more as a collection of bursars, senior tutors, and younger fellows than as a group of scholars; a good deal of their dialogue is given over to questions of who is senior fellow at the head table or which wine to choose.

For example, Dr. David Rubin, an American scientist, shows in his speech little that is American or scientific. When he does begin to talk about science, Snow gets around telling what he has to say: "To everyone's astonishment, Rubin began a long, dense and complex account of the theory of games as applied to nuclear strategy. Talk of over-simplification—this was over-complication gone mad. It was not long before Roger stopped him." [36] The conversation then turns to international politics, where instead of bypassing Rubin's dialogue with a short synopsis as before, Snow permits Rubin to have his full say. When Rubin speaks, he sounds nothing like an American. He uses phrases like "they haven't got there yet" [37] (an American would say "gotten"), and his speech patterns, such as the use or non-use of contractions, are not really American. Although Rubin uses a few American colloquialisms, this alone does not manage to convey an impression of American speech. He says, for example, "Your country cannot play in that league. As far as the economic and military side go, the sooner you get out the better. This is correct." [38] In America, a colloquialism like "play in that league" would probably be accompanied by a con-

[36] *Corridors of Power,* p. 304.   [37] *Ibid.,* p. 307.
[38] *Ibid.,* p. 305.

traction of the verb, and Americans rarely reaffirm what they have just said with the phrase "this is correct." Lapses such as these abound, both in the dialogue of Rubin and that of other characters, and very often Snow relies upon side comments from Lewis Eliot to convey the nuances of speech; he does not permit them to emerge naturally from the character's dialogue. Comments like this one about Tom Orbell exemplify this:

I was thinking that, as he explained himself to Brown, he had shown a delicate blend of the deferential and the man-to-man, beautiful to listen to. In private, out of hearing of persons in authority, few people rebelled as eloquently as Tom Orbell. In hearing of persons in authority, the eloquence remained, but the rebellion not.[39]

The reader is told about Orbell's eloquence, but in the dialogue itself he says nothing which is particularly "beautiful to listen to."

Lewis Eliot's side comments on the speeches, like his comments on the other characters in the novels, at times serve as a substitute for dialogue and characterization. Snow has named this device "commentary," which, in his words, is "any explanation or reflection upon the scene or narrative." [40] Snow feels that commentary is a great asset in the naturalistic novel:

Commentary can, in fact, give an extra dimension to novels; it is the one technical resource which can save the naturalistic novel from the cul-de-sac of the naturalistic play. For the past six or seven years several writers have been deliberately experimenting in the artistic use of commentary; it is the most hopeful contemporary experiment in the novel form.[41]

Snow would certainly include himself among the contemporary novelists who use commentary, though it is difficult to see how his use of commentary (or any other writer's, for that matter) is

[39] *The Affair*, pp. 20–21. [40] *Spec*, 185:320 (Sept. 22, 1950).
[41] *Sun Times*, June 7, 1953, p. 5.

experimental. It is also unclear how commentary can be a "hopeful" experiment in the naturalistic novel, since commentary is used, at times, instead of vivid characterization and dialogue.

Related to the idea of commentary is what Snow calls "resonance." In a note to *The Conscience of the Rich,* Snow said that the inner design of his series was based on a "resonance between what Lewis Eliot sees and what he feels. Some of the more important emotional themes he observes through others' experience, and then finds them enter into his own." [42] To some extent, Snow's concept of resonance seems to be a rationalization of the fact that in certain novels the action concerns mainly Lewis Eliot, while other books show him more as a bystander and commentator. While William Cooper has attempted to make something more profound out of the idea,[43] Snow has done very little, within the novels themselves, to show any blending or intermixture of the action Lewis experiences and that which he merely observes.

As examples of resonance Snow gives the following:

The theme of possessive love is introduced through Mr. March's relation to his son: this theme reappears in *The New Men* in Lewis's own experience, through his relation to his brother, and again, still more directly, in *Homecomings.* In the same way, through Charles March, Lewis in *The Conscience of the Rich* observes both the love of power and the renunciation of power. He observes these again, at various levels, in *The Masters, The Light and the Dark,* and *The New Men.* In *Time of Hope, Homecomings,* and a later book he goes through these experiences himself.[44]

Despite this comment, the possessive love in *The New Men* or in *Homecomings* is not at all similar to Mr. March's possessive love

----

[42] "Author's Note," *The Conscience of the Rich* (London: Macmillan, 1958), p. vii.

[43] *C. P. Snow,* p. 33.

[44] "Author's Note," *The Conscience of the Rich* (London: Macmillan, 1958), pp. vii–viii.

in *The Conscience of the Rich.* Lewis Eliot's love for his brother is neither overbearing nor particularly possessive, as was Mr. March's love for his son; and Lewis' relationships with Sheila and Margaret in *Homecomings* have nothing in common with the situations in the other two novels. It is true that Lewis observes and then experiences the love of power, but this is one of Snow's major concerns throughout his novels; since so many of Snow's characters are involved in struggles for power there is no feeling of resonance when such similarities occur.

Snow's introduction of the concept of resonance, then, seems to be an attempt to link the novels of the *Strangers and Brothers* series which concern Lewis Eliot very little with those which have Eliot as a central character; otherwise Snow could not properly consider the series a *roman-fleuve.* It is true, however, that the action in some of the novels, like *The Light and the Dark,* would not be altered considerably if the narrator were not Lewis Eliot. During the time of this novel, events which are of considerable importance to Eliot, such as the suicide of his wife, occur; yet these events are seldom alluded to in the narrative, which focuses on the life of Roy Calvert. Actually, Calvert and Eliot's wife have a good deal in common: mental illness, suicidal tendencies, and a lack of concern for the people who are in love with them. Though there are opportunities to integrate the two plots by comparing these characters, the events in each novel are kept separate. When Roy Calvert dies, Eliot makes only a veiled comment alluding to the death of his wife, though it is only four years since she has died.[45] This situation would have given Snow an excellent chance to employ the technique of resonance as he described it, but he carefully avoids making any connections between the events. This was probably a wise decision artistically, since any introduction of resonance here

---

[45] When Calvert dies, Eliot says only, "This was the second time I had known intense grief through death," hinting at, but not mentioning, the death of Sheila. See *The Light and the Dark,* p. 397.

would probably have robbed *The Light and the Dark* of a good deal of its power. Snow's use of terms like "resonance" and "commentary," however, seems to be more an afterthought than a technique which he consciously employs in his fiction.

To some extent, this is an attempt by Snow to link his own aesthetics to Proust's. Snow mentions that his wife, Pamela Hansford Johnson, did a number of studies of Proust: "Pamela Hansford Johnson, in a letter to me in 1941, some time before we met, clearly defined the problem of the novel and the anti-novel: shortly afterwards, her Proustian studies led her to find symbols for the alternatives in the persons of Proust and Joyce." [46] Snow thought enough of this idea to expand on it, and later he gave a more detailed analysis of it in the *Kenyon Review*.[47] Here and elsewhere, Snow showed great admiration, not only for Proust, but for Proust's aesthetics. Contrasting the Joycean and Proustian methods of novel writing, Snow said, "For me, even on the level of sensation, the Proustian methods work much better." [48]

Aside from the obvious link of the *roman-fleuve,* Snow's writing resembles Proust's mainly in the great amount of autobiographical matter present in the fiction. The word "resonance" might more aptly be used here than it is by Snow, for reading about Snow, the man, brings to mind detail after detail which Snow describes in the life of Lewis Eliot.

It is always dangerous to attempt to draw parallels between the life of an author and the life of his protagonist; nevertheless, the parallels between Lewis Eliot and C. P. Snow are so striking that they cannot be ignored. Because Snow has made his protagonist so very much like himself, it may be useful to examine the similarities if only to point up where they end and the dissimilarities begin.

One dissimilarity, of course, is that Snow began as a scientist

[46] *TLS,* Aug. 15, 1958, p. iii.
[47] *Kenyon Review,* 23:1 (Winter, 1961).   [48] *Ibid.,* p. 11.

and Lewis Eliot began as a lawyer; but it will be remembered that the protagonist of Snow's first important novel, *The Search,* was a scientist who decided to leave science for writing, just as Snow did. Even in this early novel there are many autobiographical details, many similarities between the author and his hero, Arthur Miles. An example occurs in the early pages of *The Search.* The young Arthur Miles, after looking at the stars with his father, had his first feelings of scientific curosity, and as soon as he got home he "took out all the eight volumes of the *Children's Encyclopaedia* and began to turn the new shiny-smelling pages in search of pictures [he] hazily remembered." [49] In an article in *Discovery,* Snow tells about his own first interest in science:

Most of us can remember the first time we heard or read something which seemed to throw a new light upon the world. In my own case, it comes back with extreme clarity. I was a child of eight or nine, and I had got hold of a bound volume of Arthur Mee's *Children's Encyclopaedia. . . .* Suddenly, for the first time, I ran across an account of how atoms were supposed to have been built up.[50]

Snow and Arthur Miles have similar experiences with the same encyclopedia, and there may be more than coincidence in the similarity of the names of the author of the encyclopedia and the hero of *The Search.*

Miles and Lewis Eliot both grow up in provincial towns similar to Leicester, where Snow was born. Like Snow, they do not do particularly brilliant work until young manhood, when they suddenly become ambitious; and having decided upon a career, they devote themselves entirely to it. Miles, like Snow, managed to do well enough as an undergraduate to win a research fellowship at Cambridge. Even the interests of the author and his protagonists are similar: none has a great interest in art or music, but

[49] *The Search,* pp. 4–5.   [50] *Discovery,* 2:161 (Apr., 1939).

all like literature; all like cricket though they do not care for many other sports; [51] and all show a fondness for the bureaucratic and administrative aspects of their respective professions. All come from rather poor families; from the little that can be learned about Snow's parents it seems that his father was mild-mannered and his mother ambitious for him, much as the parents of Miles and Eliot were. The greatest similarity between Miles and Snow is in their scientific careers and their leaving of science. Snow himself has said that a good deal of Miles's scientific career was based upon his own.[52]

Unlike Arthur Miles, Lewis Eliot does not take up writing as a career; nevertheless we are told that Lewis will, some day, end up as a writer:

I had known that sooner or later I should have some books to write; I did not worry about it; I was learning what I had to say. In trouble, that knowledge had often steadied me, and had given me a comfort greater than any other. Even after Margaret left me, in the middle of the war, when I was too busy to write anything sustained, nevertheless I could, last thing at night, read over my notebooks and add an item or two.[53]

Eliot's writing of notebooks but not publishing anything during the war corresponds exactly to events in Snow's life, as has emerged in an interview:

Interviewer: Do you keep notebooks?

Snow: Yes, the whole conception of the sequence and the whole manner of my life made that obligatory, even if I had not been disposed to. And also of course the fact that I was really quite seriously interrupted in mid-career by the first five years of the war. So that I have kept notebooks regularly almost from the beginning.[54]

[51] In his address "On Magnanimity" (*Harper's Magazine,* 225:37 [July, 1962]), Snow said that he had acquired his love of cricket from G. H. Hardy, the Cambridge mathematician. Actually, Snow was a good cricketer in secondary school; see L. Siegel, *WLB,* 28:404 (Jan., 1954).
[52] Author's note to *The Search,* p. v.   [53] *Homecomings,* p. 197.
[54] Interview, *REL,* 3:98–99 (July, 1962).

There are many obvious similarities between the lives of Snow and Lewis Eliot; actually, more than between those of Snow and Arthur Miles. Both Snow and Eliot were born in 1905; in 1927, when Eliot passed his bar examinations, Snow got his Bachelor of Science degree. Both go up to Cambridge in the early thirties and leave Cambridge to work in Whitehall during the war, work which earns them knighthoods.

These similarities have often been noted, but it is less well known how much Snow has drawn from experiences in his own life for the *Strangers and Brothers* series. The March family, described by Snow in *The Conscience of the Rich,* has a counterpart in real life. As Snow has written,

When I was very poor and very young, I was taken up by one of the rich patrician Anglo-Jewish families. It was a startling experience. I was a Gentile, and I had never seen the inside of a Jewish family before. This was my first contact with the easy, interconnected, confident world of the English ruling classes. Up to that time, cabinet ministers, high court judges, bosses of the civil service were, for me, people one read about in the newspapers. At my friends' houses I met these people: in fact, my friends' relatives occupied just such jobs.[55]

Lewis Eliot, of course, undergoes precisely the same experience, and it forms the background for an entire novel.

At times single incidents are taken from life and incorporated into the novels. Here, for example, is a passage from *Homecomings* in which Paul Lufkin, an industrialist, gives his opinion of the English honors system after hearing that he has been elevated to the House of Lords: " 'The main advantage about these tinpot honors—which I still think it's time we got rid of—' he put in, getting it both ways, as so often, 'isn't the pleasure they cause to the chaps who get them: it's the pain they cause to the

[55] Introduction by Snow to Arnold Rogow's *The Jew In a Gentile World* (New York: Macmillan, 1961), p. xv.

chaps who don't.' " [56] The basis for this incident is a remark F. A. Lindemann (Lord Cherwell) once made to Snow:

I remember talking to Lindemann one morning when the Honors List had been published. I happened to remark that the English honors system must cause far more pain than pleasure: the pleasure to those who got awards was nothing like so great as the pain of those who didn't. Miraculously Lindemann's somber heavy face lit up. With a gleeful sneer he said: "Of course it is. It wouldn't be any use getting an award if one didn't think of all the people who were miserable because they hadn't managed it." [57]

Snow often takes remarks or events from life. *The New Men,* which tells of the development of an atomic pile in England during the Second World War has many details based on actual events; Snow's spy Sawbridge, for example, is probably based on Dr. Allan Nunn May; [58] the town Barford, where the pile is located, is similar to Harwell; and many of the other scientists in the novel seem to have been drawn from life.

There is nothing unusual about a writer's using bits of life in his novels, and Snow has made no secret of the fact that this is a technique he often employs.[59] These incidents and background scenes, in addition to the obvious similarities between the lives of author and hero, do much to demonstrate that there is an autobiographical element in the novels. A number of critics have found this to be so: Alfred Kazin has written that Snow's novels are "deeply autobiographical and historical"; William Gerhardi has said that Lewis Eliot is "the author's alter ego"; and Walter Allen found "the parallel between author and character . . .

---

[56] *Homecomings,* p. 239.   [57] *Life,* 50:90 (Feb. 3, 1961).
[58] Nunn May and Sawbridge both were about the same age, born in the North of England, attended Cambridge, did work in physics, and were approved by reliable superiors for work on atomic projects. Neither Nunn May nor Sawbridge ever denied their left-wing sympathies, both remained calm during their interrogations, and neither one ever offered an explanation of why he chose to be disloyal.
[59] Interview, *REL,* 3:99 (July, 1962).

plain enough," despite the differences in professions of Snow and Eliot.[60]

Snow has defined his relationship to Lewis Eliot in the interview quoted earlier:

Interviewer: How far would you say that Lewis Eliot is yourself? Or is he a kind of literary persona?
Snow: I would have thought that in depth Lewis Eliot is myself. In a good many of his situations, a good many of his external appearances he is not me, but in any serious and interesting sense he is.[61]

In light of this admitted similarity, Snow's praise of Lewis Eliot, both in the situations in which Eliot comes off well and in the things people say about him, at times makes it seem that Snow is praising himself. This has been pointed out by Geoffrey Wagner:

Lewis Eliot is such an obnoxious *alter ego.* Snow has confessed his proximity to this character. The two were born in the same year, came from similar lower-middle-class backgrounds, and have like careers in the Civil Service and at Cambridge. But the reader cannot help being put off by the constant pats on the back Lewis gets from this character or that throughout the series. Everyone is always telling him what a good fellow he is, and in *Homecoming* he even reminds himself ("to others, I devoted myself with a lack of self-regard . . .").[62]

The self-praise is increased by the fact that Lewis Eliot is not completely autobiographical. If he is actually Snow's *alter ego,* he is an *alter ego* without the faults of the original, an uncritical self-portrait.

Lewis Eliot does have an unattractive side: his quest for

[60] William Gerhardi, *Spec,* 183:438 (Sept. 30, 1949); Alfred Kazin, *Reporter,* 20:37 (Feb. 5, 1959); Walter Allen, *Tradition and Dream,* p. 248.
[61] Interview, *REL,* 3:93 (July, 1962).
[62] Geoffrey Wagner, *Commonweal,* 65:50 (Oct. 12, 1956).

power and money, his glamorizing of materialism, and his snobbery once he begins to reach his goals; but Snow rarely sees these things as faults. Sometimes Snow even maintains a condescending attitude towards those characters whose ideals differ from Eliot's. Snow inflates the value of Lewis Eliot as a character; but even more irritating than this is Snow's conviction that the Eliots of the world are of overwhelming importance, that these bureaucrats and administrators (among whom Snow counts himself) alone have the key to the future happiness of man in their hands. This is the ultimate message which Snow attempts to convey in his speeches, and which, by example, Lewis Eliot conveys.

It is this which accounts for the tone of self-congratulation, and perhaps even of snobbery, which is to be found in Snow's writing. In *Corridors of Power,* names are dropped unselfconsciously: Eliot is intimate with Nobel Prize winners, the American ambassador, almost everyone of any importance in the government, and is ultimately a chief adviser of the prime minister himself. This novel, incidently, was published before Snow himself was given a position in the English government and a seat in the House of Lords.

The self-congratulatory tone originates in Eliot's pride in being on the "inside" of government affairs. He often uses the phrase "if one knew the language" to show that he does know the language, and then obliges the reader with an explanation: "The *Telegraph* gave bolder headlines and more space: if one knew the language, one knew they were anti-Roger." [63] Snow uses a similar tone in his Rede Lecture: "There is some evidence that Indians and other Asians are eating less, in absolute quantities, than they were a generation ago. The statistics are not reliable, and informants in the F. A. O. have told me not to put much trust in them." [64] It would seem that accurate information on food consumption in Asia were not available to just anyone; for

[63] *Corridors of Power,* p. 375.   [64] *The Two Cultures,* p. 42.

the entire story one needs highly placed friends in the government. In his effort to show that he is on the "inside" Eliot is at times inadvertently funny:

> Most of the people I met, even on the technical committees, were still ignorant about the whole uranium project. But some could not resist letting one know that they were in the secret too. In the lavatory of the Athenaeum a bald bland head turned to me from the adjacent stall.
>
> *"March 22nd,"* came the whisper and a finger rose to the lips.[65]

What could be more "inside" than getting information about a top-secret uranium project in that *sanctum sanctorum,* the men's room of the Athenaeum?

Snow seems impervious to the humor in this situation; a great fault in his novels is the seriousness with which he permits Lewis Eliot to take himself. There is very little that is funny in Snow's novels, nor does one ever encounter wit or satire. *"Satire,"* Snow has written with italics, "is cheek." [66] He never explains what is wrong with cheek.

The self-congratulation and humorlessness are based on the sense of moral superiority which Snow gives to Lewis Eliot. In one of the few instances in the novels where a character actually attempts a mild criticism of Eliot, a friend quickly defends him, and the critic must apologize: " 'I'm sorry, Lewis,' said Tom, at his jolliest and most repentant, instantaneously quick to catch the feeling of someone like Brown, 'it was absolutely monstrous of me to accuse you of that. You're frightfully good, I know you are'." [67] Tom Orbell had accused Eliot of nothing more terrible than being antireligious; but he is forced by Brown to accept the idea of Lewis Eliot's generally acknowledged goodness.

Lewis Eliot, however, is not always so moral as he appears

[65] *The New Men,* p. 97. The italics are Snow's.
[66] *Science and Government,* p. 66. In a footnote to this comment Snow says, "I owe this remark, which seems to me truer the more I think of it, to Pamela Hansford Johnson."
[67] *The Affair,* p. 20.

to be. He speaks somewhat contemptuously about the girl-chasing of characters like George Passant, Jack Cotery, and Roy Calvert; his contempt is absolute for Hannah Puchwein, who is suspected of being unfaithful to her husband. Yet Eliot himself, knowing that he is bound to make her unhappy, forces Sheila to marry him by frightening off a rival in an entirely unscrupulous manner. After marrying Sheila he spends a good amount of time mourning his wrecked career, feeling sorry for himself, and he even attempts to leave her.

After Sheila's suicide he has an affair with Margaret which ends when she accuses him of being too secretive; Lewis makes no attempt to renew the affair or to see her, and she marries someone else. After she has a child he manages to convince her to leave her husband (who is very much in love with her), obtain a divorce, and marry him.

Roy Calvert's lack of feeling for his women, George Passant's mistresses, and Hannah Puchwein's adultery are all made to seem sordid, insensitive, and tawdry. When Lewis Eliot commits the same sins himself he does not even feel any moral struggle; he accepts his actions as inevitable and leaves it at that. Here, for example, is what Lewis said to himself when, after dinner with Margaret and her husband and child, he realized that Margaret "was not free of me, any more than I of her":

In the hot room, noisy now with the boy's demands, I felt, not premonition, not responsibility, not the guilt that would have seemed ineluctable if I had seen another in my place, but an absolute exaltation, as though, all in one move, I had joy in my hands and my life miraculously simple. I did not recognize any fear mixed with the joy, I just felt happy and at one.[68]

These words end one chapter; the next one begins as follows: "It was a September afternoon when I was waiting, for the first

---

[68] *Homecomings,* p. 268.

time since her marriage, to meet Margaret alone." [69] This meeting leads to another, and ultimately to the breakdown of Margaret's first marriage; yet Snow gives absolutely no space to Lewis Eliot's thoughts between the time when he realizes that he can still attract Margaret and his decision to begin to win her again.

As Lewis admits, if he had seen another in his place his feelings about this adulterous situation would have been quite different. But Lewis spends very little time feeling guilty or in soul-searching; he and Margaret perfunctorily mention that they are doing a very bad thing and then spend most of their time worrying about what their friends will say when they learn about the affair.

By the time Lewis has been happily married for a number of years, in *Corridors of Power,* he is remote enough from his own days of intrigue to take a rather morally smug view of the extra-marital affair of Roger Quaife. Yet in many ways Roger, who is unhappily married, has as much justification for his actions as Lewis Eliot did when he renewed his affection for Margaret.

What is most striking is not so much Lewis' hypocrisy, or his readiness to forgive himself, as the absence of any real moral issue in *Homecomings.* If Snow were really as interested in morality as he has claimed he is, or if he were really a follower of George Eliot or of Dostoevsky, he would not give the few scenes where Lewis has to make some sort of moral choice such a cursory treatment. Just as he spends little time considering the morality of his actions with Margaret, Lewis decides to prevent Sheila's marriage to a man he knows can make her happier than Lewis ever will with no inner debate:

Yes. Her best chance was to marry him. I believed that I could decide it. I could bring it off—or destroy it.

[69] *Ibid.,* p. 269.

With the cruellest sense of power I had ever known, I thought that I could destroy it.[70]

He can destroy it, and he does. *Omnia vincit amor;* Lewis again feels that his actions need no explanation.

This lack of moral debate does not relate only to love affairs. In 1955 Snow wrote an article in which he said that the atomic bomb "has staggered scientists with a moral shock from which the best and most sensitive will not easily recover. . . . the mood brings scientists and novelists closer together. . . ."[71] One would think, then, that Snow was interested in examining the moral reactions of scientists to the military use of the atomic bomb.

Just before he wrote this article *The New Men* appeared, a book which dealt with this very problem: the attempt to build an atomic bomb in England during the Second World War. But Snow's scientists have very few moral qualms about building an atomic bomb; they are certain that the Nazis are engaged in similar research and their only concern is to finish a bomb before them. The English scientists in the novel never do make a bomb, because the Americans make one first. Nor do the English collaborate in the decision to use the bomb on Hiroshima; this again is done by the Americans, and the English scientists are as shocked as anyone else when they read in the newspapers about the first atomic bombs being dropped. Most of the English scientists feel not guilt but anger that the bomb has been used in this fashion.

Obviously there is no moral issue here; the English scientists have not made the bomb, nor has the English government used it. If Snow had wanted to include a moral conflict, he doubtless would have written about those English scientists who went to the United States and Canada during the Second World War, and who thus made a direct contribution to the development of

[70] *Time of Hope,* p. 352.   [71] *NYTBR,* Jan. 30, 1955, p. 29.

the bomb. This is closer to what actually occurred; the greatest part of English nuclear research at this time took place on North American soil. By being less historically accurate than he might be, Snow manages to make the English participation in the development of the bomb seem a trifle smaller; in turn, he diminishes the possibility for any real moral choice about the use of the bomb.

The only thing close to this sort of moral choice in *The New Men* comes when Martin Eliot considers sending a strongly worded letter to the *Times* in which he condemns the use of the bomb over Hiroshima; the letter says that the responsibility for this action, or some part of it, must be shared by English scientists.[72] As soon as Lewis Eliot reads his brother's letter he decides that its publication would be the end of Martin's career as a scientist. Lewis urges him not to send it, and in the end the letter is not submitted.

As Snow says, the atomic bomb has provided a new moral atmosphere for science which a novelist could profitably portray. The important issue here, as Snow has pointed out in his address "The Moral Unneutrality of Science," [73] is that the scientist cannot maintain a state of ethical neutrality; he must begin to make moral choices, especially if his work relates to the development of new weapons. That his scientists are seldom shown in moral dilemmas, that the debates dealing with the use of the bomb are not recorded in his novels is proof that morality in science, like morality in human affairs, is an area with which Snow is only superficially concerned.[74]

Instead of morality, the chief concerns of Snow's characters are mainly the hierarchical systems in which they find themselves. Should one apply for a certain position? Who is the best

[72] *The New Men*, pp. 193–94.
[73] Reprinted in *Science*, 133:256 (Jan. 27, 1961).
[74] Others who have reached similar conclusions are Bernard Bergonzi, *Twentieth Century*, 167:225 (Mar., 1960); James Ginden, *Postwar British Fiction*, pp. 210–12; Derek Stanford, *Meanjin*, 19:245 (1960).

man for another position? Might so-and-so do better if he were to choose another career? In *The Affair* it seems that there is a moral conflict: an innocent man is unjustly accused of having forged scientific evidence; but Snow is careful to show that his accusers were always under the impression that there was enough evidence to incriminate him. The novel deals not so much with a moral issue as with the siftings and resiftings of the evidence until an approximation of the truth is obtained. There is little moral conflict here, as there is little in a detective story: if a man is truly guilty of a criminal act, he must be punished; if not, he must be freed.

This is underlined by the statement which Crawford makes at the end of the novel: "In my experience sensible men usually reach sensible conclusions." [75] Justice, by however ponderous a route, has been reached; but the essential validity of the judicial system has never been questioned. It is, very often, when sensible men cannot reach a sensible conclusion that true moral dilemmas begin. This is the area which Snow avoids: the investigation of the irrational or evil side of man's nature.

Snow's characters are never devilish or angelic; their hopes and aspirations are modest, and their sins are peccadillos. They are never moral extremists, but occupy a thin grey band where good meets evil. They are not philosophers; they never question the meaning of the universe or the reasons for their own existence. Their concept of the universe is empirical and materialistic; their hope for the future is based on a deep-rooted positivism; and, like some logical positivists, they find metaphysical questions unworthy of their consideration.

Certainly Snow's heroes have nothing in common with the romantic heroes, with the Manfreds, Raskolnikovs, and Lafcadios who have dominated Western literature since the nineteenth century. This type of hero, whom F. R. Karl calls the existential-

[75] *The Affair,* p. 374.

ist hero, is not present in Snow's novels. Comparing Snow and the existential novelists, Karl says,

The existentialist, whether successful or not, sees man as a weak creature capable of a curious grandeur when faced by annihilation. Snow sets his sights considerably lower; man's grandeur is revealed when he makes a good business decision or selects a capable administrative assistant. There is no swamp, no unconscious, no cosmos.[76]

Karl finds Snow's view of man a view that most people accept, and a view that is far more comforting for the ordinary man than the existential view of the universe:

Snow's view that the will, in spite of setbacks, will ultimately give man what he wants if he is willing to persist, is comforting, especially against a background of fiction by Kafka, Beckett, Camus, Sartre, and Conrad. Snow's seems the real world of hope and desire, ambition and setbacks, will and counter-will. Life here is controllable, subject to a man's sense of his own destiny.[77]

This distinction between existential and anti-existential points of view which Karl underlines is extremely important for an understanding of Snow's position as a novelist. Both his novels and his criticism reflect his opposition to an existential point of view; as for existentialism considered purely philosophically, he has said that scientists do not care much for it, though they might respect linguistic analysis.[78] The point of view which Snow attributed to scientists seems to be as much his own as anyone else's.

Snow's rejection of existentialism consists, in his fiction, mainly in ignoring the problems which existentialists consider important. Lewis Eliot never worries about God or the problems of man's being born without an explanation for his existence; those Snow characters who do are troubled by some form of mental illness, like Howard Martineau and Roy Calvert. For

[76] *C. P. Snow*, p. 128. [77] *Ibid.*, pp. 126–27.
[78] *NS*, 52:413 (Oct. 6, 1956).

Snow, life consists not in a struggle to live in a hostile universe, but in an effort to overcome the indifference of society.

This explains why, in Snow's novels, so many second-rate men succeed, while the truly gifted and more imaginative men fail. Jago's loss to Crawford, Martin Eliot's winning of a scientific directorship from Walter Luke, the deterioration of George Passant, and the steady rise of Lewis Eliot all illustrate Snow's preference for the practical, rather than the imaginative, man. Society has rewarded these practical men: they are Nobel laureates, corporation directors, knights. The men who do not have these marks of success all have the same flaw: they are not "solid men," and though they may compete they never win.

In Snow's fiction, the men at the top are seldom evil; they may have odd prejudices, like Lord Boscastle, or curious habits, like Thomas Bevill; but in general they are decent men. No one who is really villainous, in Snow's novels, holds a place of power very long. In this way Snow subtly equates the idea of goodness with success. This type of evaluation is generally common today, as much in the capitalistic Horatio Alger view of man as in the socialist-realist view of the Marxist.

Both systems find their moral yardsticks for human beings in social instead of individual terms; both views reject asocial or apolitical existentialism.[79] The existential view is concerned with determining the place of the individual man in the universe. Opposed to this is the Marxist or Capitalist point of view which considers the needs of society before the needs of individual men within that society, and which measures success mainly in terms of social approbation.

Morality in a socially oriented system comes entirely from social sources; there is never any real dependence on a metaphysical or abstract framework of morality outside of the society itself. The immediate advantage of this system is to make

---

[79] This does not imply that some existentialists, like Sartre, could not find themselves agreeing with Marxist ideas; the point is that those who are *primarily* Marxists rarely have much use for existentialism.

society more stable by being severe with all antisocial elements within it; but ultimately it weakens society because it prevents change and discourages originality.

Snow's moral system is society-oriented in this way. He praises those values in men which are most useful socially, and even his social criticism is of the socially acceptable variety: he makes few suggestions for social change which would offend the people in power. Such a moral system must forgo abstract concepts of justice and appeal instead to ambiguous phrases like "fairness" and "decency"; these terms do not so much refer to any moral code as simply mean actions which society would approve of.

An effective moral system, whether it is founded on theology or an abstract idea of justice, refers to elements higher than, and outside of, man or society. Angus Wilson's novels, for example, have their moral foundation in Wilson's humanistic code. Snow's morality does not appeal to any higher code, and justice is reduced to fairness, morality to decency, and goodness to success.

Snow's anti-existential, socially oriented point of view is as popular in communistic countries as it is in the West; he is one of the few contemporary writers who sells well both in the United States and in Russia. This is to be expected: Snow's hero is the bureaucratic man, and by romanticizing the roles of people in essentially mundane occupations Snow has endeared himself to readers in the countries with the largest bureaucracies, regardless of their political point of view. His heroes engage in no heroic quests; they seek good incomes, but not fortunes; instead of fame they are happy with a bit of official recognition; if they have any really great ambition, it is to be able to control their fellow men. People like to read about themselves: the professional, middle-class people Snow writes about are also his greatest readers. They, like Lewis Eliot, are happy in their professions, self-satisfied because of their incomes, and totally convinced of their value to the community. Their chief fault is similar to Lewis Eliot's: an unwillingness to fight against, or even to recognize, their own essential mediocrity.

CHAPTER SIX

Conclusion
The Drawbacks of
Traditionalism

THE REACTION against experimentalism did not, of course, include all the novelists who lived in England and achieved popularity in the 1950s. William Golding, for example wrote his allegorical, symbolic novels in this period. Iris Murdoch is one of the few English novelists whose work shows even tenuous links with the absurd and existentialist writers. Muriel Spark, Lawrence Durrell, and Nigel Dennis, in their own ways, are exceptions to the general rule of anti-experimentalism. The overwhelming majority of the novelists of this time, however, did follow the rule.

The five novelists above mentioned as exceptions to the general trend, are among the finest writers of their time in England. Yet the period itself, the 1950–1960 decade, has not been a very fruitful one for the novel; few novels that could be called great were written at this time, and fewer still of the finest novels came from the anti-experimental writers.

The lack of distinction in the novel of this period was in fact one of the clichés of contemporary English criticism; it took the place of the "death of the novel" cry which was the vogue a generation before. Here, for example, is a comment from V. S. Pritchett in 1953: "Once again one has to say that nothing very remarkable has been written in the last twelve months. The good work is solidly good and gracious, but one has the impression that it is hanging on for dear life." [1] A year and a half later, Stephen Spender wrote, "What is discouraging is that with the reaction of today the achievement of works seems to have shrunk, and there is a younger generation of academic-minded writers who seem all too complacent in their aims." [2]

By 1957, most of the writers under consideration here had published at least one novel; the next comments are taken from *Declaration,* a collection of essays published in 1957 which gave some of the younger writers a chance to put forth their views on the state of contemporary literature. In this volume, Doris Lessing wrote, "We are not living in an exciting literary period but in a dull one. We are not producing masterpieces, but large numbers of small, quite lively, intelligent novels." Bill Hopkins said, "The literature of the past ten years has been conspicuous for its total lack of direction, purpose, and power. It has opened no new roads of imagination, created no monumental characters, and contributed nothing whatever to the vitality of the written word." [3]

In the 1960s, the tone of the comments still was the same. Bernard Bergonzi wrote, "On the whole it is true to say that most contemporary novelists have in practice, but not in theory, sold out. Though they subscribe in principle to the notion of originality at all costs, and avoid overt plagiarism, they are still broadly content to write much the same kind of novel as many other novelists." [4] This opinion was echoed by many other

[1] *NYTBR,* Jan. 25, 1953, p. 26.   [2] *Ibid.,* Aug. 1, 1954, p. 2.
[3] *Declaration,* edited by Tom Maschler, p. 22 (Lessing); p. 133 (Hopkins).
[4] *List,* 70:416 (Sept. 19, 1963).

critics, as a statement of G. S. Fraser's shows: "It has been a general critical comment that English fiction in the 1950s has shown a very high average level of technical intelligence, but that it has not produced masters: the novelist as a great man, as oracle, sage, or prophet, as lonely dedicated artist, of the type of James, Conrad, Joyce, Lawrence, seems no longer to exist." [5]

The novelists of the 1950s have not produced fiction which approaches the quality of the novels of the writers whom they have imitated. Nor, for that matter, is their work as good as the fiction of the writers whom they have rejected; as Anthony Quinton says,

There is no one among the leading novelists of the last thirteen years who has managed to evoke any sustained and passionate partisanship one way or the other; they are tractable and commodious figures who can be fitted into our lives without disrupting them. No one has made the sort of claims for the importance of his work made by, or on behalf of, Joyce, Lawrence, or even Virginia Woolf.[6]

A principal complaint of these critics is that the new English novel lacks originality; but at the same time it seems as though the aesthetics of the movement and the literary ideas put forward by the newer writers are designed to stifle originality before it has a chance to develop. The critical mood in England has produced a climate in which traditional novels can flourish and anything out of the ordinary is given the denigrating label "experimental" and neglected. The critics who have brought about this mood have forgotten the maxim that today's traditional art was experimental in its own time. As F. R. Karl says,

To decry the new is certainly prevalent among popular critics who defend with exemplary energy what worked well in the past. Like political reactionaries, they applaud what they recognize and reject what looks foreign. For the serious reader, however, the experimen-

[5] G. S. Fraser, *The Modern Writer and His World*, p. 166.
[6] *Lon M*, 5:13–14 (Nov., 1958).

tal novel signifies that something adventurous is being undertaken and that the art is healthy. All truly great novels are experimental in some way—whether in content or technique—and possibly the reason why many major contemporary novels disappoint is that the novelist has in the main disdained experiment.[7]

The greatest fear of the English contemporary novelist is to commit a *faux pas;* every step taken is within prescribed limits; and the result is intelligent, technically competent, but ultimately mediocre. When a novelist goes outside the set limits, he can expect no help from the critics, no matter how good his work.

William Golding is a case in point. Golding's *Lord of the Flies* is certainly one of the best and most original novels to appear in the 1950–1960 decade. When it was published, the reviews were of the variety which send a book to oblivion: according to the *New York Times Book Review,* "it received lukewarm-to-unfavorable reviews and its sale was small." After the publication of a paperback edition, however, "it began winning a devoted following as a rousing adventure tale with deep philosophical implications. Some critics believe it is a minor, modern classic." [8]

Walter Allen (whose review of *Lucky Jim* helped to make it an instant success) is one of the critics whose reviews were lukewarm. Here is a paragraph from it:

Lord of the Flies is like a fragment of nightmare, for all that it is lightly told. It commands a reluctant assent: yes, doubtless it could be like that, with the regression from choir school to Mau Mau only a step. The difficulty begins when one smells allegory. "There's not a child so small and weak But has his little cross to take." These children's crosses, it seems to me, were altogether too unnaturally heavy for it to be possible to draw conclusions from Mr. Golding's novel, and if that is so, it is, however skillfully told, only a rather unpleasant and too-easily affecting story.[9]

[7] *A Reader's Guide to the Contemporary English Novel,* p. 15.
[8] *NYTBR,* Dec. 10, 1961, p. 56.   [9] *NS,* 48:370 (Sept. 25, 1954).

Ten years later, when *Lord of the Flies* had become a success in spite of the poor reviews, Allen wrote the following:

The brilliance of *Lord of the Flies* can scarcely be exaggerated, and horrific as it is, it cannot be dismissed merely as a horror-comic of high literary merit, as a "sick" comment on R. M. Ballantyne's nineteenth-century views on the nature of British boyhood. The fact is, its apprehension of evil is such that it touches the nerve of contemporary horror as no English novel of its time has done; it takes us, with the greatest dramatic power and through the most poignant symbolism, into a world of active, proliferating evil which is seen, one feels, as the natural condition of man and which is bound to remind the reader of the vilest manifestations of Nazi regression.[10]

This is not intended to be a comment on the critical intelligence of Walter Allen; Allen is an astute and perceptive critic, honest enough to revise an original judgment when he thought it had been unfair. The indictment here is against the entire school of English reviewers of contemporary fiction, who as Karl says, "applaud what they recognize and reject what looks foreign." The novelist like Golding, who can succeed in spite of bad reviews, is rare; when the critical climate is unvaried enough to be predictable, writers who know they will get bad reviews must either conform or stop writing.

The successful novelist in England becomes, too quickly, a part of the London literary establishment. Between novels, he supports himself by reviewing for the weeklies and quarterlies and by giving broadcasts over the B.B.C. All too often, he uses his position as a critic to endorse the type of fiction he himself is writing and to attack those whose approach is different.[11]

The English literary situation is not entirely gloomy; recently a few novelists have appeared who have moved in a somewhat unconventional direction. Andrew Sinclair, for example, has left

[10] Walter Allen, *Tradition and Dream*, p. 289.
[11] This situation has been described in detail by Stephen Spender, *NYTBR*, Aug. 28, 1960, p. 1.

behind the dull, realistic style of the previous decade; his writing has a new freshness and liveliness. Anthony Burgess has even attempted an experimental novel, *A Clockwork Orange,* which uses a good deal of neologistic slang. But most English novelists, like the president of the Royal Academy of Arts who preferred eighteenth-century dress, still seem content to live in the past.

Bibliography

This bibliography is divided into four parts: one each for Amis, Wilson, and Snow, and a general bibliography. The first three lists are comprehensive bibliographies; the fourth, selective. Each individual bibliography is divided into three sections: the first contains books written by the novelist (arranged chronologically); the second, articles by the novelist (entered, in chronological order, under the name of the periodical in which the article appears, or under the name of the author or editor of the book in which it appears); the last section contains critical articles about the novelist, and is selective.

In instances where the title of a book review is not specific, the title of the book under discussion, rather than the title of the review, has been used.

The general bibliography, arranged alphabetically by author, consists of a list of general critical articles dealing with the English novel in the 1950s.

KINGSLEY AMIS, b. 1922

I. Books Written or Edited by Amis

Bright November. London: Fortune Press, 1947. Poems.

Oxford Poetry, 1949. Edited by Amis and J. Michie. Oxford: Blackwell, 1949.

A Frame of Mind. Reading: School of Art, University of Reading, 1953. Poems.

Kingsley Amis. Number 22, Fantasy Poets Series. Oxford: Fantasy Press, 1954.

Lucky Jim. London: Gollancz, 1954; New York: Viking, 1959.

That Uncertain Feeling. London: Gollancz, 1955; New York: Harcourt Brace, 1956.

A Case of Samples. Poems, 1945–1956. London: Gollancz, 1956; New York: Harcourt Brace, 1957.

Socialism and the Intellectuals. London: The Fabian Society, 1957.

I Like It Here. London: Gollancz; New York: Harcourt Brace, 1958.

New Maps of Hell: A Survey of Science Fiction. New York: Harcourt Brace, 1960; London: Gollancz, 1961.

Take a Girl Like You. London: Gollancz, 1960; New York: Harcourt Brace, 1961.

Spectrum: A Science Fiction Anthology. Edited by Amis and Robert Conquest. London: Gollancz, 1961; New York: Harcourt Brace, 1962.

Penguin Modern Poets II: Kingsley Amis, Dom Moraes, Peter Porter. London: Penguin Books, 1962.

My Enemy's Enemy. London: Gollancz; New York: Harcourt Brace, 1962.

Spectrum II: A Second Science Fiction Anthology. Edited by Amis and Robert Conquest. London: Gollancz, 1962; New York, Harcourt Brace, 1963.

The Evans Country. Oxford: Fantasy Press, 1963. Poems.

Spectrum III: A Third Science Fiction Anthology. Edited by Amis and Robert Conquest. London: Gollancz, 1963; New York: Harcourt Brace, 1964.

One Fat Englishman. London: Gollancz, 1963; New York: Harcourt Brace, 1964.

A Question About Hell. Television play, presented on ITV (London), April 27, 1964.

Spectrum IV. Edited by Amis and Robert Conquest. New York: Harcourt, Brace, and World, 1965.

The James Bond Dossier. New York: The New American Library, 1965

The Egyptologists. London: Jonathan Cape, 1965. A novel by Kingsley Amis and Robert Conquest.

The Anti-Death League. London: Gollancz, 1966.

II. Essays, Articles, and Book Reviews by Amis

Butler, Samuel, *Erewhon.* New York: New American Library (Signet), 1960. Afterword by Amis.

Encounter: Novels by Moravia, Greene, and others (review). 4:75 (April, 1955). "My Enemy's Enemy." 4:51 (June, 1955). Story. "Lone Voices: Views of the Fifties." 15:6 (July, 1960). "Going into Europe." 19:56 (Dec., 1962). "One Fat Englishman." 21:30 (Nov., 1963). An excerpt from the novel. "No More Parades." 22:23 (Feb., 1964).

Essays in Criticism: "The Curious Elf. A Note on Rhyme in Keats." 1:189 (April, 1951). "Emily Colored Primulas." 2:338 (July, 1952). By Amis and Geoffrey Nokes. "Ulster Bull: The Case of W. R. Rodgers." 3:470 (Oct., 1953). "Communication and the Victorian Poet." 4:386 (Oct., 1954). *C. Day Lewis,* by C. Dyment (review). 5:394 (Oct., 1955).

Harper's: "Delights of Literary Lecturing." 219:180 (Oct., 1959).

Listener: "Good Brave Causes?" 65:1087 (June 22, 1961).

Mademoiselle: "Decade of New Heartbreakers." 50:74 (Jan., 1960). "Sexy Defects; or Why Henrietta Maria Kept Her Eyes Open." 51:88 (Oct., 1960). "Psyche of the Future." 54:40 (Jan., 1962).

Nation: "How To Get Away with It." 182:514 (June 16, 1956).
New Republic: "Dodos Less Darling." 135:27 (Oct. 15, 1956).
New Statesman: "Red Dragon Blues." 61:298 (Feb. 24, 1961). "Definitions of Culture." 61:880 (June 2, 1961). *Previous Convictions,* by Cyril Connolly (review). 66:386 (Dec. 6, 1963). Novels by Ian Fleming and others (review). 67:453 (March 20, 1964).
New World Writing: "You That Love England; or, Limey, Stay Home." 16:135 (1960).
New York Times Book Review: "Laughter's To Be Taken Seriously." July 7, 1957, p. 1.
Observer: Jazz Criticism. In issues of April 13, July 20, Aug. 17, and Sept. 21, 1958.

"Where Novelists Fear To Tread. The Case for Science Fiction." Nov. 29, 1959, p. 8.   Science fiction (review). Dec. 13, 1959, p. 23.

"How Not To Talk to a Texan." Jan. 3, 1960, p. 8.   Science fiction (review). March 20, 1960, p. 21.   Science fiction (review). April 10, 1960, p. 21.   Science fiction (review). May 15, 1960, p. 25.   *Casanova's Chinese Restaurant,* by Anthony Powell (review). June 19, 1960, p. 26.   Novels by H. E. Bates, Emanuel Litvinoff, and others (review). July 17, 1960, p. 28.   Novels by David Lytton, D. J. Enright, and others (review). July 31, 1960, p. 20.   Science fiction novels (review). Aug. 21, 1960, p. 26.   Novels by Brian Moore, Honor Tracy, and others (review). Aug. 28, 1960, p. 26.   Novels by Gabriel Fielding and others (review). Sept. 25, 1960, p. 23.   *The Custard Boys,* by John Rae (review). Oct. 9, 1960, p. 23.   Science fiction (review). Oct. 16, 1960, p. 22.   Juvenile science fiction (review). Dec. 4, 1960, p. 28.

Science fiction (review). Jan. 15, 1961, p. 29.   Two novels by William Cooper (review). Jan. 29, 1961, p. 28.   "The Threat of the Practical." Feb. 26, 1961, p. 21.   Science fiction (review). April 9, 1961, p. 30.   *Through the Fields of Clover,* by Peter DeVries (review). June 11, 1961, p. 27. Science fiction in paperback (review). Sept. 3, 1961, p. 24. Books by and dealing with P. G. Wodehouse (review). Oct. 15, 1961, p. 28.

Novels by Anthony Burgess and Edna O'Brien (review). May 13, 1962, p. 29.   Science fiction novels (review). May 20, 1962, p. 25.   Science fiction novels (review). Oct. 7, 1962, p. 24.

"What's Left for Patriotism?" Jan. 20, 1963, p. 21.   *The Drowned World,* by J. G. Ballard (review). Jan. 27, 1963, p. 22.   Fantasy by Ray Bradbury and others (review). Feb. 24, 1963, p. 24.   Science fiction magazines (review). March 17, 1963, p. 24.   Science fiction (review). July 7, 1963, p. 22.   Science fiction (review). Dec. 8, 1963, p. 24.

Becket and other films (review). March 29, 1964, p. 20. *The Chalk Garden* and other films (review). April 5, 1964, p. 24.   *Seven Days in May* and other films (review). April 19, 1964, p. 25.   *The Big Snatch* and other films (review). May 3, 1964, p. 24.   *The Girl with the Green Eyes* and other films (review). May 17, 1964, p. 23.   *Three Lives of Thomasina* and other films (review). May 24, 1964, p. 29.

Punch: "In Defence of Illiteracy." 239:364 (Sept. 14, 1960). "Hemingway in Space." 239:895 (Dec. 21, 1960).

Ray, Cyril, editor. *The Compleat Imbiber: An Entertainment.* London: Vista Books, 1959. Includes "The 2003 Claret," by Amis.

Saturday Evening Post: "All the Blood within Me." 236:40 (April 6, 1963). Story.

Show Magazine: "A Great Poet in a Paradise Island." 2:78 (Dec., 1962). On Robert Graves.

Spectator: Novels by James Thurber and P. G. Wodehouse (review). 191:595 (Nov. 20, 1953).   *The Incredible Mizeners,* by Alva Johnston (review). 191:676 (Dec. 4, 1953).

Novels by John Prebble and others (review). 192:160 (Feb. 5, 1954).   Novels by Amos Tutuoala and others (review). 192:244 (Feb. 26, 1954).   Novels by Jane Gillespie and others (review). 192:336 (March 19, 1954). Novels by Pierre Boulle and others (review). 192:444 (April 9, 1954). Novels by Robie Macaulay and others (review). 192:528 (April 30, 1954). Novels by Saul Bellow and others (review). 192:626 (May 21, 1954). *Under the Net,* by Iris Murdoch, and other novels (review). 192:722 (June 11, 1954). *Sense of Humour,* by Stephen Potter (review). 192:787 (June 25, 1954). Novels by Igor Gouzenko and others (review). 193:42 (July 2, 1954). *I Play as I Please,* by Humphrey Lyttelton (review). 193:66 (July 9, 1954). *A Cool Million,* by Nathaniel West, and other novels (review). 193:126 (July 23, 1954). "Where Tawe Flows." 193:190 (Aug. 13, 1954). Novels by John Lodwick and others (review). 193:210 (Aug. 13, 1954). Novels by Edward Crankshaw and others (review). 193:267 (Aug. 27, 1954). Novels by Erich Maria Remarque, J. B. Priestley, and others (review). 193:350 (Sept. 17, 1954). *Parade of Pleasure,* by Geoffrey Wagner (review). 193:407 (Oct. 1, 1954). *A Proper Marriage,* by Doris Lessing, and other novels (review). 193:450 (Oct. 8, 1954). Novels by H. E. Bates, Eudora Welty, and others (review). 193:532 (Oct. 29, 1954). Novels by Nigel Balchin and others (review). 193:643 (Nov. 19, 1954). "School for Spastics." 193:702 (Dec. 3, 1954). Novels by James Courage and others (review). 193:764 (Dec. 10, 1954). *Byron: A Selection,* by A. S. B. Glover (review). 193:831 (Dec. 31, 1954).

Private View, by Jocelyn Brooke (review). 194:152 (Jan. 14, 1955). *Glorious Life,* by D. Barton, and other novels (review). 194:108 (Jan. 28, 1955). Novels by T. A. G. Hungerford and others (review). 194:198 (Feb. 18, 1955). *Homer's Daughter,* by Robert Graves, and other novels (review). 194:298 (March 11, 1955). *Satchmo,* by Louis Armstrong (review). 194:332 (March 18, 1955). Books by T. L. Peacock (review). 194:402 (April 1, 1955). *Swift: An Introduction,* by Ricardo Quintana (review). 194:474 (April 15, 1955). Books dealing with Hans Christian Andersen (review). 194:590 (May 6, 1955). Two novels by Anthony Powell (review). 194:619 (May 13, 1955). Books by Laurie Lee and Peter Mayne (review). 194:774 (June 17, 1955). *Officers and Gentlemen,* by Evelyn Waugh (review). 195:56 (July 8, 1955). *A Prospect of the Sea,* by Dylan Thomas (review). 195:227 (Aug. 12, 1955). *The Whispering Gallery,* by John Lehmann (review). 195:459 (Oct. 7, 1955). *On Modern Literature,* by W. P. Ker (review). 195:594 (Nov. 4, 1955). Books on jazz (review). 195:668 (Nov. 18, 1955). "Mind We Don't Quarrel." 195:762 (Dec. 2, 1955). *Children's Comics: A Guide for Parents and Teachers,* by G. H. Pumphrey (review). 195:894 (Dec. 30, 1955).

Dickens and His Readers: Aspects of Novel-Criticism since 1836, by G. H. Ford (review). 196:22 (Jan. 6, 1956). *Song at the Year's Turning,* by R. S. Thomas (review). 196:56 (Jan. 13, 1956). *An Illustrated History of English Literature,* Vol. III, by A. C. Ward (review). 196:89 (Jan. 20, 1956). "Lusitanian Liquors." 196:109 (Jan. 27, 1956). *Selected Literary Criticism,* by D. H. Lawrence (review). 196:156 (Feb. 3, 1956). *Sweet and Sour,* by John O'Hara (review). 196:193 (Feb. 10, 1956). *Heaven and Hell,* by Aldous Huxley (review). 196:338 (March 16, 1956). *The Deprived Child and the Community,* by Donald Ford (review). 196:384 (March 23, 1956). *Predilections,* by Marianne Moore (review). 196:552 (April 20, 1956). *The English Sense of Humour,* by Harold Nicolson (review). 196:625 (May 4, 1956). *Unprofessional Essays,* by J. M. Murray (review). 196:663 (May 11, 1956). *Anglo-Saxon Attitudes,* by Angus Wilson (review). 196:764 (June 1, 1956). *The Outsider,* by Colin Wilson (review). 196:830 (June 15, 1956). *Welsh Short Stories,* ed. by Gwyn Jones (review). 197:33 (July 6, 1956). *The Craft of Letters in England: A Symposium,* ed. by John Lehmann (review). 197:68 (July 13, 1956). *The Queen's Wales: South Wales,* by H. L. V. Fletcher (review). 197:101 (July 20, 1956). *A Study of*

George Orwell, by Christopher Hollis (review). 197:292 (Aug. 31, 1956).   "At the Jazz Band Ball." 197:409 (Sept. 28, 1956).   *More Comic and Curious Verse,* ed. by J. M. Cohen (review). 197:461 (Oct. 5, 1956).   *Pincher Martin,* by William Golding (review). 197:656 (Nov. 9, 1956). "Court of Inquiry." 197:730 (Nov. 23, 1956).   *Shelley at Work,* by Neville Rogers (review). 197:908 (Dec. 21, 1956).

Catastrophe and Imagination: An Interpretation of Recent English and American Literature, by John McCormick (review). 198:179 (Feb. 8, 1957).   *The Uses of Literacy,* by Richard Hoggart (review). 198:285 (March 1, 1957). *Beowulf,* tr. by David Wright (review). 198:445 (April 5, 1957).   *Angel,* by Elizabeth Taylor (review). 198:784 (June 14, 1957).   *Family and Kinship in East London,* by Michael Young and Peter Willmott (review). 198:818 (June 21, 1957).   *The Collected Poems of Norman Cameron* (review). 199:112 (July 19, 1957).   "Cock o' the Forth." 199:269 (Aug. 30, 1957).   *A Family Party,* by John O'Hara (review). 199:371 (Sept. 20, 1957).   *Pnin,* by Vladimir Nabokov (review). 199:403 (Sept. 27, 1957). *Mansfield Park,* by Jane Austen (review). 199:439 (Oct. 4, 1957).   *A Bit Off the Map and Other Stories,* by Angus Wilson (review). 199:521 (Oct. 18, 1957).   *The British,* by Drew Middleton (review). 199:550 (Oct. 25, 1957). *Scotland the Brave,* by Iain Hamilton (review). 199:650 (Nov. 15, 1957).   *Keats,* by Sidney Colvin (review). 199:699 (Nov. 22, 1957).   "Evening with Dylan Thomas." 199:737 (Nov. 29, 1957).   *The Bodley Head Leacock,* ed. by J. B. Priestley (review). 199:808 (Dec. 6, 1957).

"City Ways." 200:255 (Feb. 28, 1958).   *The Family Life of Old People,* by Peter Townsend (review). 200:398 (March 28, 1958).   Five novels by West Indian and Indian authors (review). 200:565 (May 2, 1958).   Works by and dealing with George Gissing (review). 201:19 (July 4, 1958).   *The Comic Tradition in America,* ed. by K. S. Lynn (review).

201:448 (Oct. 3, 1958).   *The Blush and Other Stories,* by Elizabeth Taylor (review). 201:708 (Nov. 21, 1958).

"Slightly More of a Plague on One of Your Houses" (politics). 203:431 (Oct. 2, 1959).   *Lolita,* by Vladimir Nabokov (review). 203:635 (Nov. 6, 1959).   *The Bodley Head Scott Fitzgerald,* Vol. III (review). 203:719 (Nov. 20, 1959).

Love in Action: The Sociology of Sex, by Fernando Henriques (review). 204:19 (Jan. 1, 1960).   *The Status Seekers,* by Vance Packard (review). 204:186 (Feb. 5, 1960).   *The American Imagination* (review). 205:30 (July 1, 1960). Articles from *TLS.   Don't Tell Alfred,* by Nancy Mitford (review). 205:661 (Oct. 28, 1960).   "Something Strange." 205:821 (Nov. 25, 1960). Story.   *Conversations with Max,* by S. N. Behrman (review). 205:845 (Nov. 25, 1960).

Love and Death in the American Novel, by Leslie Fiedler (review). 206:47 (Jan. 13, 1961).   *Somerset Maugham,* by Richard Cordell (review). 207:23 (July 7, 1961).   *Unconditional Surrender,* by Evelyn Waugh (review). 207:581 (Oct. 27, 1961).

Down There on a Visit, by Christopher Isherwood (review). 208:309 (March 9, 1962).   "All the Blood Within Me." 208:399 (March 30, 1962). Story.   Books on British education and communications (review). 208:554 (April 27, 1962). Comments after a meeting with Yevtushenko. 209:13 (July 6, 1962).   Plays by Arnold Wesker (review). 209:190 (Aug. 10, 1962).   "Trouble in Pennsylvania." 209:522 (Oct. 5, 1962). Preprint from the novel, *One Fat Englishman.* "Something Does Not Work with My Car." 209:789 (Nov. 23, 1962). Story.

"Holiday Preference." 210:113 (Jan. 25, 1963).   *Aniara,* by Harry Martinson (review). 210:267 (March 1, 1963).
Twentieth Century: "One World and Its Way." 158:168 (Aug., 1955).   "Age-old Ceremony at Mumbles." 160:558 (Dec., 1956).   "My Kind of Comedy." 170:46 (July, 1961).

III. Essays and Articles Dealing with Amis

Allen, Walter. *Reading a Novel* (London: Phoenix House, 1956), esp. pp. 61–64.

——— *Tradition and Dream* (London: Phoenix House, 1964), esp. pp. 278–82.

Allsop, Kenneth. *The Angry Decade.* London: Peter Owen, 1958.

Bergonzi, Bernard. "Reputations IX: Kingsley Amis," *Lon M,* 3:50 (Jan., 1964).

Caplan, Ralph. "Kingsley Amis," in *Contemporary British Novelists,* ed. by Charles Shapiro. Carbondale: Southern Illinois University Press, 1965.

Chase, Richard. "Middlebrow England: The Novels of Kingsley Amis," *Com,* 22:263 (Sept., 1956).

Colby, Vineta. "Biographical Sketch," *WLB,* 32:618 (May, 1958).

Colville, Derek. "The Sane New World of Kingsley Amis," *Bucknell Review,* 9:46 (1960).

Conquest, Robert. "Christian Symbolism in *Lucky Jim,*" *Critical Quarterly,* 7:87 (June, 1965).

Fraser, G. S. *The Modern Writer and His World.* Rev. ed. Baltimore: Penguin Books, 1964.

Ginden, James. "Kingsley Amis' Funny Novels," in *Postwar British Fiction* (Berkeley: University of California Press, 1961), pp. 34–50.

——— "The Reassertion of the Personal," *Tex Q,* 4:126 (No. 1, 1958).

Green, Martin. "Amis and Salinger: The Latitude of Private Conscience," *Chicago Review,* 11:20 (Winter, 1958).

——— "British Decency," *Ken R,* 21:505 (Fall, 1959).

——— "British Comedy and the British Sense of Humour: Shaw, Waugh, and Amis." *Tex Q,* 4:217 (No. 3, 1961).

——— *A Mirror for Anglo-Saxons.* New York: Harper and Brothers, 1960.

Harvey, W. T. "Have You Anything To Declare? or, Angry Young

Men: Facts and Fictions," in *International Literary Annual,* ed. by John Wain (London: John Calder, 1958), p. 47.

Hilton, Frank. "Britain's New Class," *Enc,* 10:59 (Feb. 1958).

Hurrell, John D. "Class and Conscience in John Braine and Kingsley Amis," *Critique,* 2:39 (Spring-Summer, 1958).

Hynes, Samuel. "The Poor Sod as Hero," *Commonweal,* 64:51 (April 13, 1956).

Kalb, B. "Three Comers," *Sat R,* 38:22 (May 7, 1955).

Karl, F. R. "The Angries: Is There a Protestant in the House?", in *A Reader's Guide to the Contemporary English Novel* (New York: Noonday Press, 1962), p. 220.

Lebowitz, Naomi. "Kingsley Amis: The Penitent Hero," *Perspective,* 10:129 (Summer-Autumn, 1958).

Lodge, David. "The Contemporary Novel and All That Jazz," *Lon M,* n.s. 2:73 (Aug., 1962).

——— "The Modern, the Contemporary, and the Importance of Being Amis," *Critical Quarterly,* 5:335 (Winter, 1963). Reprinted in *Language of Fiction.* London: Routledge and Kegan Paul; New York: Columbia University Press, 1966.

Moberg, George. "Structure and Theme in Amis's Novels," *CEA Critic,* March, 1963, p. 7.

O'Connor, William Van. *The New University Wits.* Carbondale: Southern Illinois University Press, 1963.

Parker, R. B. "Farce and Society: The Range of Kingsley Amis," *WSCL,* 2:27 (No. 3, 1961).

Peschmann, Herman. "The Nonconformists, Angry Young Men, Lucky Jims, and Outsiders," *English* (London) 13:12 (1960).

"Portrait Gallery," *Sun Times,* Jan. 26, 1958, p. 5. Short biography of Amis.

Pritchett, V. S. "These Writers Couldn't Care Less," *NYTBR,* April 28, 1957, p. 1.

Procter, Mortimer R. *The English University Novel* (Berkeley and Los Angeles: University of California Press, 1957), esp. pp. 175–76.

"Profile. Kingsley Amis," *Obs,* Jan. 14, 1962, p. 13.

Quinton, Anthony, *et al.* "The New Novelists: An Enquiry." *Lon M,* 5:13 (Nov., 1958). Symposium.

Snow, C. P. "Italo Svevo: Forerunner of Cooper and Amis," in *Essays and Studies by Members of the English Association,* 14:7 (1961).

"The Uses of Comic Vision." *TLS,* Sept. 9, 1960, p. ix.

Weatherby, W. J. "Mr. Sellers and Mr. Amis: A Conversation Reported by W. J. Weatherby," *Guardian,* April 27, 1961, p. 9.

Wilson, Colin. "The Writer and Publicity." *Enc,* 13:8 (Nov., 1959).

ANGUS WILSON, b. 1913

I. Books by Wilson

The Wrong Set and Other Stories. London: Secker and Warburg, 1949; New York: Morrow, 1950.

Such Darling Dodos and Other Stories. London: Secker and Warburg, 1950; New York: Morrow, 1951.

Émile Zola: An Introductory Study of His Novels. London: Secker and Warburg; New York: Morrow, 1952.

Hemlock and After. London: Secker and Warburg; New York: Viking Press, 1952.

For Whom the Cloche Tolls: A Scrap-Book of the Twenties. London: Methuen, 1953; New York: British Book Centre, 1954.

The Mulberry Bush (play). London: Secker and Warburg, 1956.

Anglo-Saxon Attitudes. London: Secker and Warburg; New York, Viking, 1956.

A Bit Off the Map and Other Stories. London: Secker and Warburg; New York: Viking, 1957.

The Middle Age of Mrs. Eliot. London: Secker and Warburg, 1958; New York: Viking, 1959.

After the Show (television play, produced but not published, 1959).

The Stranger (television play, produced but not published, 1960).

The Old Men at the Zoo. London: Secker and Warburg; New York: Viking, 1961.

The Seven Deadly Sins, by Angus Wilson and others (series of essays from the London *Sunday Times*). London and New York: Morrow, 1962.

The Wild Garden, or Speaking of Writing (Ewing Lectures at UCLA). Berkeley: University of California Press, 1963.

The Invasion (television play, produced but not published, 1963).

Late Call. New York: The Viking Press, 1964.

Tempo. London: Studio Vista Books, 1964.

II. Essays, Articles, and Book Reviews by Wilson

American Mercury: "Letter from London." 72:571 (May, 1951). "Revolution in British Reading." 73:47 (Dec., 1951).
Atlantic Monthly: "The Revolt of Samuel Butler." 200:190 (Nov., 1957).
Bonnard, G. A., editor. *English Studies Today.* Second series. Berne: Francke Verlag, 1961. Includes "The Novelist and the Narrator," by Wilson.
Commentary: Sprightly Running, by John Wain (review). 37:74 (June, 1964).
Critical Quarterly: "Charles Dickens: A Haunting." 2:101 (Summer, 1960).
Encounter: The World in the Evening, by Christopher Isherwood (review). 3:62 (Aug., 1954).

Night Rider, by Robert Penn Warren (review). 4:75 (May, 1955). *Utopian Fantasy,* by Richard Gerber (review). 4:73 (June, 1955). *The Genius and the Goddess,* by Aldous Huxley (review). 5:73 (July, 1955). *The Opposing Self,* by Lionel Trilling (review). 5:79 (Aug., 1955). *Exploring English Character,* by Geoffrey Gorer (review). 5:84 (Sept., 1955).

The Expansion of Elizabethan England, by A. L. Rowse (review). 6:86 (Jan., 1956). *Beaverbrook: A Study in Power and Frustration,* by Tom Driberg (review). 6:88 (Feb., 1956). *The Domestic Servant Class in Eighteenth Century England,* by J. J. Hecht (review). 6:76 (March, 1956). *Dickens and His Readers,* by G. H. Ford (review). 6:75 (April, 1956). *The Lisbon Earthquake,* by T. D. Kendrick (review). 6:91 (June, 1956). Novels by William Cooper, Irwin Shaw, and others (review). 7:83 (Aug., 1956). *A Historian's Approach to Religion,* by Arnold Toynbee (review). 7:80 (Oct., 1956). *Suicide in London,* by Peter Saintsbury (review). 7:82 (Dec., 1956).

Past Finding Out, by G. K. Balleine (review). 8:81 (Feb., 1957). *Modern Japanese Literature,* ed. by Donald Keene (review). 8:83 (April, 1957). *Votes for Women,* by Roger Fulford (review). 9:84 (July, 1957). "A Conversation with E. M. Forster." 9:52 (Nov., 1957). "Some Japanese Observations." 9:49 (Dec., 1957).

"The Intellectual on the Aisle." 12:68 (June, 1959). *Ronald Knox,* by Evelyn Waugh (review). 14:78 (Jan., 1960). *The Dandy,* by Ellen Moers (review). 14:74 (May, 1960). *Apologies to the Iroquois,* by Edmund Wilson (review). 15:82 (Aug., 1960).

"Fourteen Points." 18:10 (Jan., 1962). *On the Contrary,* by Mary McCarthy (review). 18:71 (June, 1962).

"Going into Europe." 20:53 (Jan., 1963).
Guardian: An Unofficial Rose, by Iris Murdoch (review). June 8, 1962, p. 6.
Holiday: "The World's Greatest Museum." 18:48 (Sept., 1955). "The Jolliest Resort in the World." 24:46 (Aug., 1958). "Confessions of a Zoo-Lover." 35:12 (June, 1964).
Horizon (London): "Totentanz." 19:337 (May, 1949). Story.
Kronenberger, Louis, editor. *Novelists on Novelists* (New York: Doubleday and Co. [Anchor Books], 1962), p. 137: "Zola," by Wilson.
Listener: "Realpolitik." 40:423 (Sept. 16, 1948). Story.

"What Do Hippos Eat?" 41:673 (April 21, 1949). Story. *A Writer's Notebook,* by W. S. Maugham (review). 42:639 (Oct. 13, 1949).

Novels by Anna Sebastian, Merle Miller, and others (review). 43:261 (Feb. 9, 1950). Novels by Vera Panova, Alfred Hayes, and others (review). 43:357 (Feb. 23, 1950). Novels by Denton Welch, H. E. Bates, and others (review). 43:444 (March 9, 1950). Novels by William Cooper, Harold Acton, and others (review). 43:577 (March 30, 1950). Novels by F. L. Green, H. S. Davies, and others (review).

43:621 (April 6, 1950).   Books of short stories by Truman Capote, Gabriel Chevallier, and others (review). 43:758 (April 27, 1950).   *Nothing,* by Henry Green, and other novels (review). 43:801 (May 4, 1950).   "Sense and Sensibility in Recent Writing." 44:279 (Aug. 24, 1950).

"Broken Promise." 45:575 (April 12, 1951). *The Denton Welch Journals,* ed. by Jocelyn Brooke (review). 48:941 (Dec. 4, 1952).

"Higher Standards." 49:107 (Jan. 15, 1953). Story.   "The Bicentenary of the British Museum—II: The Reading Room." 49:1005 (June 18, 1953).   *Émile Zola,* by F. W. J. Hemmings (review). 49:1065 (June 25, 1953).

"The Future of the English Novel." 51:746 (April 29, 1954).

Literature and Western Man, by J. B. Priestley (review). 63:405 (March 3, 1960).

The Garnett Family, by Carolyn Heilbrun (review). 66:181 (Aug. 3, 1961).

The Essay Prize, by John Bowen (review). 68:327 (Aug. 30, 1962).

"Evil in the English Novel." 1. "Richardson and Jane Austen." 68:1079 (Dec. 27, 1962). 2. "George Eliot to Virginia Woolf." 69:15 (Jan. 3, 1963). 3. "Outside the Central Tradition." 69:63 (Jan. 10, 1963). 4. "Evil and the Novelist Today." 69:115 (Jan. 17, 1963).

London Magazine: "Arnold Bennett's Novels." 1:59 (Oct., 1954). "Oscar Wilde." 2:71 (Feb., 1955).   "Ivy Compton-Burnett." 2:64 (July, 1955).   *Crome Yellow* and *Those Barren Leaves,* by Aldous Huxley (review). 2:53 (Aug., 1955). *Confessions of Felix Krull, Confidence Man,* by Thomas Mann (review). 3:69 (May, 1956).   "The Living Dead IV— Bernard Shaw." 3:53 (Dec., 1956).   "Mood of the Month III." 5:40 (April, 1958).   *The Picaresque Saint,* by R. W. B. Lewis, and *Camus,* by Germaine Bree (review). 7:71

(April, 1960). *The Last Hours of Sandra Lee,* by William Sansom (review). n.s. 1:89 (Dec., 1961).
Month: "Dickens and the Divided Conscience." n.s. 3:349 (May, 1963).
New Statesman: Novels by Anthony Rhodes and others (review). 38:226 (Aug. 27, 1949). Novels by Arthur Miller and Ernest Frost (review). 38:336 (Sept. 24, 1949). Books by Frances Towers and Christopher Sykes (review). 38:435 (Oct. 15, 1949). Books by Elizabeth Bowen, Jean Paul Sartre, Delmore Schwartz, and others (review). 38:656 (Dec. 3, 1949). *The Mind of Proust,* by F. C. Green (review). 38:760 (Dec. 24, 1949).

Letters to a Friend, by Marcel Proust, tr. by A. E. Henderson (review). 39:312 (March 18, 1950). *Letters of Marcel Proust,* tr. by Mina Curtiss (review). 40:434 (Nov. 11, 1950). "The Old, Old Message." 40:648 (Dec. 23, 1950). Story.

Hugh Walpole, by Rupert Hart-Davis (review). 43:312 (March 15, 1952). Collections of short stories by Robert Penn Warren, Wallace Stegner, Irwin Shaw, and others (review). 43:738 (June 21, 1952). *Mary Wollstonecraft,* by R. M. Wardle (review). 44:382 (Oct. 4, 1952). *The Devils of Loudun,* by Aldous Huxley (review). 44:516 (Nov. 1, 1952).

Francis Younghusband, by George Seaver (review). 45:347 (March 21, 1953). "Throughout the Country." 45:696 (June 13, 1953). Collections of short stories by J. D. Salinger, Gwyn Jones, and J. B. Priestley (review). 46:187 (Aug. 15, 1953).

Collections of short stories by Walter de la Mare, Eudora Welty, and H. E. Bates (review). 50:679 (Nov. 19, 1955).

An Introduction to Anglo-Saxon England, by P. H. Blair (review). 51:159 (Feb. 11, 1956). "Reassessments: Galsworthy's *Forsyte Saga.*" 51:187 (March 3, 1956). *The Hero in Eclipse in Victorian Fiction,* by Mario Praz (review). 51:426 (April 21, 1956).

Margaret the First, by Douglas Grant (review). 53:109 (Jan. 26, 1957).   *A Mirror of Witchcraft,* by Christina Hole (review). 53:282 (March 2, 1957).   *The Twenties,* by John Montgomery (review). 53:491 (April 13, 1957).

"Vision, Vision; Mr. Woocock." 60:298 (Sept. 3, 1960).

Courage, by Lord Beaverbrook (review). 63:374 (March 16, 1962).   *To Deprave and Corrupt,* ed. by John Channing (review). 64:50 (July 13, 1962).   "John Cowper Powys." 64:588 (Oct. 26, 1962).

New Yorker: "More Friend than Lodger." 33:28 (Aug. 10, 1957). Story.   "Once a Lady." 33:23 (Aug. 31, 1957). Story.

New York Times Book Review: "If It's New and Modish, Is It Good?" July 2, 1961, p. 1.

Nouvelles Littéraires: "L'écrivain dans l'Angleterre d'aujourd'hui." 12:1 (Dec., 1957).

Observer: Novels by Bettina Lynn, Francis King, and others (review). Jan. 26, 1958, p. 16.   Novels by Alfred Hayes, Anthony Burgess, and others (review). Feb. 9, 1958, p. 15. Novels by Sylvia Ashton-Warner and others (review). March 9, 1958, p. 16.   Novels by Robin Jenkins, May Sarton, and others (review). March 23, 1958, p. 16.   Books by Adriaan van der Veen, W. J. White, and others (review). April 6, 1958, p. 14.   *By Love Possessed,* by J. G. Cozzens (review). April 13, 1958, p. 17.   Novels by Rex Warner and others (review). June 8, 1958, p. 17.   Novels by Mary Crawford, Angela Thirkell, and others (review). June 22, 1958, p. 17.   *Two Women,* by Alberto Moravia, and other novels (review). July 6, 1958, p. 17.   Novels by J. P. Marquand and others (review). July 20, 1958, p. 15.   Novels by Roger Vailland, Peter De Vries, and others (review). Aug. 3, 1958, p. 10.   *Culture and Society, 1780–1950,* by Raymond Williams (review). Oct. 19, 1958, p. 21.   Criticism of the play, *West Side Story,* by Leonard Bernstein and Stephen Sondheim. Dec. 14, 1958, p. 15.   Criticism of *Cinderella* and other plays. Dec. 21, 1958, p. 11.

Criticism of the television program, "Billy Bunter's Mystery Christmas." Jan. 4, 1959, p. 13. Criticism of the play, *The Long and the Short and the Tall,* by Willis Hall. Jan. 11, 1959, p. 17. Criticism of *Valmouth,* by Sandy Wilson (based on Ronald Firbank's novel), and other plays. Feb. 1, 1959, p. 17. Criticism of *Prince Genji,* by William Cooper. Feb. 8, 1959, p. 19. Criticism of *A Taste of Honey,* by Shelagh Delaney. Feb. 15, 1959, p. 19. "Strindberg in a Comic Vein." March 22, 1959, p. 25. *The Broken Mirror,* ed. by Pawel Mayewski (review). May 31, 1959, p. 25. *Marcel Proust: A Biography,* by George D. Painter (review). Sept. 20, 1959, p. 22. *Dickens Incognito,* by Felix Aylmer (review). Nov. 29, 1959, Christmas Book Section, p. 1.

Bridge of the Brocade Sash, by Sacheverell Sitwell (review). Jan. 3, 1960, p. 16. *The Wayward Wife,* by Alberto Moravia (review). Jan. 17, 1960, p. 21. *A Hermit Disclosed,* by Raleigh Trevalyan (review). March 13, 1960, p. 20. *A Voice from the Cell,* by Saverio Montalto (review). April 10, 1960, p. 21. *Memoirs of a Fox-Hunting Man,* by Siegfried Sassoon (review). July 31, 1960, p. 21. *For Love or Money,* by Richard Rees (review). Aug. 14, 1960, p. 20.

New Maps of Hell, by Kingsley Amis (review). March 12, 1961, p. 28. Guidebooks dealing with Suffolk (review). April 23, 1961, p. 31. *A Clean, Well-lighted Place,* by Kathleen Nott (review). June 25, 1961, p. 25. *Branwell Bronte,* by Winifred Gérin (review). July 23, 1961, p. 20. *The Imagination of Charles Dickens,* by A. O. J. Cockshut (review). Aug. 27, 1961, p. 18. *The Mighty and Their Fall,* by Ivy Compton-Burnett (review). Sept. 17, 1961, p. 30. *Riders in the Chariot,* by Patrick White (review). Oct. 29, 1961, p. 30. *Godliness and Good Learning,* by David Newsome (review). Dec. 3, 1961, p. 29.

Novels by Patrick van Rensburg and Myrna Blumberg (review). Jan. 21, 1962, p. 31. *The Moral and the Story,* by

Ian Gregor and Brian Nicholas (review). Feb. 4, 1962, p. 31. *Down There on a Visit,* by Christopher Isherwood (review). March 4, 1962, p. 30.   *The Strangled Cry,* by John Strachey (review). June 17, 1962, p. 25.   Novels by Jack London (review). July 8, 1962, p. 24.   *Dickens and Crime,* by Phillip Collins (review). Aug. 5, 1962, p. 14.   *The Little Ottleys,* by Ada Leverson (review). Aug. 19, 1962, p. 17. *Sprightly Running,* by John Wain (review). Sept. 16, 1962, p. 22.   *Margin Released,* by J. B. Priestley (review). Sept. 23, 1962, p. 28.   *Ship of Fools,* by Katherine Anne Porter (review). Oct. 28, 1962, p. 27.   *Sum Total,* by Ray Gosling (review). Nov. 11, 1962, p. 25.   Books of criticism dealing with Dostoevsky (review). Nov. 25, 1962, p. 29.

Time of Arrival, by Dan Jacobson (review). March 31, 1963, p. 27.   Books dealing with Ada Leverson, Lord Alfred Douglas, and Oscar Wilde (review). May 26, 1963, p. 27. *Selected Writings of Truman Capote* (review). July 7, 1963, p. 22.   *Cat and Mouse,* by Günter Grass, and *After the Banquet,* by Yukio Mishima (review). Aug. 25, 1963, p. 18. *The New Look,* by Harry Hopkins (review). Sept. 22, 1963, p. 24.   *Dickens and Education,* by Phillip Collins (review). Dec. 22, 1963, p. 16.

Kipling's Mind and Art, ed. by Andrew Rutherford (review). March 29, 1964, p. 23.   *Beginning Again,* by Leonard Woolf (review). May 10, 1964, p. 26.   *Science: The Glorious Entertainment,* by Jacques Barzun (review). May 31, 1964, p. 27.   *The English Garden,* by Edward Hyams (review). July 5, 1964, p. 26.

Partisan Review: "Life and Letters" and "Et Dona Ferentes." 16:982 (Oct., 1949). Stories.   "New Playwrights." 26:631 (Fall, 1959).   "Whites in South Africa." 28:612 (Sept., 1961).

Queen: Television criticism, 1962–63.

Review of English Literature: "Heroes and Heroines of Dickens." 2:9 (July, 1961).   "Mythology in John Cowper Powys's Novels." 4:9 (Jan., 1963).

Spectator: Books by Margaret Lane, Jean Stafford, and C. S. Forester (review). 193:401 (Oct. 1, 1954). *O Rare Amanda,* by Jack Loudan (review). 193:726 (Dec. 3, 1954).

The Best S. F., ed. by Edmund Crispin (review). 194:160 (Feb. 11, 1955). *Memoirs of Catherine the Great,* ed. by Dominique Maroger (review). 194:261 (March 4, 1955). *Dearest Bess,* by D. M. Stuart, and *Three Howard Sisters,* ed. by Maud, Lady Leconfield (review). 194:410 (April 1, 1955). *A Train of Powder,* by Rebecca West (review). 194:711 (June 3, 1955). *Modern Italian Short Stories,* ed. by W. J. Strachan (review). 194:748 (June 10, 1955). Science fiction (review). 195:64 (July 8, 1955). *Hogarth's Progress,* by Peter Quennell (review). 195:129 (July 22, 1955). *Elinor Glyn,* by Anthony Glyn (review). 195:284 (Aug. 26, 1955). *The Trouble with Cinderella,* by Artie Shaw (review). 195:342 (Sept. 9, 1955). *The Capel Letters,* ed. by the Marquess of Anglesey (review). 195:679 (Nov. 18, 1955). *Alicella,* by Averil Stewart (review). 195:772 (Dec. 2, 1955).

"Bexhill and After." 200:583–84 (May 9, 1958). Reminiscences of schooldays.

Nabokov's Dozen, by Vladimir Nabokov (review). 202:412 (March 20, 1959). *Edward Marsh,* by Christopher Hassall (review). 202:861 (June 12, 1959). "Room at the Topism." 204:435 (Oct. 2, 1959). *The Prof,* by R. F. Harrod (review). 203:479 (Oct. 9, 1959).

Stand on Me, by Robert Norman (review). 204:46 (Jan. 8, 1960). *Weekend in Dinlock,* by Clancy Sigal (review). 204:140 (Jan. 29, 1960). "Albert Camus, Humanist." 204:293 (Feb. 26, 1960). *The Jews in Our Time,* by Norman Bentwick (review). 204:586 (April 22, 1960). *Nancy Astor,* by Maurice Collis (review). 204:668 (May 6, 1960). *A Bundle of Sensations,* by Goronwy Rees (review). 205:138 (July 22, 1960). Japanese fiction (review). 211:22 (July 5, 1963).

Texas Quarterly: "My Husband Is Right." 4:139 (Autumn, 1961). Story.
Times [London] *Literary Supplement:* "Diversity and Depth." Aug. 15, 1958, Special Section, p. viii.
World Review: "The Novels of William Godwin." 28:37 (June, 1951).
Zola, Émile. *The Kill,* tr. from the French *La Curée* by A. Teixeira de Mattos. New York: Farrar, Straus, and Young, 1954. Introduction by Wilson.

III. Essays and Articles Dealing with Wilson

Allen, Walter. *Tradition and Dream* (London: Phoenix House, 1964), esp. pp. 270–74.
Bittner, W. "Hemlock and Piltdown," *Nat,* 183:311 (Oct. 13, 1956).
Bowen, John. "One Man's Meat: The Idea of Individual Responsibility," *TLS,* Aug. 7, 1959, Special Section, p. xii.
Burgess, Anthony. "The Powers That Be," *Enc,* 24:71 (Jan., 1965).
Cockshut, A. O. J. "Favoured Sons: The Moral World of Angus Wilson." *E in C,* 9:50 (1959).
Cox, C. B. "The Humanism of Angus Wilson: A Study of *Hemlock and After,*" *Critical Quarterly,* 3:227 (Fall, 1961).
———— *The Free Spirit: A Study of Liberal Humanism in the Novels of George Eliot, Henry James, E. M. Forster, Virginia Woolf, and Angus Wilson.* London: Oxford University Press, 1963.
Fraser, G. S. *The Modern Writer and His World.* Rev. ed. Baltimore: Penguin Books, 1964.
Ginden, James. "The Reassertion of the Personal," *Tex Q,* 1:126 (No. 4, 1958).
———— "Angus Wilson's Qualified Nationalism," in *Postwar British Fiction* (Berkeley: University of California Press, 1961), p. 145.
Halio, Jay L. "The Novels of Angus Wilson," *Modern Fiction Studies,* 8:171 (1962).

—————— *Angus Wilson.* London: Oliver and Boyd, 1964.

Jenkins, A. "Hemlock—and Before," *Spec,* 193:331 (Sept. 17, 1954).

Karl, F. R. "The Still Comic Muse of Humanity: The Novels of Anthony Powell, Angus Wilson, and Nigel Dennis," in *A Reader's Guide to the Contemporary English Novel* (New York: Noonday Press, 1962), esp. pp. 238–53.

Kermode, Frank. "Myth, Reality, and Fiction," *List,* 68:311 (Aug. 30, 1962).

—————— "Mr. Wilson's People," in *Puzzles and Epiphanies* (London: Routledge and Kegan Paul, 1962), p. 193.

—————— "The House of Fiction: Interviews with Seven English Novelists," *Partisan Review,* 30:68 (Spring, 1963).

Mandel, Siegfried "Biographical Sketch," *Sat R,* 39:22 (Oct. 6, 1956).

Mander, John. "The Short Stories of Angus Wilson," in *The Writer and Commitment* (London: Secker and Warburg, 1961), p. 111.

Millgate, Michael "Angus Wilson's Guide to Modern England," *N Repub,* 137:17 (Nov. 25, 1957).

—————— "Angus Wilson (The Art of Fiction, XX)," *Paris Review,* No. 17 (Autumn-Winter, 1957), p. 89.

Procter, M. R. *The English University Novel* (Berkeley and Los Angeles: University of California, 1957), esp. pp. 176–77.

Scott-Kilvert, Ian. "Angus Wilson," *REL,* 1:42 (April, 1960).

Symons, Julian. "Politics and the Novel," *Twentieth Century,* 170:147 (Winter, 1962).

"The Workaday World that the Novelist Never Enters," *TLS,* Sept. 9, 1960, Special Section, p. vii.

C. P. SNOW, b. 1905

I. Books Written or Edited by Snow

Translations into foreign languages and scientific publications are not included.

Death Under Sail. London: Heinemann, 1932 (rev. reprint, 1959); New York: Doubleday Doran, 1932.

New Lives for Old (published anonymously). London: Gollancz, 1933.

The Search. London: Macmillan, 1934 (rev. reprint, 1958); New York: Scribner, 1959.

Richard Aldington: An Appreciation. London: Heinemann, 1938.

The Cambridge Library of Modern Science, C. P. Snow, editor. Snow was editor for a number of books in this series *circa* 1940.

Strangers and Brothers. London: Faber and Faber, 1940; Macmillan, 1953; New York: Scribner, 1960.

The Light and the Dark. London: Faber and Faber, 1947; New York: Macmillan, 1948; Scribner, 1961.

Time of Hope. London: Faber and Faber, 1949; Macmillan, 1960; New York: Macmillan, 1950.

View over the Park (a play). Produced at the Lyric Theater, Hammersmith, 1950.

A Series of One-Act Plays (*The Supper Dance, Family Party, Spare the Rod, To Murder Mrs. Mortimer, The Pigeon with the Silver Foot, Her Best Foot Forward*) by Pamela Hansford Johnson and C. P. Snow. London: Evans Brothers, Ltd., 1951.

The Masters. London and New York: Macmillan, 1951.

The New Men. London: Macmillan, 1954; New York: Scribner, 1955.

Homecomings (published in America as *Homecoming*). London: Macmillan, 1956; New York: Scribner, 1956.

The Conscience of the Rich. London and New York: Macmillan, 1958; New York: Scribner, 1958.

The Two Cultures and the Scientific Revolution (Rede Lecture, Cambridge, 1959). Cambridge: Cambridge University Press, 1959; New York: Cambridge University Press, 1961.

The Affair. London: Macmillan, 1960; New York: Scribner, 1960; St. Martin's Press, 1960.

Science and Government (Godkin Lectures, Harvard, 1960). Oxford: Oxford University Press; Cambridge: Harvard University Press, 1961.

The Affair (play by Ronald Millar from the novel by C. P. Snow. Presented at the Strand Theater, London, 1961). New York: Scribner, 1962.

Winter's Tales Number 7 (stories from modern Russia). Edited and introduced by C. P. Snow and Pamela Hansford Johnson. London: Macmillan; New York: St. Martin's Press, 1961.

Recent Thoughts on the Two Cultures (oration delivered at Birkbeck College [of the University of London], 12th December 1961, in celebration of the 138th anniversary of the foundation of the college). London: Birkbeck College, 1961.

A Postscript to Science and Government (published in America as *An Appendix to Science and Government*). Oxford: Oxford University Press, 1962; Cambridge: Harvard University Press, 1962.

The New Men (play by Ronald Millar from the novel of C. P. Snow). Presented at the Strand Theater, London, September, 1962.

The Two Cultures: and a Second Look. Cambridge: Cambridge University Press, 1963.

The Masters (play by Ronald Millar from the novel of C. P. Snow). Presented at the Savoy Theater, London, May, 1963.

Corridors of Power. New York: Scribner, 1964.

II. Essays, Articles, and Book Reviews by Snow

Atlantic Monthly: "The Age of Rutherford." 202:76 (Nov., 1958).
Author: "Illiteracy." 64:32 (Winter, 1953). "Monthlies and the Less Frequent." 66:4 (Autumn, 1955).

Brinton, Crane C., editor. *The Fate of Man.* New York: Braziller, 1961. Includes "The Literati and the Scientists," by Snow.

Bryant, Arthur, T. R. Glover, *et al. Imaginary Biographies.* London: G. Allen and Unwin, Ltd., 1936. Includes "The Original of the Mona Lisa," by Snow.

Commentary: "Western Values and Total War." 32:277 (Oct., 1961). A symposium with Sidney Hook, H. Stuart Hughes, and Hans Morgenthau.

Discovery (edited by Snow from 1938 to 1940): *"Discovery* Comes to Cambridge." n.s. 1:1 (April, 1938). "The Progress of *Discovery."* 1:103 (June, 1938). "Science and the Modern World." 1:317 (Oct., 1938). "Answer to a Letter from Richard Aldington." 1:422 (Dec., 1938).

"Scientific Prophecies." 2:1 (Jan., 1939). "Blueprint of Future Science." 2:107 (March, 1939). "The First Excitement that Knowledge Gives." 2:161 (April, 1939). "Science and Air Warfare." 2:215 (May, 1939). "Race, Nation, Class: Lessons of Genetics." 2:271 (June, 1939). "A New Attempt To Explain Modern Physics." 2:329 (July, 1939). "A New Means of Destruction?" 2:443 (Sept., 1939). "The Fate of Homo Sapiens." 2:449 (Oct., 1939). "Against Destructiveness." 2:557 (Nov., 1939). "The Truth of Genetics." 2:617 (Dec., 1939).

"Stretches of Time." 3:1 (Jan., 1940). "Scientists and War Discoveries." 3:59 (Feb., 1940). "The End of *Discovery."* 3:117 (March, 1940).

Encounter: "The Two Cultures and the Scientific Revolution." Part I: 12:17 (June, 1959); Part II: 13:22 (July, 1959). *The House of the Intellect,* by Jacques Barzun (review). 13:66 (Nov., 1959). "The 'Two Cultures' Controversy—Afterthoughts." 14:64 (Feb., 1960). "Conversation Piece: Muggeridge and Snow." 18:90 (Feb., 1962).

Essays and Studies by Members of the English Association: "Italo Svevo: Forerunner of Cooper and Amis." 14:7 (1961).

Evergreen Review: "The Moral Unneutrality of Science" (excerpt). No. 17 (March–April 1961), p. 1.

Harper's Magazine: "Which Side of the Atlantic?" 219:163 (Oct., 1959). "On Magnanimity" (reprint of an address). 225:37 (July, 1962).

Holiday: "Men of Fission." 23:94 (April, 1958).

Kenyon Review: "Science, Politics, and the Novelist." 23:1 (Winter, 1961).

Life: "Whether We Live or Die." 50:90 (Feb. 3, 1961).

Listener: "The Corridors of Power." 57:619 (April 18, 1957).

London Magazine: "Reply to Sir Herbert Read's Comment on His Rede Lecture." 6:57 (no. 10, 1959).

Look: "The Quarter Century: Its Great Delusions." 25:116 (Dec. 19, 1961). "Churchill." 27:26 (Feb. 26, 1963).

Mademoiselle: "The Changing Nature of Love." 46:105 (Feb., 1958).

Meanjin: "An Object of Love." 9:229 (Sept., 1960). Excerpt from a novel.

Moderna Sprak (Stockholm): "The English Realistic Novel, 1957." 51:265 (1957).

Nation: "The Irregular Right." 182:238 (March 24, 1956). "The Future of Man." 187:124 (Sept. 13, 1958).

New Republic: Science and Human Values, by Jacob Bronowski (review). 139:26 (Aug. 18, 1958). *Brighter than a Thousand Suns,* by Robert Jungk (review). 139:18 (Oct. 27, 1958).

New Statesman: Books on science and industry (review). 47:374 (March 20, 1954). "The Well Endowed." 48:850 (Dec. 25, 1954).

The Life of Ludwig Mond, by J. M. Cohen (review). 51:702 (June 16, 1956). *I Am a Mathematician,* by Norbert Wiener (review). 52:219 (Aug. 25, 1956). "New Minds for the New World." 52:279 (Sept. 6, 1956). Published anonymously. "The Two Cultures." 52:413 (Oct. 6, 1956).

Sir Richard Gregory, by W. H. G. Armytage (review). 53:175 (Feb. 9, 1957). "London Diary." 53:226 (Feb. 23, 1957). "London Diary." 53:266 (March 2, 1957). *Dickens at*

Work, by J. E. Butt and K. M. Tillotson (review). 54:119 (July 27, 1957).

Brighter than a Thousand Suns, by Robert Jungk (review). 55:771 (June 14, 1958).   "Which Side of the Atlantic: The Writer's Choice." 56:287 (Sept. 6, 1958).   *World Without War,* by J. D. Bernal (review). 56:698 (Nov. 15, 1958).

The Victoria History of the County of Cambridge, Vol. III (review). 57:406 (March 21, 1959).   *The Prof,* by R. F. Harrod (review). 58:398 (Sept. 26, 1959).

Albert Einstein, Philosopher-Scientist, ed. by P. A. Schlipp (review). 59:453 (March 26, 1960).

Science and Human Values, by Jacob Bronowski (review). 61:630 (April 21, 1961).   *The Democratic Intellect,* by G. E.

Dovie (review). 62:186 (Aug. 11, 1961).

"Education and Sacrifice." 65:746 (May 17, 1963).
Newsweek: "Adding Up Einstein." 55:82 (April 11, 1960).
New York Herald Tribune Book Review: The Flying Trapeze: Three Crises for Physicists, by J. R. Oppenheimer (review). Nov. 29, 1964, p. 3.
New York Times Book Review: "Storytellers for the Atomic Age." Jan. 30, 1955, p. 1.   "Englishmen of Power and Place on the Road that Led to Munich." Dec. 24, 1961, p. 3.
Observer: "Man in Society." July 13, 1958, p. 12.
Partisan Review: "The Cold War and the West." 29:81 (Winter, 1962).
Political Quarterly: "Careers." 15:310 (Oct., 1944).
Rogow, Arnold. *The Jew in a Gentile World.* New York: Macmillan, 1961. Introduction by Snow.
Saturday Book: "The Mathematician on Cricket." 8:65 (1948). "The Wisdom of Niels Bohr." 9:180 (1949).
Saturday Evening Post: "The Conflict of Cultures." 232:28 (Sept. 12, 1959).
School and Society: "On American Education." 90:209 (May 5, 1962).

Science: "The Moral Unneutrality of Science." 133:256 (Jan. 27, 1961); 133:1272 (April 21, 1961).

Senior Scholastic: "Pat on the Back." 82:4 (March 20, 1963). Summary of an address.

Spectator: "The Enjoyment of Science." 156:1074 (June 12, 1936). "A False Alarm in Physics." 157:628 (Oct. 16, 1936). "What We Need from Applied Science." 157:904 (Nov. 20, 1936). "Superfluity of Particles." 157:984 (Dec. 4, 1936).

"The Humanity of Science." 158:702 (April 16, 1937). "Controlling Reproduction." 159:678 (Oct. 22, 1937).

"The Brightest Things in the Universe." 160:124 (Jan. 28, 1938).

Books by Henry Green and William Gerhardi (review). 185:320 (Sept. 22, 1950).

Novels by Ada Leverson and Ronald Firbank (review). 186:82 (Jan. 19, 1951). *Simpson,* by E. Sackville-West (review). 187:136 (July 27, 1951).

West-African Explorers, ed. by Clare Howard (review). 188:554 (April 25, 1952).

Time and the Novel, by A. A. Mendilow (review). 190:254 (Feb. 27, 1953).

"Reflections on Mr. Dean's Report [*Report on the Atom*]." 192:283 (March 12, 1954). *Government and Science: Their Dynamic Relation in American Democracy,* by Don K. Price (review). 193:29 (July 2, 1954). *Prospect of Canada,* by Ernest Watkins (review). 193:406 (Oct. 1, 1954).

Sunday Times (London): *Collected Work of William Gerhardi* (review). June 6, 1948, p. 3.

Novels by Kenneth Roberts and others (review). Jan. 9, 1949, p. 3. Novels by H. E. Bates, P. H. Newby, and others (review). Jan. 16, 1949, p. 3. Novels by Edwin Gilbert and others (review). Jan. 23, 1949, p. 3. Novels by Alex

Comfort and others (review). Jan. 30, 1949, p. 3. Novels by Herman Hesse and others (review). May 15, 1949, p. 3. Novels by Compton Mackenzie and others (review). May 29, 1949, p. 3. Novels by Marc Bernard and others (review). June 12, 1949, p. 3. Novels by Nigel Balchin and others (review). June 19, 1949, p. 3. Novels by Georges Simenon, Ivy Compton-Burnett, and others (review). June 26, 1949, p. 3. *The River Line,* by Charles Morgan (review). July 10, 1949, p. 3. Novels by Alberto Moravia and others (review). July 17, 1949, p. 3. Novels by Nancy Mitford and F. Scott Fitzgerald (review). July 31, 1949, p. 3. Books by Woodrow Wyatt and others (review). Aug. 14, 1949, p. 3. Novels by Emyr Humphreys and others (review). Aug. 28, 1949, p. 3. Novels by William McFee and others (review). Sept. 11, 1949, p. 3. Books by Robert Graves and others (review) Oct. 2, 1949, p. 3. Novels by William Faulkner and others (review). Oct. 16, 1949, p. 3. Novels by Joyce Cary and others (review). Oct. 30, 1949, p. 3. Novels by Irwin Shaw and others (review). Nov. 13, 1949, p. 3. Novels by J. G. Cozzens and others (review). Nov. 20, 1949, p. 3. Novels by Eric Linklater, Rex Warner, and others (review). Nov. 27, 1949, p. 3. Novels by J. P. Marquand and others (review). Dec. 4, 1949, p. 3. Novels by Sholem Asch and others (review). Dec. 11, 1949, p. 3. Novels by Ernest Raymond and others (review). Dec. 18, 1949, p. 3. Novels by Mary J. Ward and others (review). Dec. 25, 1949, p. 3.

Novels by Isabel Bolton and others (review). Jan. 1, 1950, p. 3. Novels by C. L. Philippe and others (review). Jan. 8, 1950, p. 3. Novels by L. P. Hartley, P. J. Newby, and others (review). Jan. 22, 1950, p. 3. Novels by George Buchanan and others (review). Feb. 5, 1950, p. 3. Novels by Alexander Baron and others (review). Feb. 19, 1950, p. 3. *Scenes from Provincial Life,* by William Cooper, and other novels (review). March 5, 1950, p. 3. Novels by Denton Welch and others (review). March 19, 1950, p. 3. Novels by Charles Jackson and others (review). April 2, 1950, p. 3. "Changes in the Detective Story." April 9, 1950, p. 3.   Novels by Francis MacManus and others (review). April 16, 1950, p. 3.   Novels by Rupert Croft-Cooke and others (review). April 30, 1950, p. 3.   *Nothing,* by Henry Green, and other novels (review). May 14, 1950, p. 3.   Novels by James Hanley and C. S. Forester (review). May 28, 1950, p. 3. Novels by François Mauriac, Nevil Shute, and others (review). June 11, 1950, p. 3.   Novels by Jerome Weidman and others (review). June 25, 1950, p. 3.   Novels by Wallace Stegner and others (review). July 9, 1950, p. 3.   Novels by Jane Lane and others (review). July 16, 1950, p. 3.   *Such Darling Dodos,* by Angus Wilson, and other books (review). July 23, 1950, p. 3.   *Iron in the Soul,* by J. P. Sartre, and other books (review). Aug. 6, 1950, p. 3.   Novels by Ardyth Kennelly and others (review). Aug. 29, 1950, p. 3. Novels by Hugh McGraw and others (review). Sept. 3, 1950, p. 3.   Novels by Angela Thirkell, George Barker, and others (review). Sept. 17, 1950, p. 3.   Novels by Dennis Parry and others (review). Oct. 1, 1950, p. 3.   Novels by Liam O'Flaherty and others (review). Nov. 5, 1950, p. 3.   Novels by John Pudney and others (review). Nov. 19, 1950, p. 3. Novels by Jon Godden and others (review). Dec. 3, 1950, p. 3.   Books by Tennessee Williams and others (review). Dec. 17, 1950, p. 3.   Novels by David Devine and others (review). Dec. 31, 1950, p. 3.

Novels by N. B. Morrison and others (review). Jan. 14, 1951, p. 3.   Novels by Frederic Morton and others (review). Jan. 28, 1951, p. 3.   Novels by François Mauriac and others (review). Feb. 11, 1951, p. 3.   Books by Frank O'Connor and others (review). Feb. 25, 1951, p. 3.   Novels by Emyr Humphreys and others (review). March 11, 1951, p. 3. Novels by Alberto Moravia, Henry Morton Robinson, and others (review). March 18, 1951, p. 3.   Novels by Margaret Penn and others (review). March 25, 1951, p. 3.   Novels by Doris Lessing and others (review). April 8, 1951, p. 3.

Books by William Sansom and others (review). April 22, 1951, p. 3. Novels by Kathleen Farrell and others (review). May 6, 1951, p. 3. Novels by Julian Green and others (review). May 20, 1951, p. 3. Novels by Nigel Balchin and Wallace Stegner (review). June 3, 1951, p. 3. Novels by Francis King and others (review). June 17, 1951, p. 3. Books by H. E. Bates and others (review). July 1, 1951, p. 3. Novels by Millie Toole and others (review). July 15, 1951, p. 3. Novels by Daphne du Maurier and others (review). July 29, 1951, p. 3. Novels by Elizabeth Sewell and others (review). Aug. 12, 1951, p. 3. Novels by John Wyndham and others (review). Aug. 26, 1951, p. 3. Novels by Olivia Manning and others (review). Sept. 9, 1951, p. 3. Novels by Margery Fisher and others (review). Sept. 23, 1951, p. 3. Novels by Marnix Gijsen and others (review). Nov. 4, 1951, p. 3. Novels by Edith de Born and others (review). Nov. 18, 1951, p. 3. Novels by Walter Baxter and others (review). Dec. 2, 1951, p. 3. Novels by Irwin Shaw and others (review). Dec. 16, 1951, p. 3. Novels by N. C. Hunter and others (review). Dec. 30, 1951, p. 3.

Novels by Mary McCarthy and others (review). Jan. 13, 1952, p. 3. Novels by Mervyn Jones and others (review). Jan. 27, 1952, p. 3. Novels by Norman Mailer, James Jones, and others (review). Feb. 3, 1952, p. 3. Novels by Riccardo Bacclelli and others (review). Feb. 24, 1952, p. 3. Novels by Alberto Moravia and others (review). March 9, 1952, p. 3. Novels by H. F. M. Prescott and others (review). March 23, 1952, p. 3. Novels by François Mauriac and others (review). April 6, 1952, p. 3. Novels by Thomas Mann and others (review). April 20, 1952, p. 3. Novels by Gwyn Thomas, Wallace Stegner, and others (review). May 4, 1952, p. 6. *Mr. Nicholas,* by Thomas Hinde, and other novels (review). May 18, 1952, p. 9. Novels by Robert Neumann and others (review). June 1, 1952, p. 8. Novels by Roger Lemelin and others (review).

June 15, 1952, p. 11. Novels by Richard Church and others (review). June 29, 1952, p. 5. Novels by James Hanley and others (review). July 13, 1952, p. 3. Novels by Storm Jameson and others (review). July 27, 1952, p. 5. Novels by Wolf Mankowitz and others (review). Aug. 10, 1952, p. 3. Novels by John Masters and others (review). Aug. 24, 1952, p. 5. Novels by Dorothy Charques and others (review). Sept. 7, 1952, p. 5. Novels by Emyr Humphreys and others (review). Sept. 21, 1952, p. 5. Novels by H. E. Bates and others (review). Oct. 5, 1952, p. 5. Novels by A. T. W. Simeons and others (review). Oct. 19, 1952, p. 5. Novels by Doris Lessing and others (review). Nov. 2, 1952, p. 5. Novels by Eric Lambert and others (review). Nov. 16, 1952, p. 5. Novels by Henri Troyat and others (review). Nov. 30, 1952, p. 5. Novels by Richard Brooks and others (review). Dec. 14, 1952, p. 5. "Valedictory." Dec. 28, 1952, p. 5.

The Weeping and the Laughter, by Julian Maclaren-Ross (review). May 17, 1953, p. 7. *Some Principles of Fiction,* by Robert Liddell (review). June 7, 1953, p. 5. *Notes on André Gide,* by Roger Martin du Gard (review). July 12, 1953, p. 5. *A Decade of Decision,* by Fred Hoyle (review). Oct. 11, 1953, p. 5. "New Trends in First Novels." Dec. 27, 1953, p. 3.

George Eliot, by Robert Speaight (review). Jan. 17, 1954, p. 5. Books by Gordon Dean and Robert Jungk (review). Jan. 31, 1954, p. 5. *The Magicians,* by J. B. Priestley (review). Feb. 21, 1954, p. 5. *The Craft of Fiction,* by Percy Lubbock (review). July 18, 1954, p. 5. *The Corner-stone,* by Zoe Oldenbourg (review). Nov. 14, 1954, p. 5. *The English Novel: A Short Critical History,* by Walter Allen (review). Dec. 5, 1954, p. 4. "Novels of 1954: Counter-Revolution." Dec. 26, 1954, p. 5.

"Reply to W. S. Maugham" (letter). Jan. 18, 1956. *The George Eliot Letters,* ed. by G. S. Haight (review). June 17, 1956, p. 4. "Books of the Year." Dec. 30, 1956, p. 11.

"The Two Cultures." Part I: March 10, 1957; Part II: March 17, 1957.   *Thoughts in the Wilderness,* by J. B. Priestley (review). Nov. 17, 1957, p. 8.   *The Castle of Fratta,* by Ippolito Nievo, tr. by L. F. Edwards (review). Nov. 24, 1957, p. 8.   "Mr. Cozzens Hits the Jackpot." Dec. 8, 1957, p. 8.

"New Men for a New Era." Aug. 24, 1958, p. 12.   *J. B. Priestley,* by David Hughes (review). Nov. 9, 1958, p. 16. "Books of the Year." Dec. 28, 1958, p. 11.

"Billiard Room Talks." March 6, 1960, p. 18.

"A Secret War of Whitehall." Part I: March 12, 1961, p. 25; Part II: March 19, 1961, p. 27; Part III: March 26, 1961, p. 25.   "The Scientist in Government." April 2, 1961, p. 23. "The Great Delusions. An Open Letter to an American Friend." Dec. 31, 1961, p. 13.

"C. P. Snow on Magnanimity" (rectorial address at the University of St. Andrews). April 22, 1962, p. 17.

Time: "Bring on the Scientists" (excerpt from an address). 76:40 (Dec. 12, 1960).

Time and Tide: The World of Somerset Maugham, by Clark Jonas (review). 40:303 (March 14, 1959).

Times (London) *Literary Supplement:* "Challenge to the Intellect." Aug. 15, 1958, p. iii.   *The Writer's Dilemma* [a collection of articles from *TLS*] (review). June 9, 1961, p. 351.   "The Two Cultures: A Second Look." Oct. 25, 1963, p. 839.

Weintraub, Stanley, editor. *C. P. Snow: A Spectrum.* New York: Scribner, 1963. Contains essays, articles, and excerpts from novels by Snow.

III. Books, Essays, and Articles Dealing with Snow

Adams, Robert. "Pomp and Circumstance: C. P. Snow," *Atlantic Monthly,* 214:95 (Nov., 1964).

Allen, Walter. *Reading a Novel.* London: Phoenix House, 1956.

———— "Mr. Leavis Pays His Respects to Mr. Snow," *NYTBR,* April 1, 1962, p. 10.

———— *Tradition and Dream* (London: Phoenix House, 1964), esp. pp. 248–51.

Bergonzi, Bernard. "The World of Lewis Eliot," *Twentieth Century,* 167:214 (March, 1960).

Brady, Charles A. "The British Novel Today," *Thought,* 30:518 (Winter, 1959–60).

"Chubb Fellow," *NY,* 37:44 (Dec. 16, 1961).

Cooper, William, pseud., *see* Hoff, Harry.

Corke, Hilary "The Dog that Didn't Bark," *N Repub,* 148:27 (April 13, 1963).

Cornelius, David K., and Edwin St. Vincent. *Cultures in Conflict: Perspectives on the Snow-Leavis Controversy.* Chicago: Scott, Foresman, 1964.

Davis, Robert G. *C. P. Snow.* New York: Columbia University Press, 1965.

Dennis, Nigel. "Under the Combination Room," *Enc,* 17:51 (Dec., 1961).

Gardner, A. "A Literary Owl Who Doesn't Give a Hoot," *Sat R,* 44:53 (March 4, 1961).

Gerhardi, William, *et al.* "Sir Charles Snow, Dr. F. R. Leavis, and The Two Cultures: Comments by William Gerhardi, J. D. Scott, Dame Edith Sitwell, Lord Boothby, Susan Hill, Denis Lant, Stephen Toulmin, G. Reichardt, Anthony Storr, Ronald Millar, G. S. Fraser, Peter Jay, C. R. Jones, M. S. Deal, Sir Oliver Scott, A. L. Haskell, and Gavin Ewart," *Spec,* 208:329 (March 16, 1962).

Ginden, James. *Postwar British Fiction* (Berkeley: University of California Press, 1961), esp. pp. 207–15.

Greacen, Robert. "Profile of C. P. Snow," *Humanist,* 73:9 (Oct., 1958).

———— "The World of C. P. Snow," *Tex Q,* 4:266 (Autumn, 1961).

———— *The World of C. P. Snow.* With a bibliography by Bernard Stone. London: Scorpion Press, 1962.

Green, Martin. "A Literary Defense of *The Two Cultures*," *Critical Quarterly*, 4:155 (Summer, 1962). Reprinted in *Ken R*, 24:731 (Autumn, 1962).

———— "Lionel Trilling and the Two Cultures," *E in C*, 13:375 (Oct., 1963).

———— *Science and the Shabby Curate of Poetry*. London: Longmans, 1964.

Halio, Jay L. "C. P. Snow's Literary Limitations," *Northwest Review*, (Winter, 1962), p. 97.

Hall, William F. "The Humanism of C. P. Snow," *WSCL*, 4:199 (1963).

Heppenstall, Raynor. *The Fourfold Tradition* (London: Barrie and Rockliff, 1961), esp. pp. 224–43.

Hoff, Harry. "The World of C. P. Snow" (by William Cooper, pseud.). *Nation*, 184:104 (Feb. 2, 1957).

Hoff, Harry. *The World of C. P. Snow* (by William Cooper, pseud.). London: Longmans, for the British Council and National Book League, 1959.

Huxley, Aldous. *Literature and Science*. London: Chatto and Windus, 1963.

"Interview with C. P. Snow," *REL*, 3:91 (July, 1962).

Johnson, Pamela Hansford (Lady Snow). "With Prejudice," *Windmill*, 1:1 (1944).

———— "Three Novelists and the Drawing of Character: C. P. Snow, Joyce Cary, and Ivy Compton-Burnett," in *English Association Essays and Studies*, n.s., vol. 3 (1950).

Karl, F. R. "The Politics of Conscience: The Novels of C. P. Snow," in *A Reader's Guide to the Contemporary English Novel* (New York: Noonday Press, 1962), p. 62.

———— *C. P. Snow: The Politics of Conscience*. With a preface by Harry T. Moore. Carbondale: Southern Illinois University Press, 1963.

Kazin, Alfred. "A Gifted Boy from the Midlands," *The Reporter*, 20:37 (Feb. 5, 1959). Reprinted in a collection of Kazin's essays, *Contemporaries* (Boston: Little, Brown, and Co., 1962).

Kermode, Frank. "Beckett, Snow, and Pure Poverty," *Enc*, 14:73 (July, 1960). Reprinted in a collection of Kermode's essays,

Puzzles and Epiphanies (London: Routledge and Kegan Paul, 1962).

————— "Myth, Reality, and Fiction," *List,* 68:311 (Aug. 30, 1962).

————— "The House of Fiction: Interviews with Seven English Novelists," *Partisan Review,* 30:74 (Spring, 1963).

Leavis, F. R. "The Significance of C. P. Snow," *Spec,* 208:297 (March 9, 1962).

————— *Two Cultures? The Significance of C. P. Snow: Being the Richmond Lecture, 1962.* With an essay on Sir Charles Snow's Rede Lecture by Michael Yudkin. London: Chatto and Windus, 1962.

————— "Two Cultures? The Significance of C. P. Snow." *Melbourne Critical Review,* 5:90 (1962).

Lehan, Richard. "The Divided World: *The Masters* Examined," in *Six Contemporary Novels: Six Introductory Essays in Modern Fiction,* ed. by William Sutherland. Austin: University of Texas Department of English, 1962.

Lloyd, Quentin. "My Relationship with C. P. Snow. Ronald Millar Interviewed by Quentin Lloyd," *Time and Tide,* 43:16 (Sept. 13–20, 1962).

Lovell, A. C. B., *et al.* "The Two Cultures: A Discussion of C. P. Snow's Views." Comments by Lovell, Walter Allen, Sir John Cockcroft, Bertrand Russell, Michael Ayrton, J. H. Plumb, and David Riesman. *Enc,* 13:67 (Aug., 1959).

"The Many-sided Life of Sir Charles Snow," *Life,* 50:134 (Apr. 7, 1961).

Marcus, Steven. "Intellectuals, Scientists, and the Future," *Com,* 28:165, (Feb., 1960).

Martin, Graham. "Novelists of Three Decades: Evelyn Waugh, Graham Greene, C. P. Snow," in *The Modern Age,* ed. by Boris Ford. Baltimore: Penguin Books, 1963.

Mayne, Richard. "The Club Armchair," *Enc,* 21:76 (Nov., 1963).

Millar, Ronald, *see* Lloyd, Quentin.

Millgate, Michael. "Structure and Style in the Novels of C. P. Snow," *REL,* 1:34 (April, 1960).

Miner, E. "C. P. Snow and the Realistic Novel," *Nat,* 190:554 (June 25, 1960).

Nott, Kathleen. "The Type to Which the Whole Creation Moves? Further Thoughts on the Snow Saga," *Enc*, 18:87 (Feb., 1962).

―――― "Whose Culture?", *List*, 67:631 (April 12, 1962); 67:677 (April 19, 1962).

"The Observer Profile: Sir Charles Snow," *Obs*, April 9, 1961, p. 12.

Phelps, Gilbert. "The Novel Today," in *The Modern Age,* ed. by Boris Ford. Baltimore: Penguin Books, 1963.

Procter, Mortimer R. *The English University Novel* (Berkeley and Los Angeles: University of California Press, 1957), esp. pp. 150, 178–80.

Putt, S. G. "Technique and Culture: Three Cambridge Portraits," *Essays and Studies by Members of the English Association,* 14:17 (1961).

―――― "Snow-Leavis Rumpus," *Antioch Review,* 23:299 (Fall, 1963).

"A Question of Brains," *TLS,* March 23, 1962, p. 201.

Read, Herbert. "Mood of the Month—10." *Lon M,* 6:39 (no. 8, 1959). Comment on Snow's Rede Lecture.

Seigel, Leila "Biographical Sketch," *WLB,* 28:404 (Jan., 1954).

Stanford, Derek. "C. P. Snow: The Novelist as Fox," *Meanjin,* 19:236 (1960).

―――― "A Disputed Master: C. P. Snow and his Critics," *Month,* 29:91 (Feb., 1963).

Stanford, Raney. "Personal Politics in the Novels of C. P. Snow," *Critique* (Minneapolis), 2:16 (Spring-Summer, 1958).

―――― "The Achievement of C. P. Snow," *Western Humanities Review,* 16:43 (1962).

Thale, Jerome. "C. P. Snow: The Art of Worldliness," *Ken R,* 22:621 (Fall, 1960).

―――― *C. P. Snow.* (The Writers and Critics Series.) London: Oliver and Boyd, 1964.

Tindall, William Y. *Forces in Modern British Literature* ([rev. ed.] New York: Vintage Books, 1956), esp. p. 210.

Trilling, Lionel. "The Novel Alive or Dead," in *A Gathering of Fugitives.* Boston: Beacon Press, 1956.

———— "Science, Literature, and Culture: A Comment on the Leavis-Snow Controversy," *Com*, 33:461 (June, 1962).

Vogel, Albert W. "The Academic World of C. P. Snow," *Twentieth Century Literature*, 9:143 (1963).

Waddington, C. H. "Humanists and Scientists: A Last Comment on C. P. Snow," *Enc*, 14:72 (Jan., 1960).

Wagner, Geoffrey. "The Writer in the Welfare State," *Commonweal*, 65:49 (Oct. 12, 1956).

———— "Sociology and Fiction," *Twentieth Century*, 167:108 (Feb., 1960).

Wall, Stephen. "Reputations 10: The Novels of C. P. Snow," *Lon M*, n.s., 4:68 (Apr., 1964).

Watson-Watt, R. "The Truth about Churchill's Aide: A Rebuttal to the Godkin Lectures by C. P. Snow at Harvard," *Sat R*, 44:49 (March 4, 1961).

West, Paul. *The Modern Novel*. London: Hutchinson, 1963.

Wilson, Angus. "If It's New and Modish Is It Good?", *NYTBR*, July 2, 1961, p. 1.

Wilson, Edmund. "An Interview with Edmund Wilson," *NY*, June 2, 1962, p. 118. This article also appeared in the London *Sunday Times*, Sept. 2, 1962, p. 21.

"The Workaday World the Novelist Never Enters," *TLS*, Sept. 9, 1960, p. vii.

Yudkin, Michael, see Leavis, F. R., *Two Cultures?*

SELECTED GENERAL CRITICAL WORKS

Allen, Walter. *The Novel Today*. London: Longman's, for the British Council and National Book League, 1955.
—— *Reading a Novel*. London: Phoenix House, 1956.
—— "The Newest Voice in English Lit Is from the Working Class," *NYTBR*, Dec. 20, 1959, p. 4.
—— "A Literary Letter from London," *NYTBR*, Sept. 17, 1961, p. 40.
—— "London Literary Letter," *NYTBR*, Sept. 22, 1963, p. 38.
—— *Tradition and Dream* (published in America as *The Modern Novel*). London: Phoenix House; New York: Dutton, 1964.
Allsop, Kenneth. *The Angry Decade*. London: Peter Owen, 1958.
Alvarez, A. *The New Poetry*. Harmondsworth: Penguin Books, 1962.
Barzun, Jacques. *Romanticism and the Modern Ego*. Boston: Little, Brown, and Co., 1943.
Bateson, F. W. "Organs of Critical Opinion, 4: The *T.L.S.*," *E in C*, 7:349 (1957).
Becker, George J. *Documents of Modern Literary Realism*. Princeton: Princeton University Press, 1963.
Bergonzi, Bernard. "The Novel No Longer Novel," *List* 70:415 (Sept. 19, 1963).
Bowen, Elizabeth. "English Fiction at Midcentury," *N Repub*, 129:15 (Sept. 21, 1953).
Bowen, John. "One Man's Meat: The Idea of Individual Responsibility," *TLS*, Aug. 7, 1959, p. xii.
Bradbury, Malcolm. "Literary Culture in England Today," *List* 68:209 (Aug. 9, 1962).
—— "Recent English Novels," *Critical Survey*, 1:138 (Autumn, 1963).
——, and Dudley Andrew. "The Sugar-Beet Generation: A Note in English Intellectual History," *Tex Q*, 3:38 (1960).
Braine, John. "The Fog Lifts," *Spec*, 201:188 (Aug. 8, 1958).

———— Review of novels by William Cooper, *Sun Times,* Jan. 22, 1961, p. 28.

————, *see also* Sykes, Adam.

The British Imagination: A Critical Survey from the Times Literary Supplement. New York: Atheneum, 1961.

Brophy, Brigid. "The Novel as Take-over Bid," *List,* 70:501 (Oct. 3, 1963).

Buckley, Vincent. *Poetry and Morality: Studies on the Criticism of Matthew Arnold, T. S. Eliot, and F. R. Leavis.* London: Chatto and Windus, 1959.

Burgess, Anthony. "The Corruption of the Exotic," *List,* 70:465 (Sept. 26, 1963).

Churchill, Randolph S. "Portrait of the 'Artist' as an Angry Young Gentleman," *Enc,* 10:66 (1958).

Conquest, Robert, ed. *New Lines: An Anthology.* London: Macmillan, 1956.

Cooper, William, pseud., *see* Hoff, Harry.

Cox, C. B. *The Free Spirit.* London: Oxford University Press, 1963.

The Critical Moment: Essays on the Nature of Literature. London: Faber and Faber, 1963. From the *Times Literary Supplement.*

Cruttwell, Patrick. "Fiction Chronicle," *Hudson Review,* 15:588 (1962).

Current-Garcia, Eugene, and Walton R. Patrick. *Realism and Romanticism in Fiction.* Chicago: Scott, Foresman, and Co., 1961.

Daiches, David. "How to Criticize a Novel," *List,* 48:468 (Sept. 18, 1952).

———— *The Present Age from 1920.* London: The Cresset Press, 1958.

Davie, Donald. "Is There a London Literary Racket?", *Twentieth Century,* 155:540 (June, 1954).

Derry, T. K., and T. L. Jarman. *The Making of Modern Britain.* New York: New York University Press, 1956.

"The English and the American Novel," *TLS,* Aug. 29, 1952, p. xii.

Esslin, Martin. *The Theater of the Absurd.* Garden City: Anchor Books, 1961.

Evans, B. Ifor. "The Victorian Revival," *Britain Today,* Feb., 1948, p. 20.

Evashova, V. "The Struggle Continues: Some Comments on English Modernist Esthetics," *Zeitschrift für Anglistik und Amerikanistik,* 8:409 (1960).

"Experience of a Lifetime," *TLS,* June 20, 1958, p. 345.

"Experiment in Prose," *TLS,* Aug. 17, 1956, p. ii.

Faverty, Frederic. *The Victorian Poets: A Guide to Research.* Cambridge: Harvard University Press, 1956.

Feldman, Gene, and Max Gartenberg, eds. *The Beat Generation and the Angry Young Men.* New York: Citadel, 1958.

Fiedler, Leslie A. "Class War in British Literature," *Esquire,* 49:79 (April, 1958).

Fielding, Gabriel. "Four Cheers for the Novelist," *Sun Times,* Nov. 3, 1963, p. 37.

Ford, Boris, ed. *The Modern Age.* Baltimore: Penguin, 1963.

Fraser, G. S. *Poetry Now: An Anthology.* London: Faber and Faber, 1956.

――― *The Modern Writer and His World.* Rev. ed. Baltimore: Penguin Books, 1964.

Fyvel, T. R. "Problems of the Modern Novelist," *List,* 53:708 (April 21, 1955).

Ginden, James. *Postwar British Fiction: New Accents and Attitudes.* Berkeley: University of California Press, 1961.

Glicksberg, Charles I. "The Literature of the Angry Young Men," *Colorado Quarterly,* 8:293 (Spring, 1960).

Golding, William. "On the Crest of the Wave," *TLS,* June 17, 1960, p. 387.

Gransden, K. W. "Thoughts on Contemporary Fiction," *REL,* 1:7 (April, 1960).

Green, Martin. "Room at the Middle." *Commonweal,* 72:38 (April 8, 1960).

――― *A Mirror for Anglo-Saxons.* New York: Harper and Brothers, 1960.

Hartley, Anthony. "Philistine to Philistine?", in *International Liter-*

ary Annual No. 2, ed. by John Wain. London: John Calder, 1959.

Hartley, L. P. "The Novelist and His Material," *TLS*, Aug. 15, 1958, p. iv.

Harvey, W. T. "Have You Anything To Declare? or, Angry Young Men: Facts and Fictions," in *International Literary Annual*, ed. by John Wain. London: John Calder, 1958.

Heppenstall, Rayner. "Outsiders and Others," *Twentieth Century*, 158:453 (Nov., 1955).

———— *The Fourfold Tradition*. London: Barrie and Rockliff, 1961.

Hilton, Frank. "Britain's New Class." *Enc*, 10:59 (Feb., 1958).

Hobson, Harold. "Lunch with Iris Murdoch," *Sun Times*, March 11, 1962, p. 28.

Hoff, Harry (pseud., William Cooper). "Reflections on some Aspects of the Experimental Novel," in *International Literary Annual No. 2*, ed. by John Wain. London: John Calder, 1959.

———— "Novel and Anti-novel," *Sun Times*, Dec. 17, 1961, p. 21.

Hoffman, Frederick J. *Freudianism and the Literary Mind*. Baton Rouge: Louisiana State University Press, 1945.

Hoggert, Richard. *The Uses of Literacy*. Harmondsworth: Penguin Books, 1963.

———— "Classes and Masses: Class and Cultural Change in Mid-Century Britain," *Tex Q*, 3:1 (Winter, 1960).

Holloway, John. "Tank in the Stalls: Notes on the 'School of Anger,' " *Hudson Review*, 10:424 (Autumn, 1957).

Hope, Francis. "Joking in Earnest," *Obs*, April 28, 1963, p. 26.

Hopkins, Harry. *The New Look: A Social History of the Forties and Fifties in Britain*. Boston: Houghton Mifflin Co., 1964.

Hough, Graham. *Reflections on a Literary Revolution*. Washington, D.C.: Catholic University of America Press, 1960.

———— "The Nature of a Revolution," *Audience*, 8:39 (Winter, 1961).

Humphreys, Emyr. "A Protestant View of the Modern Novel," *List*, 49:557 (April 2, 1953).

Huxley, Aldous. *Literature and Science*. New York: Harper and Row, 1963.

Hynes, Sam. "The 'Poor Sod' as Hero," *Commonweal*, 64:51 (April 13, 1956).

"In the Picture," *Obs*, Jan. 14, 1962, p. 25. On Thomas Hinde.

Jarman, T. L. *A Short History of Twentieth-Century England*. New York: New American Library (Mentor Books), 1963.

Jarrett, James L., and Sterling M. McMurrin, eds. *Contemporary Philosophy*. New York: Henry Holt and Co., 1957.

Jennings, Elizabeth, ed. *An Anthology of Modern Verse, 1940–1960*. London: Methuen and Co., 1961.

Johnson, Pamela Hansford. "With Prejudice," *Windmill* (No. 1, 1944), p. 1.

———— "The Sickroom Hush over the English Novel," *List*, 42:235 (Aug. 11, 1949).

———— "The Debate about the Novel," *NS*, 56:172 (Aug. 9, 1958).

———— *Proust Recaptured*. Chicago: University of Chicago Press, 1958.

———— "Modern Fiction and the English Understatement," *TLS*, Aug. 7, 1959, p. iii.

Karl, F. R. *A Reader's Guide to the Contemporary English Novel*. New York: Noonday Press, 1962.

Kermode, Frank. "Counter-Revolution," *Spec*, 205:25 (July 1, 1960).

———— *Puzzles and Epiphanies*. London: Routledge and Kegan Paul, 1962.

———— "The House of Fiction: Interviews with Seven English Novelists," *Partisan Review*, 30:61 (Spring, 1963).

Kitchin, Lawrence. *Mid-Century Drama*. London: Faber and Faber, 1960.

Kostelonetz, Richard, ed. *On Contemporary Literature*. New York: Avon Books, 1964.

Larkin, Philip. "The Writer in his Age." *Lon M*, 4:46 (May, 1957).

Leavis, F. R. *The Great Tradition*. New York: Doubleday, 1954.

Lehmann, John. "English Letters in the Doldrums?", *Tex Q*, 4:56 (Autumn, 1961)

————, ed. *The Craft of Letters in England.* London: The Cresset Press, 1956. See especially Francis Wyndham, "Twenty-five Years of the Novel," p. 44, and Phillip Toynbee, "Experiment and the Future of the Novel," p. 60.

Lodge, David. "The Contemporary Novel and All That Jazz," *Lon M,* 2:73 (Aug., 1962).

———— "The Modern, the Contemporary, and the Importance of Being Amis." *Critical Quarterly,* 5:335 (Winter, 1963). Reprinted in *Language of Fiction.* London: Routledge and Kegan Paul; New York: Columbia University Press, 1966.

Longaker, Mark, and Edwin C. Bolles. *Contemporary English Literature.* New York: Appleton-Century-Crofts, 1953.

Lucas, F. L. *The Decline and Fall of the Romantic Ideal.* Cambridge: Cambridge University Press, 1963.

Lukács, George. *The Meaning of Contemporary Realism.* New York: The Merlin Press, 1962.

———— *Studies in European Realism.* New York: Grosset and Dunlap, 1964.

McElroy, D. D. *Existentialism and Modern Literature.* New York: Philosophical Library, 1963.

Mander, John. *The Writer and Commitment.* London: Secker and Warburg, 1961.

Manning, Olivia. "Notes on the Future of the Novel," *TLS,* Aug. 15, 1958, p. vi.

Marwick, Arthur. *The Explosion of British Society, 1914–62.* London: Pan Books, 1963.

Maschler, Tom. *Declaration.* London: MacGibbon and Kee, 1957.

Mayersberg, Paul. "The Writer as Spaceman," *List,* 70:607 (Oct. 17, 1963).

Murdoch, Iris. "The Existentialist Hero." *List,* 43:523 (March 23, 1950).

———— "A House of Theory," *Partisan Review,* 26:17 (Winter, 1959).

———— "The Sublime and the Beautiful Revisited," *Yale Review,* 49:247 (Dec., 1959).

———— "Against Dryness: A Polemical Sketch," *Enc,* 16:16 (Jan. 1961).

Neill, S. Diana. *A Short History of the English Novel*. Rev. ed. New York: Collier Books, 1964.

Newby, P. H. *The Novel, 1945–1950*. London: Longman's, for the British Council, 1951.

"The Novelist's World," *TLS*, Sept. 6, 1957, p. 553.

O'Connor, Frank. *The Mirror in the Roadway: A Study in the Modern Novel*. New York: Knopf, 1956.

O'Connor, William Van. *The New University Wits*. Carbondale: Southern Illinois University Press, 1963.

Osborne, John. "The Writer in His Age," *Lon M*, 4:47 (May, 1957).

Paloczi-Horvath, George. *The Writer and the Commissar*. London: The Bodley Head, 1960.

Pendry, E. D. *The New Feminism of English Fiction: A Study in Contemporary Women Novelists*. Tokyo: Kenkyusha, Ltd., 1957.

Pinter, Harold. "Writing for Myself," *Twentieth Century*, 169:172 (Feb., 1961).

Powell, Anthony. "Taken from Life," *Twentieth Century*, 170:50 (July, 1961).

Pritchett, V. S. "A Literary Letter from London," *NYTBR*, Jan. 25, 1953, p. 26.

———— "An English Letter on Books and Their Authors," *NYTBR*, Sept. 13, 1953, p. 18.

———— "Books in General," *NS*, 49:76 (Jan. 15, 1955).

———— "Books in General: Joyce's *Ulysses*," *NS*, 51:75 (Jan. 21, 1956).

———— "These Writers Couldn't Care Less," *NYTBR*, April 28, 1957, p. 1.

———— "The Current Scene, Great Britain," *NYTBR*, Nov. 3, 1957, p. 50.

Procter, Mortimer R. *The English University Novel*. Berkeley and Los Angeles: University of California Press, 1957.

Quinton, Anthony. "A Refusal to Look," *List*, 52:138 (July 22, 1954).

———— "Masculine, Feminine, and Neuter, or Three Kinds of the Contemporary Novel," *Lon M*, 7:63 (April, 1960).

—— *et al.* "The New Novelists: An Enquiry," *Lon M,* 5:13 (Nov., 1958).

Raleigh, John H. "Victorian Morals and the Modern Novel," *Partisan Review,* 25:241 (Spring, 1958).

Ricks, Christopher. "The Epicene," *NS,* 65:496 (April 5, 1963). On Anthony Burgess.

Scott-James, R. A. *Fifty Years of English Literature, 1900–1950.* London: Longmans, Green, 1951.

Shapiro, Charles, ed. *Contemporary British Novelists.* Carbondale and Edwardsville: Southern Illinois University Press, 1965.

Sillitoe, Alan. "Both Sides of the Street," *TLS,* July 8, 1960, p. 435.

—— Introduction to Arnold Bennett's *The Old Wives' Tale.* London: Pan Books, 1964.

Simon, W. M. *European Positivism in the Nineteenth Century.* Ithaca: Cornell University Press, 1963.

Snow, C. P. "Italo Svevo: Forerunner of Cooper and Amis," in *Essays and Studies by Members of the English Association,* 14:7 (1961).

Snow, Lady Pamela, *see* Pamela Hansford Johnson.

Spark, Muriel. "My Conversion," *Twentieth Century,* 170:58 (Autumn, 1961).

Spender, Stephen. "A Literary Letter from London," *NYTBR,* Jan. 10, 1954, p. 14.

—— "The Current Scene in Great Britain," *NYTBR,* May 9, 1954, p. 24.

—— "Speaking of Books," *NYTBR,* Aug. 1, 1954, p. 2.

—— "When the Angry Young Men Grow Older," *NYTBR,* July 20, 1958, p. 1.

—— "Literary London: A Tight Little Isle," *NYTBR,* Aug. 28, 1960, p. 1.

—— "In the Overlap," *Spec,* 209:532 (Oct. 5, 1962).

—— "The Obsessive Situation: Moderns and Contemporaries," *List,* 68:555 (Oct. 11, 1962).

—— *The Struggle of the Modern.* London: Hamish Hamilton, 1963.

Stanford, Derek. "Thoughts on Contemporary Literature," *Contemporary Review,* 191:234 (April, 1957).

———— "Report from London," *Western Review*, 21:293 (Summer, 1957).

———— "Beatniks and Angry Young Men," *Meanjin*, 17:413 (1958).

Stevenson, Lionel, ed. *Victorian Fiction, a Guide to Research.* Cambridge: Harvard University Press, 1964.

Storey, David. "Journey through a Tunnel," *List*, 70:159 (Aug. 1, 1963).

Sykes, Adam. "How I Write My Novels: John Braine Interviewed by Adam Sykes," *Time and Tide*, 43:23 (Oct. 4–11, 1962).

Taylor, John Russell. *Anger and After*. London: Methuen, 1962.

Tertz, Abram [pseud. of Andrei Sinyavsky]. *On Socialist Realism.* New York: Pantheon Books, 1960.

Tillyard, E. M. W. *The Epic Strain in the English Novel.* London: Chatto and Windus, 1963.

Tindall, William Y. *Forces in Modern British Literature.* Rev. ed. New York: Vintage Books, 1956.

T.L.S. 1962: Essays and Reviews from the Times Literary Supplement. London: Oxford University Press, 1963.

T.L.S.: Essays and Reviews from the Times Literary Supplement, 1963. London: Oxford University Press, 1964.

Toynbee, Phillip. "Dragons and Dragon Killers," *Obs*, Dec. 20, 1959, p. 16.

———— "Art and Catastrophe." *Obs*, May 19, 1963, p. 23.

"Two Views of Fiction," *TLS*, Nov. 7, 1958, p. 641.

"Uncommitted Talents," *TLS*, Aug. 29, 1952, p. iii.

Wain, John. *Preliminary Essays.* London: Macmillan, 1957.

———— "Instrument of Communication," *TLS*, Aug. 15, 1958, p. xxii.

————, ed. *International Literary Annual No. 1.* London: John Calder, 1958.

————, ed. *International Literary Annual No. 2.* London: John Calder, 1959.

———— "Shadow of an Epic," *Spec*, 204:360 (March 11, 1960).

———— "London Letter," *Hudson Review*, 15:253 (Summer, 1960).

————— *Sprightly Running: Part of an Autobiography.* London: Macmillan, 1962.

————— "Modernism Revisited," *Obs,* March 3, 1963, p. 22.

————— "Notes on Imagination and Judgment," *TLS,* July 26, 1963, p. 561.

————— "21 Years with Dr. Leavis," *Obs,* Oct. 27, 1963, p. 25.

—————, ed. *Anthology of Modern Poetry.* London: Hutchinson, 1963.

————— *Essays on Literature and Ideas.* London: Macmillan, 1963.

Ward, A. C. *Twentieth-Century English Literature, 1901–1960.* New York: Barnes and Noble, 1964.

Watson, George, ed. *The Concise Cambridge Bibliography of English Literature.* Cambridge: Cambridge University Press, 1965.

Wesker, Arnold. "Art Is Not Enough," *Twentieth Century,* 169:190 (Feb., 1961).

West, Paul. *The Modern Novel.* London: Hutchinson, 1963.

Whitehead, Frank. "A Postscript on the 1950's," in *English Literature of the Twentieth Century,* by A. S. Collins. London: University Tutorial Press, 1962.

Widmer, Kingsley. *The Literary Rebel.* Carbondale: Southern Illinois University Press, 1965.

Wiemann, Robert. "Die Literatur der *Angry Young Men.* Ein Beitrag zur Deutung englischer Gegenwartsliteratur." *Zeitschrift für Anglistik und Amerikanistik,* 7:117 (1959).

Williams, Raymond. "Realism and the Contemporary Novel," *Partisan Review,* 26:200 (Spring, 1959).

————— "A Changing Social History of English Writing," *Audience,* 8:76 (Winter, 1961).

————— *The Long Revolution.* New York: Columbia University Press, 1961.

Wilson Edmund. "An Interview with Edmund Wilson," *NY,* 38:118 (June 2, 1962).

The Writer's Dilemma: Essays First Published in the Times Literary Supplement under the Heading, "Limits of Control." London: Oxford University Press, 1961.

Acknowledgments

The author is indebted to the publishers, authors, literary agents, and other owners of rights who have allowed him to reprint passages from books and periodicals under copyright. The donors listed below are thanked for permission to quote from the works indicated.

The Atlantic Monthly:
Angus Wilson, "The Revolt of Samuel Butler."
The British Broadcasting Corporation:
Writers on Themselves.
From *The Listener:*
Bernard Bergonzi, "The Novel No Longer Novel."
Emyr Humphries, "A Protestant View of the Modern Novel."
Pamela Hansford Johnson, "The Sick-room Hush over the English Novel."
Angus Wilson, "Sense and Sensibility in Recent Writing"; "Evil in the English Novel."
The British Council:
Walter Allen, *The Novel Today.*
William Cooper, *C. P. Snow.*
From *Britain Today:*
B. Ifor Evans, "The Victorian Revival" (Feb., 1948).

Calder and Boyars, Ltd.:
John Wain, ed., *International Literary Annual,* nos. 1 and 2.
University of California Press:
James Ginden, *Postwar British Fiction.*
Angus Wilson, *The Wild Garden.*
Cambridge University Press:
C. P. Snow, *The Two Cultures: and a Second Look.*
Mrs. Frances W. Chase:
Richard Chase, "Middlebrow England: the Novels of Kingsley Amis."
Columbia University Press:
David Lodge, *Language of Fiction.*
Commentary:
Richard Chase, "Middlebrow England: the Novels of Kingsley Amis." Reprinted from *Commentary,* copyright © 1956 by the American Jewish Committee.
Commonweal:
Geoffrey Wagner, "The Writer in the Welfare State."
Contemporary Review:
Derek Stanford, "Thoughts on Contemporary Literature."
The Critical Quarterly:
David Lodge, "The Modern, the Contemporary, and the Importance of Being Amis."
Angus Wilson, "Charles Dickens: A Haunting."
Curtis Brown, Ltd. (London):
Kingsley Amis, *A Case of Samples; New Maps of Hell; One Fat Englishman.*
G. S. Fraser, *The Modern Writer and His World.*
C. P. Snow, *Death Under Sail.*
John Wain, *The Contenders.*
Angus Wilson, *Anglo-Saxon Attitudes; The Middle Age of Mrs. Eliot.*
Discovery:
C. P. Snow, "The First Excitement that Knowledge Gives."
Doubleday and Company, Inc.:
Arnold Bennett, *The Old Wives' Tale* (American edition).
E. P. Dutton and Co., Inc.:

Walter Allen, *The Modern Novel.*
Encounter:
Kathleen Nott, "The Type to which the Whole Creation Moves?"
Angus Wilson, quotations from book reviews, 1956.
The English Association:
Pamela Hansford Johnson, "Three Novelists and the Drawing of Character."
The Fabian Society:
Kingsley Amis, *Socialism and the Intellectuals.*
Farrar, Straus and Giroux, Inc.:
F. R. Karl, *A Reader's Guide to the Contemporary English Novel,* copyright © 1962 by Frederick Karl.
Victor Gollancz, Ltd.:
Kingsley Amis, *I Like It Here.*
Kingsley Amis and Robert Conquest, *Spectrum 4.*
Harcourt, Brace and World, Inc.:
Kingsley Amis, *I Like It Here; New Maps of Hell; One Fat Englishman.*
Kingsley Amis and Robert Conquest, *Spectrum 4.*
Harvard University Press:
C. P. Snow, *Science and Government.*
Lionel Stevenson, ed., *Victorian Fiction: A Guide to Research.*
David Higham Associates, Ltd.:
Walter Allen, *Tradition and Dream.*
The Hudson Review:
John Holloway, "Tank in the Stalls," copyright © 1957 by The Hudson Review, Inc.
Mr. Alfred Kazin:
"A Gifted Boy from the Midlands."
Kennikat Press, Inc.:
Kenneth Allsop, *The Angry Decade.*
The Kenyon Review:
C. P. Snow, "Science, Politics, and the Novelist."
Mr. Frank Kermode:
"The House of Fiction: Interviews with Seven English Novelists."
London Magazine:
Bernard Bergonzi, "Kingsley Amis."

Anthony Quinton, "The New Novelists: An Enquiry."
Stephen Wall, "The Novels of C. P. Snow."
Angus Wilson, "Arnold Bennett's Novels"; "The House Party Novels"; "Ivy Compton-Burnett"; "Mood of the Month III."
Longmans, Green, and Co.:
    From *A Review of English Literature,*
    Michael Millgate, "An Interview with C. P. Snow."
Macgibbon and Kee, Ltd.:
    Tom Maschler, ed., *Declaration.*
Macmillan and Co., Ltd. (London):
    C. P. Snow, *Time of Hope; The Light and the Dark; The New Men; Homecomings; The Conscience of the Rich; The Affair.*
    John Wain, *Preliminary Essays; Essays on Literature and Ideas.*
The Macmillan Company (New York):
    Arnold Rogow, *The Jew in a Gentile World.*
    C. P. Snow, *Time of Hope.*
The Macmillan Company of Canada, Ltd. (Toronto):
    John Wain, *Preliminary Essays; Essays on Literature and Ideas;* excerpts reprinted by permission of Macmillan and Co., Ltd. London and the Macmillan Company of Canada Limited.
Harold Matson Company, Inc.:
    Stephen Spender, *The Struggle of the Modern.*
Meanjin:
    Derek Stanford, "C. P. Snow: The Novelist as Fox."
Professor Michael Millgate:
    "An Interview with C. P. Snow."
Moderna Sprak:
    C. P. Snow, "The English Realistic Novel, 1957."
William Morrow and Company, Inc.:
    Angus Wilson, *Émile Zola.*
The Nation:
    William Cooper, "The World of C. P. Snow."
The New Statesman:
    Walter Allen, extracts from a book review.
    Pamela Hansford Johnson, "The Debate about the Novel."
    Angus Wilson, "Reassessments: Galsworthy's *Forsyte Saga.*"
The New York *Times:*

Walter Allen, "London Literary Letter."
Kingsley Amis, "Laughter's To Be Taken Seriously."
Anonymous reviewer, Dec. 12, 1961, p. 56.
V. S. Pritchett, "A Literary Letter from London."
C. P. Snow, "Story Tellers for the Atomic Age."
Stephen Spender, "Speaking of Books."
Angus Wilson, "If It's New and Modish, Is It Good?"
All of the articles above are held in copyright © by The New York Times Company.
The New Yorker:
"Chubb Fellow," Dec. 16, 1961.
The Observer:
Kingsley Amis, book review, July 17, 1960.
Interview with Iris Murdoch, June 25, 1961.
John Wain, "21 Years with Dr. Leavis."
Angus Wilson, "The Challenge of Kipling."
Oliver and Boyd:
Jay Halio, *Angus Wilson.*
Oxford University Press:
C. B. Cox, *The Free Spirit.*
Pan Books, Ltd.:
Arnold Bennett, *The Old Wives' Tale.*
Arthur Marwick, *The Explosion of British Society, 1914–62.*
The Paris Review:
Interview with Angus Wilson, Autumn-Winter, 1957.
Partisan Review:
Frank Kermode, "The House of Fiction: Interviews with Seven English Novelists," © 1963 by *Partisan Review.*
Angus Wilson, "New Playwrights," © 1959 by *Partisan Review.*
Penguin Books:
Boris Ford, ed., *The Modern Age.*
A. D. Peters and Co.:
Stephen Spender, *The Struggle of the Modern.*
Routledge and Kegan Paul, Ltd.:
David Lodge, *Language of Fiction.*
St. Martin's Press, Inc.:
John Wain, *Preliminary Essays; Essays on Literature and Ideas.*

Charles Scribner's Sons:
C. P. Snow, *The Search; The Light and the Dark; The New Men; Homecoming; The Conscience of the Rich; The Affair; Corridors of Power.*
Martin Secker and Warburg, Ltd.:
John Mander, *The Writer and Commitment.*
Angus Wilson, *Émile Zola.*
Lord Snow:
Recent Thoughts on the Two Cultures; "Science, Politics, and the Novelist."
Southern Illinois University Press:
F. R. Karl, *C. P. Snow: The Politics of Conscience.*
William Van O'Connor, *The New University Wits.*
The Spectator:
Kingsley Amis, book reviews published in 1953, 1954, 1955, 1956, 1957, 1958, 1959, 1960, and 1962.
C. P. Snow, "Books and Writers."
The Sunday Times (London):
Anonymous articles, June 7, 1953; May 1, 1955; Jan. 1, 1956.
J. B. Priestley, Jan. 2, 1955.
C. P. Snow, book reviews published in 1949, 1950, 1951, 1952, 1953, 1954, 1956, 1957, 1960.
Texas Quarterly:
Martin Green, "British Comedy and the British Sense of Humor: Shaw, Waugh, and Amis."
The Times (London):
Anonymous review, Aug. 29, 1952.
C. P. Snow, "Challenge to the Intellect."
Angus Wilson, "Diversity and Depth."
The Twentieth Century:
Kingsley Amis, "My Kind of Comedy."
Geoffrey Wagner, review, Feb., 1960.
The Viking Press, Inc.:
Angus Wilson, *Anglo-Saxon Attitudes,* © 1956 by Angus Wilson; *The Middle Age of Mrs. Eliot,* © 1958 by Angus Wilson.
A. P. Watt and Son:
Arnold Bennett, *The Old Wives' Tale* (English edition).

Mr. Angus Wilson:
"New Playwrights"; "A Revolution in British Reading"; "Charles Dickens: A Haunting"; "Diversity and Depth."
The Yale Review:
Iris Murdoch, "The Sublime and the Beautiful Revisited."

Index

Chaucer, Geoffrey, 6, 30, 58
Cheever, John, 51
Chekhov, Anton, 15, 110
Childhood: vision and, 94; Snow
treatment of, 144
Children's Encyclopaedia, 151
Christian Gauss Seminars in Criticism (Princeton University), 54
"Christmas Day in the Workhouse" (Wilson), 91
Churchill, Winston, 22, 128
Cities: nature and, 68–70
Clarity, 5–6, 123–25, 133
Clockwork Orange, A (Burgess), 171
Cockshut, A. O. J., cited, 95
Comfort, Alex, 125
Commentary (stylistic device), 147–48, 150
Common Reader, The (Woolf), 66
"Communication and the Victorian Poet" (Amis), 14n, 45
Communism, 28–29. *See also* Marxism
"Companion of Literature" honors, 128
Compton-Burnett, Ivy, 39, 80, 116; craftsmanship, 8, 47–48, 78
Comte, Auguste Le, 33, 108, 110
Conquest, Robert, 48, 49, 54n; quoted, 30
Conrad, Joseph, 115, 163, 168
Conscience of the Rich, The (Snow), 131n, 148–49, 153
Conservatism, 62, 77, 87–88, 89; "extreme reaction" charge, 100
Contenders, The (Wain), 17–18
Cooper, William, 2, 8–9, 12, 16, 30, 34; quoted, 6–7, 31, 32, 105, 132–33, 134; Wells and, 19; Wilson on, 78, 79; Snow on, 116–17, 126; "resonance" and, 148
Corridors of Power (Snow), 106, 129, 130, 145, 156, 159
Countryside, 68–70
Cowper, William, 69
Cox, C. B.: cited, 86n; quoted, 84–85
Cozzens, J. G., 120–21, 125, 131

"Credo" (Snow), 97
Crime and Punishment (Dostoevsky), Raskolnikov of, 45
Criticism, 12–16, 34–37, 166–69; Marxist, 28–29, 118–19, 122n, 126; Amis approach to, 36, 39–42, 43, 48, 51–53, 54; Wilson approach to, 36, 64–67, 73; Leavis approach to, 80–81, 114; Snow approach to, 36, 97–127, 131, 135–36, 163. *See also individual critics and specific critical work*
Culture, *see* Society

Dachau, 31
Daisy Miller (James), 72
Darwin, Charles, 112
Davie, Donald, 48
Death Under Sail (Snow), 99, 129–30
Declaration (Maschler, ed.), 167
Defoe, Daniel, 21
Delancy, Shelagh, 17, 25, 27, 79
Dennis, Nigel, 36, 166
Detective fiction, 99, 129–30
Determinism, 141–42
Dialogue, 131, 132, 145–48
Dickens, Charles, 5, 6, 12, 112n; scholarly works on, 13, 14, 64, 66n, 108; influence of, 14, 15, 16, 21, 45, 67, 68, 69, 70–72, 75, 83, 94, 95, 104, 110, 117
Disquiet and Peace (Cooper), 79n
Dividing Stream, The (King), 123
Donne, John, 39
Dos Passos, John, 121
Dostoyevsky, Fyodor, 15, 45, 112n; Snow and, 101, 104, 108, 109–10, 159
Drama, 8, 9, 12, 90; class attitudes and, 25, 27, 28, 79; Marxism and, 86–87
Dujardin, Édouard, 99, 112
Du Maurier, Daphne, 122
Durrell, Lawrence, 5, 9, 36–37, 103, 166

East Anglia, University of, 66n
East Europe, 28

48 | 1023609